T0178685

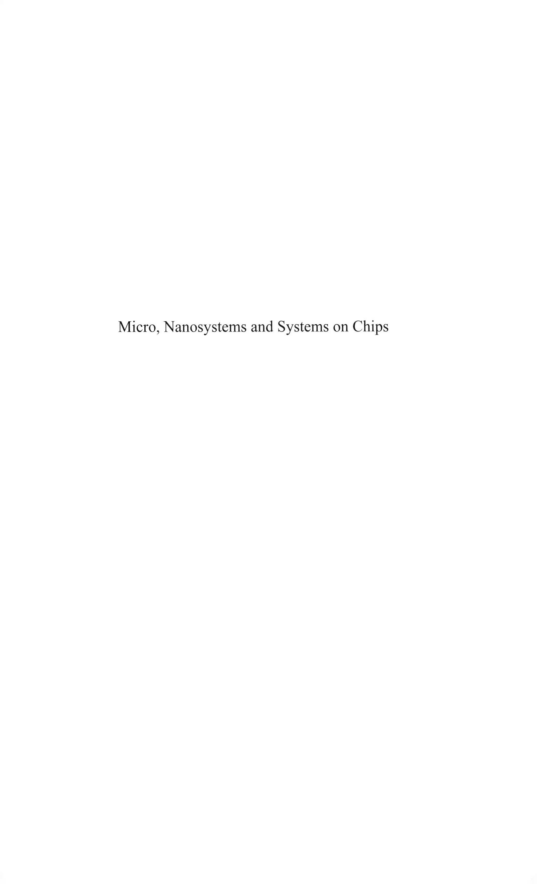

Micro, Nanosystems and Systems on Chips

To Anaïs and Raphaël

Micro, Nanosystems and Systems on Chips

Modeling, Control and Estimation

Edited by
Alina Voda

First published 2010 in Great Britain and the United States by ISTE Ltd and John Wiley & Sons, Inc.

ISTE Ltd
27-37 St George's Road
London SW19 4EU
UK

www.iste.co.uk

John Wiley & Sons, Inc.
111 River Street
Hoboken, NJ 07030
USA

www.wiley.com

© ISTE Ltd 2010

Library of Congress Cataloging-in-Publication Data

Micro, nanosystems, and systems on chips : modeling, control, and estimation / edited by Alina Voda.
 p. cm.
 Includes bibliographical references and index.
 ISBN 978-1-84821-190-2
 1. Microelectromechanical systems. 2. Systems on a chip. I. Voda, Alina.
 TK7875.M532487 2010
 621.381--dc22

2009041386

British Library Cataloguing-in-Publication Data
A CIP record for this book is available from the British Library
ISBN 978-1-84821-190-2

Printed and bound in Great Britain by CPI Antony Rowe, Chippenham and Eastbourne

Contents

Chapter 5. Controller Design and Analysis for High-performance STM . . 121
Irfan AHMAD, Alina VODA, Gildas BESANÇON

Introduction

Micro and nanosystems represent a major scientific and technological challenge, with actual and potential applications in almost all fields of human activity. From the first physics and philosophical concepts of atoms, developed by classical Greek and Roman thinkers such as Democritus, Epicurus and Lucretins some centuries BC at the dawn of the scientific era, to the famous Nobel Prize Feynman conference 50 years ago ("There is plenty of room at the bottom"), phenomena at atomic scale have incessantly attracted the human spirit. However, to produce, touch, manipulate and create such atomistic-based systems has only been possible during the last 50 years as the appropriate technologies became available.

Books on micro- and nanosystems have already been written and continue to appear. They focus on the physics, chemical, technological and biological concepts, problems and applications. The dynamical modeling, estimation and feedback control are not classically addressed in the literature on miniaturization. However, these are innovative and efficient approaches to explore and improve; new small-scale systems could even be created.

The instruments for measuring and manipulating individual systems at molecular and atomic scale cannot be imagined without incorporating very precise estimation and feedback control concepts. On the other hand, to make such a dream feasible, control system methods have to adapt to unusual systems governed by different physics than the macroscopic systems. Phenomena which are usually neglected, such as thermal noise, become an important source of disturbances for nanosystems. Dust particles can represent obstacles when dealing with molecular positioning. The influence of the measuring process on the measured variable, referred to as back action, cannot be ignored if the measured signal is of the same order of magnitude as the measuring device noise.

This book is addressed to researchers, engineers and students interested in the domain of miniaturized systems and dynamical systems and information treatment at this scale. The aim of this book is to present how concepts from dynamical control systems (modeling, estimation, observation, identification and feedback control) can be adapted and applied to the development of original very small-scale systems and to their human interfaces.

All the contributions have a model-based approach in common. The model is a set of dynamical system equations which, depending on its intended purpose, is either based on physics principles or is a black-box identified model or an energy (or potential field) based model. The model is then used for the design of the feedback control law, for estimation purposes (parameter identification or observer design) or for human interface design.

The applications presented in this book range from micro- and nanorobotics and biochips to near-field microscopy (Atomic Force and Scanning Tunneling Microscopes), nanosystems arrays, biochip cells and also human interfaces.

The book has three parts. The first part is dedicated to mini- and microsystems, with two applications of feedback control in micropositioning devices and microbeam dynamic shaping.

The second part is dedicated to nanoscale systems or phenomena. The fundamental instrument which we are concerned with is the microscope, which is either used to analyze or explore surfaces or to measure forces at an atomic scale. The core of the microscope is a cantilever with a sharp tip, in close proximity to the sample under analysis. Several chapters of the book treat different aspects related to the microscopy: force measurement at nanoscale is recast as an observer design, fast and precise nano-positioning is reached by feedback control design and cantilever arrays can be modeled and controlled using a non-standard approach. Another domain of interest is the field of biochips. A chapter is dedicated to the identification of a non-integer order model applied to such an electrochemical transduction/detection cell.

The third part of the book treats aspects of the interactions between the human and nanoworlds through haptic interfaces, telemanipulation and virtual reality.

Alina Voda
Grenoble
January 2010

PART I

Mini and Microsystems

Chapter 1

Modeling and Control of Stick-slip Micropositioning Devices

The principle of stick-slip motion is highly appreciated in the design of micro-positioning devices. Indeed, this principle offers both a very high resolution and a high range of displacement for the devices. In fact, stick-slip motion is a step-by-step motion and two modes can therefore be used: the stepping mode (for coarse positioning) and the sub-step mode (for fine positioning). In this chapter, we present the modeling and control of micropositioning devices based on stick-slip motion principle. For each mode (sub-step and stepping), we describe the model and propose a control law in order to improve the performance of the devices. Experimental results validate and confirm the results in the theoretical section.

1.1. Introduction

In microassembly and micromanipulation tasks, i.e. assembly or manipulation of objects with submillimetric sizes, the manipulators should achieve a micrometric or submicrometric accuracy. To reach such a performance, the design of microrobots and micromanipulators is radically different from the design of classical robots. Instead of using hinges that may introduce imprecision, active materials are preferred. Piezoelectric materials are highly prized because of the high resolution and the short response time they can offer.

In addition to the high accuracy, a large range of motion is also important in microassembly/micromanipulation tasks. Indeed, the pick-and-place of small objects

Chapter written by Micky RAKOTONDRABE, Yassine HADDAB and Philippe LUTZ.

may require the transportation of the latter over a long distance. To execute tasks with high accuracy and over a high range of displacement, micropositioning devices and microrobots use embedded (micro)actuators. According to the type of microactuators used, there are different motion principles that can be used e.g. the stick-slip motion principle, the impact drive motion principle and the inch-worm motion principle. Each of these principles provides a step-by-step motion. The micropositioning device analyzed and experimented upon in this chapter is based on the stick-slip motion principle and uses piezoelectric microactuators.

Stick-slip micropositioning devices can work with two modes of motion: the coarse mode which is for long-distance positioning and the sub-step mode which is for fine positioning. This chapter presents the modeling and the control of the micropositioning device for both fine and coarse modes.

First we describe the micropositioning device. The modeling and control in fine mode are then analyzed. We then present the modeling in coarse mode, and end the chapter by describing control of the device in coarse mode.

1.2. General description of stick-slip micropositioning devices

1.2.1. *Principle*

Figure 1.1a explains the functioning of the stick-slip motion principle. In the figure, two microactuators are embedded onto a body to be moved. The two microactuators are made of a smart material. Here, we consider piezoelectric microactuators.

If we apply a ramp voltage to the microactuators, they slowly bend. As the bending acceleration is low, there is an adherence between the tips of the microactuators and the base (Figure 1.1b). If we reset the voltage, the bending of the legs is also abruptly halted. Because of the high acceleration, sliding occurs between their tips and the base. A displacement Δx of the body is therefore obtained (Figure 1.1c). Repeating the sequence using a sawtooth voltage signal makes the body perform a step-by-step motion. The corresponding motion principle is called stick-slip. The amplitude of a step is defined by the sawtooth voltage amplitude and the speed of the body is defined by both the amplitude and the frequency. The step value indicates the positioning resolution.

While the step-by-step motion corresponds to the coarse mode, it is also possible to work in sub-step mode. In this case, the rate of the applied voltage is limited so that the legs never slide (Figure 1.1d). In many cases, this mode is used when the error between the reference position and the present position of the device is less than one step. This mode is called fine mode.

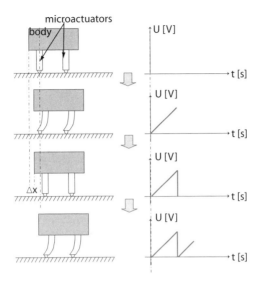

Figure 1.1. *Stick-slip principle: (a–c) stepping mode and (d) scanning mode*

1.2.2. *Experimental device*

The positioning device experimented upon in this paper, referred to as triangular RING (TRING) module, is depicted in Figure 1.2. It can perform a linear and an angular motion on the base (a glass tube) independently. Without loss of generality, our experiments are carried out only in linear motion. To move the TRING-module, six piezoelectric microactuators are embedded. Details of the design and development of the TRING-module are given in [RAK 06, RAK 09] while the piezoelectric microactuators are described in [BER 03].

To evaluate the step of the device, we apply a sawtooth signal to its microactuators. The measurements were carried out with an interferometer of 1.24 nm resolution. Figure 1.3a depicts the resulting displacement at amplitude 150 V and frequency 500 Hz. We note that the step is quasi-constant during the displacement. Figure 1.3b is a zoomed image of one step. The oscillations during the stick phase are caused by the dynamics of the microactuators and the mass of the TRING-module. The maximal step, obtained with 150 V, is about 200 nm. Decreasing the amplitude will decrease the value of the step and increase the resolution of the micropositioning device. As an example, with $U = 75$ V the step is approximatively 70 nm. However, the step efficiency is constant whatever the value of the amplitude. It is defined as the ratio of the gained step to the amplitude of the sawtooth voltage [DRI 03]:

$$\eta_{\text{step}} = \frac{\text{step}}{\Delta \text{amp}} \approx 0.7. \tag{1.1}$$

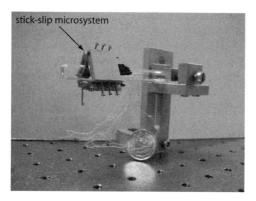

Figure 1.2. *A photograph of the TRING-module*

As introduced above, two modes of displacement are possible: the fine and the coarse modes. In the next sections, the fine mode of the TRING-module is first modeled and controlled. After that, we will detail the modeling and the control in coarse mode, all with linear motion.

1.3. Model of the sub-step mode

The sub-step modeling of a stick-slip micropositioning device is highly dependent upon the structure of microactuators. This in turn depends upon the required number of degrees of freedom and their kinematics, the structure of the device where they will be integrated and the structure of the base. For example, [FAT 95] and [BER 04] use two kinds of stick-slip microactuators to move the MICRON micropositioning device (5-dof) and the MINIMAN micropositioning device (3-dof). Despite this dependence of the model on the microactuator's structure, as long as the piezoelectric microactuator is operating linearly, the sub-step model is still linear [RAK 09].

During the modeling of the sub-step mode, it is of interest to include the state of the friction between the microactuators and the base. For example, it is possible to control it to be lower than a certain value to ensure the stick mode. There are several models of friction according to the application [ARM 94], but the elastoplastic model [DUP 02] is best adapted to the sub-step modeling. The model of the sub-step mode is therefore linear and has an order at least equal to the order of the microactuator model.

1.3.1. *Assumptions*

During the modeling, the adhesion forces between the foot of the microactuators and the base are assumed to be insignificant relative to the preload charge. The

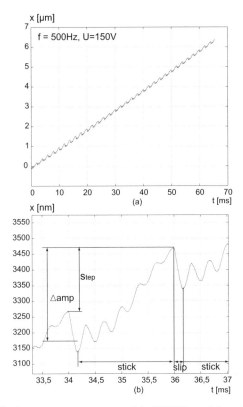

Figure 1.3. *Linear displacement measurement of the TRING-module using an interferometer: (a) a series of stick-slip motion obtained with $U = 150\,V$ and $f = 500\,Hz$ and (b) vibrations inside a step obtained with $U = 150\,V$ and $f = 60\,Hz$*

preload charge is the vertical force that maintains the device on the base. The base is considered to be rigid and we assume that no vibration affects it because we work in the stick mode. Indeed, during this mode, the tip of the microactuator and the base are fixed and shocks do not cause vibration.

To model the TRING micropositioning device, a physical approach has been applied [RAK 09]. While physical models of stick-slip devices strongly depend upon their structure and characteristics and on their microactuators, the structure of these models does not vary significantly. Assuming the piezoelectric microactuators work in the linear domain, the final model is linear. The order of the model is equal to the microactuator's model order added to the model order of the friction state. The sub-step modeling can be separated into two stages: the modeling of the microactuator (electromechanical part) and the inclusion of the friction model (mechanical part).

1.3.2. *Microactuator equation*

The different microactuators and the positioning device can be lumped into one microactuator supporting a body (Figure 1.4).

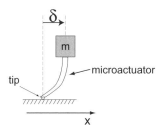

Figure 1.4. *Schematic of the microactuator*

If the microactuator works in a linear domain, a second-order lumped model is:

$$a_2 \ddot{\delta} + a_1 \dot{\delta} + \delta = d_p U + s_p F_{\text{piezo}} \tag{1.2}$$

where δ is the deflection of the microactuator, a_i are the parameters of the dynamic parts, d_p is the piezoelectric coefficient, s_p is the elastic coefficient and F_{piezo} is the external force applied to the microactuator. It may be derived from external disturbance (manipulation force, etc.) or internal stresses between the base and the microactuator.

1.3.3. *The elastoplastic friction model*

The elastoplastic friction model was proposed by Dupont *et al.* [DUP 02] and is well adapted for stick-slip micropositioning devices. Consider a block that moves along a base (Figure 1.5a). If the force F applied to the block is lower than a certain value, the block does not move. This corresponds to a stick phase. If we increase the force, the block starts sliding and the slip phase is obtained.

In the elastoplastic model, the contact between the block and the base are lumped in a medium asperity model (Figure 1.5b). Let G be the center of gravity of the block and x its motion. During the stick phase, the medium asperity bends. As there is no sliding ($\dot{w} = 0$), the motion of the block corresponds only to the deflection x_{asp} of the asperity: $x = x_{\text{asp}}$. This motion is elastic; when the force is removed, the deflection becomes null.

When the external force F exceeds a value corresponding to $x_{\text{asp}} = x_{\text{asp}}^{\text{ba}}$ (referred to as break-away), the tip of the asperity starts sliding and its displacement is given by

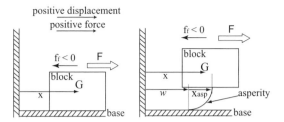

Figure 1.5. *(a) A block that moves along a base and (b) the contact between the block and the base can be approximated by a medium asperity*

w. While $\dot{w} \neq 0$, the deflection x_{asp} continues to vary. This phase is elastic because of x_{asp} but also plastic because of w.

If F is increased further, x_{asp} tends to a saturation called $x_{\mathrm{asp}}^{\mathrm{ss}}$ (steady state) and the speed $\dot{x}$ of the block is equal to $\dot{w} \neq 0$. This phase is called plastic because removing the force will not reset the block to its initial position.

The equations describing the elastoplastic model are:

$$
\begin{aligned}
x &= x_{\mathrm{aps}} + w \\
f_f &= -N\left(\rho_0 x_{\mathrm{asp}} + \rho_1 \dot{x}_{\mathrm{asp}} + \rho_2 x\right) \\
\dot{x}_{\mathrm{asp}} &= \dot{x}\left(1 - \alpha\left(x_{\mathrm{asp}}, \dot{x}\right) \frac{x_{\mathrm{asp}}}{x_{\mathrm{asp}}^{\mathrm{ss}}(\dot{x})}\right)
\end{aligned}
\tag{1.3}
$$

where N designates the normal force applied to the block, ρ_0 and ρ_2 are the Coulomb and the viscous parameters of the friction, respectively, ρ_1 provides damping for tangential compliance and $\alpha\left(x_{\mathrm{asp}}, \dot{x}\right)$ is a function which determines the phase (stick or slip). Figure 1.6 provides an example of allure of α.

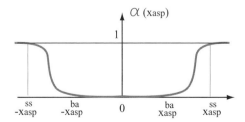

Figure 1.6. *An example of allure of α*

For stick-slip devices working in the sub-step mode, there is no sliding and so $\dot{w} = 0$. In addition, the coefficients ρ_1 and ρ_2 are negligible because the friction is dry (there is no lubricant). Assuming that the initial value is $w = 0$, the friction equations of stick-slip devices in the stick mode are:

$$
\begin{aligned}
f_f &= -N\rho_0 x_{\mathrm{asp}} \\
x &= x_{\mathrm{asp}} \\
\dot{x} &= \dot{x}_{\mathrm{asp}}.
\end{aligned}
\tag{1.4}
$$

1.3.4. *The state equation*

To compute the model of the stick-slip micropositioning device in a stick mode, the deformation of the microactuator (equation (1.2)) and the friction model (equation (1.4)) are used. Figure 1.7 represents the same image as Figure 1.4 with the contact between the tip of the microactuator and the base enlarged. According to the figure, the displacement x_{sub} can be determined by combining the microactuator equation δ and the friction state x_{asp} using dynamic laws [RAK 09].

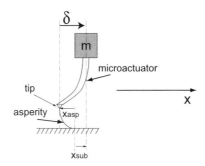

Figure 1.7. *An example of allure of α*

The state equation of the TRING-module is therefore:

$$
\frac{d}{dt}
\begin{bmatrix}
\delta \\
\dot{\delta} \\
x_{\mathrm{asp}} \\
\dot{x}_{\mathrm{asp}}
\end{bmatrix}
=
\begin{bmatrix}
0 & 1 & 0 & 0 \\
A_{21} & A_{22} & A_{23} & 0 \\
0 & 0 & 0 & 1 \\
A_{41} & A_{42} & A_{43} & 0
\end{bmatrix}
\begin{bmatrix}
\delta \\
\dot{\delta} \\
x_{\mathrm{asp}} \\
\dot{x}_{\mathrm{asp}}
\end{bmatrix}
+
\begin{bmatrix}
0 \\
B_2 \\
0 \\
B_4
\end{bmatrix}
U
\tag{1.5}
$$

where the state vector is composed of:

– the states of the electromechanical part: the deflection δ of the piezoelectric microactuator and the corresponding derivative $\dot{\delta}$; and

– the states of the friction part: the deflection of a medium asperity x_{asp} and the corresponding derivative $\dot{x}_{asp}$.

The following values have been identified and validated for the considered system [RAK 09]:

$$
\begin{aligned}
A_{21} &= -1,023,243,521 \\
A_{22} &= -204,649 \\
A_{23} &= 44,183,761,041 \\
A_{41} &= 1,021,647,707 \\
A_{42} &= 204,330 \\
A_{43} &= -1,624,646,063,889
\end{aligned}
\tag{1.6}
$$

and

$$
\begin{aligned}
B_2 &= 0.969 \\
B_4 &= -0.9674
\end{aligned}
\tag{1.7}
$$

1.3.5. *The output equation*

The output equation is defined as

$$
\begin{bmatrix} T \\ x_{sub} \end{bmatrix} = \begin{bmatrix} C_{11} & C_{12} & C_{13} & 0 \\ 1 & 0 & 1 & 0 \end{bmatrix} \begin{bmatrix} \delta \\ \dot{\delta} \\ x_{asp} \\ \dot{x}_{asp} \end{bmatrix} + \begin{bmatrix} D_1 \\ 0 \end{bmatrix} U
\tag{1.8}
$$

where T is the friction and x_{sub} is the displacement of the mass m during the stick mode. x_{sub} corresponds to the fine position of the TRING device. The different parameters are defined:

$$
\begin{aligned}
C_{11} &= -1,596 \\
C_{12} &= -0.32 \\
C_{13} &= -1,580,462,303 \\
D_1 &= -1.5 \times 10^{-6}.
\end{aligned}
\tag{1.9}
$$

1.3.6. *Experimental and simulation curves*

In the considered application, we are interested in the control of the position. We therefore only consider the output x_{sub}. From the previous state and output equations, we derive the transfer function relating the applied voltage and x_{sub}:

$$G_{x_{\text{sub}}U} = \frac{x_{\text{sub}}(s)}{U(s)} = \frac{1.5 \times 10^{-3} \left(s^2 + 1.01 \times 10^{15}\right)}{\left(s + 1.94 \times 10^5\right)\left(s + 5133\right)\left(s^2 + 5735s + 1.63 \times 10^{12}\right)}$$

(1.10)

where s is the Laplace variable.

To compare the computed model $G_{x_{\text{sub}}U}$ and the real system, a harmonic analysis is performed by applying a sine input voltage to the TRING-module. The chosen amplitude of the sine voltage is 75 V instead of 150 V. Indeed, with a high amplitude the minimum frequency from which the drift (and then the sliding mode) starts is low. In the example of Figure 1.8, a frequency of 2250 Hz leads to a drift when the amplitude is 150 V while a frequency of 5000 Hz does not when amplitude is 75 V. The higher the amplitude, the higher the acceleration is and the higher the risk of sliding (drift). When the TRING-module slides, the sub-step model is no longer valuable.

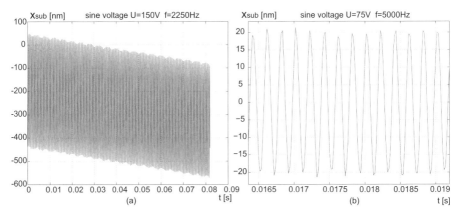

Figure 1.8. *Harmonic experiment: (a) outbreak of a drift of the TRING positioning system (sliding mode) and (b) stick mode*

Figure 1.9 depicts the magnitude of the simulation (equation (1.10)) and the experimental result. It shows that the structure of the model and the identified parameters correspond well.

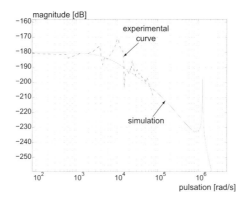

Figure 1.9. *Comparison of the simulation of the developed model and the experimental results*

1.4. PI control of the sub-step mode

The aim of the sub-step control is to improve the performance of the TRING-module during a highly accurate task and to eliminate disturbances (e.g. manipulation force, adhesion forces and environmental disturbances such as temperature). Indeed, when positioning a microcomponent such as fixing a microlens at the tip of an optical fiber [GAR 00], the manipulation force can disturb the positioning task and modify its accuracy. In addition, the numerical values of the model parameters may contain uncertainty. We therefore present here the closed-loop control of the fine mode to introduce high stability margins.

The sub-step functioning requires that the derivative dU/dt of the voltage should be inferior to a maximum slope $\dot{U}_{\max}$. To ensure this, we introduce a rate limiter in the controller scheme as depicted in Figure 1.10.

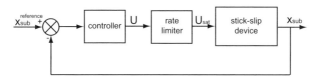

Figure 1.10. *Structure of the closed-loop system*

To ensure a null static error, we choose a proportional-integral (PI) controller. The parameters of the controller are computed to ensure a phase margin of $60°$, required for stability in residual phase uncertainty.

First, we trace the Black–Nichols diagram of the open-loop system $G_{x_{\text{sub}}U}$, as depicted in Figure 1.11.

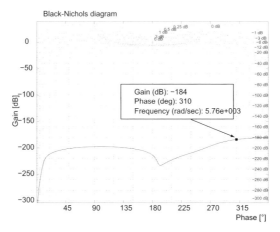

Figure 1.11. *Black–Nichols diagram of $G_{x_{\text{sub}}U}$*

Let

$$K_{\text{PI}} = K_p \times \left(1 + K_i \times \frac{1}{s} \right)$$

be the transfer function of the controller, where K_p and $K_i = 1/T_i$ are the proportional and the integrator gains, respectively. The $60°$ of phase margin is obtained if the new open-loop transfer function $K_{\text{PI}} \times G_{xU}$ has a Black–Nichols diagram which cuts the $0\,\text{dB}$ horizontal axis at $240°$. This can be obtained by computing a corrector K_{PI} that adjusts the data depicted in Figure 1.11 to that required. Using the computation method presented in [BOU 06], we find:

$$
\begin{aligned}
K_p &= 383,749,529 \\
K_i &= 7,940.
\end{aligned}
\tag{1.11}
$$

The controller has been implemented following that depicted in Figure 1.10. The reference displacement is a step input signal $x_{\text{sub}}^{\text{ref}} = 100\,\text{nm}$. Figure 1.12a shows the experimental response of the TRING-module and the quasi-instantaneous response of the closed-loop system. The accuracy is about $\pm 5\,\text{nm}$ and the vibrations are due to the high sensitivity of the measurement to the environment. Such performances are of great interest in micromanipulation/microassembly.

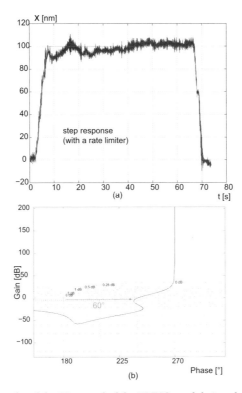

Figure 1.12. *Results of the PI control of the TRING-module in sub-step functioning*

Figure 1.12b shows the Black–Nichols diagram of the closed-loop system and indicates the margin phase. According to the figure, the margin gain is 50 dB. These robustness margins are sufficient to ensure the stability of the closed-loop system regarding the uncertainty of the parameters and of the structure of the developed model. Finally, the closed-loop control ensures these performances when external disturbances occur during the micromanipulation/microassembly tasks. A disturbance may be of an environmental type (e.g. temperature variation) or a manipulation type (e.g. manipulation force).

1.5. Modeling the coarse mode

When scanning over a large distance (e.g. pick-and-place tasks in microassembly), the micropositioning device should work in coarse mode. The applied voltage is no longer limited in slope as for the fine mode, but has a sawtooth form. The resulting displacement is a succession of steps. This section, which follows that of [BOU 06], discusses the modeling and control of the coarse mode. The presented results are applicable to stepping systems.

1.5.1. *The model*

First, let us study one step. For that, we first apply a ramp input voltage up to U. If the slope of the ramp is weak, there is no sliding between the tip of the microactuators and the base. Using the model in the stick mode, the displacement of the device is defined:

$$x_{\text{sub}}(s) = G_{x_{\text{sub}}U}(s) \times U(s). \tag{1.12}$$

To obtain a step, the voltage is quickly reduced to zero. The resulting step x_{step} is smaller than the amplitude x_{sub} that corresponds to the last value of U (Figure 1.13a). We denote this amplitude x_{sub}^U. We then have:

$$x_{\text{step}} = x_{\text{sub}}^U - \Delta_{\text{back}}. \tag{1.13}$$

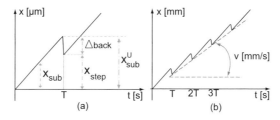

Figure 1.13. *(a) Motion of a stick-slip system and (b) speed approximation*

If we assume that backlash Δ_{back} is dynamically linear relative to the amplitude U, the step can be written as:

$$x_{\text{step}}(s) = G_{\text{step}}(s) \times U(s) \tag{1.14}$$

where G_{step} is a linear transfer function. When the sequence is repeated with a frequency $f = 1/T$, i.e. a sawtooth signal, the micropositioning device works in the stepping mode (coarse mode). During this mode, each transient part inside a step is no longer important. Instead, we are interested in the speed performance of the device over a large distance. To compute the speed, we consider the final value of a step:

$$x_{\text{step}} = \alpha \times U \tag{1.15}$$

where $\alpha > 0$ is the static gain of G_{step}.

From Figure 1.13b and equation (1.15), we easily deduce the speed:

$$v = \frac{x_{\text{step}}}{T} = x_{\text{step}} \times f. \tag{1.16}$$

The speed is therefore bilinear in relation to the amplitude U and the frequency f of the sawtooth input voltage:

$$v = \alpha f U. \tag{1.17}$$

However, the experiments show that there is a deadzone in the amplitude inside which the speed is null. Indeed, if the amplitude U is below a certain value U_0, the micropositioning system does not move in the stepping mode but only moves back and forth in the stick mode. To take into account this threshold, equation (1.15) is slightly modified and the final model becomes:

$$\begin{cases} v = 0 & \text{if} \quad |U| \leq U_0 \\ v = \alpha f \left(U - \text{sgn}(U) U_0 \right) & \text{if} \quad |U| > U_0. \end{cases} \tag{1.18}$$

1.5.2. *Experimental results*

The identification on the TRING-module gives $\alpha = 15.65 \times 10^{-7} \text{mm V}^{-1}$ and $U_0 = 35\,\text{V}$. Figure 1.14 summarizes the speed performances of the micropositioning system: simulation of the model using equation (1.18) and experimental result. During the experiments, the amplitude U is limited to $\pm 150\,\text{V}$ in order to avoid the destruction of the piezoelectric microactutors. Figure 1.14a depicts the speed versus amplitude for three different frequencies. It shows that the experimental results fit the model simulation well. Figure 1.14b depicts the speed versus frequency. In this, the experimental results and the simulation curve correspond up to $f \approx 10\,\text{kHz}$; above this frequency there are saturations and fluctuations.

1.5.3. *Remarks*

To obtain equation (1.14), we made the assumption that the backlash Δback was linear relative to the amplitude U, such that in the static mode we have $\Delta\text{back} = K_{\text{back}} U$ where K_{back} is the static gain of the backlash. In fact, the backlash is pseudo-linear relative to U because K_{back} is dependent upon U.

Let $x_{\text{sub}}^{U} = G_{x_{\text{sub}}U}(0)\,U$ be the static value of x_{sub} in the sub-step mode obtained using equation (1.12) and corresponding to an input U, where $G_{x_{\text{sub}}U}(0)$ is a static gain. Substituting it into equation (1.13) and using equation (1.16), we have:

$$v = f \left(G_{x_{\text{sub}}U}(0)\,U - K_{\text{back}} U \right). \tag{1.19}$$

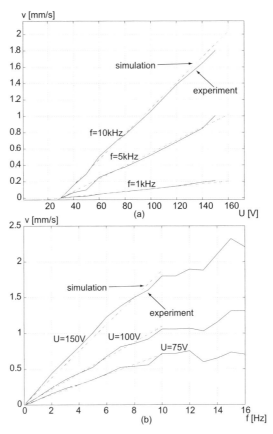

Figure 1.14. *Speed performances of the micropositioning system (experimental results in solid lines and simulation of equation (1.18) in dashed lines): (a) speed versus the amplitude U and (b) speed versus the frequency f*

Comparing equation (1.19) and the second equation of equation (1.18), we demonstrate the pseudo-linearity of the backlash in relation to U:

$$K_{\text{back}} = G_{x_{\text{sub}}U}(0) - \alpha \left(1 - \frac{U_0 \text{sgn}(U)}{U}\right). \tag{1.20}$$

1.6. Voltage/frequency (U/f) proportional control of the coarse mode

The micropositioning device working in coarse mode is a two-inputs-one-output system. The input variables are the frequency and the amplitude of the sawtooth voltage while the output is the displacement.

A stick-slip device is a type of stepping motor, and so stepping motor control techniques may be used. The easiest control of stepping motors is the open-loop counter technique. This consists of applying the number of steps necessary to reach a final position. In this, no sensor is necessary but the step value should be exactly known. In stick-slip micropositioning devices, such a technique is not very convenient. In fact, the friction varies along a displacement and the step is not very predictible. Closed-loop controllers are therefore preferred.

In closed-loop techniques, a natural control principle is the following basic algorithm:

$$\text{WHILE } |x_c - x| \geq \text{step DO}$$

apply 1 step

$$\text{ENDWHILE} \tag{1.21}$$

where x_c and x are the reference and the present positions of the stick-slip devices, respectively, and step is the value of one step. The resolution of the closed-loop system is equal to 1 step. If the accuracy of the sensor is lower than 1 step, a slight modification can be made:

$$\text{WHILE } |x_c - x| \geq n \times \text{step DO}$$

apply $n \times$ step

$$\text{ENDWHILE.} \tag{1.22}$$

It is clear that for very precise positioning, the basic algorithm must be combined with a sub-step controller (such as the PI controller presented in the previous section). In that case, equation (1.21) is first activated during the coarse mode. When the error position $x_c - x$ is lower than the value of a step, the controller is switched into the sub-step mode.

In order to avoid the use of two triggered controllers for coarse mode and fine mode, Breguet and Clavel [BRE 98] propose a numerical controller where the frequency f of the sawtooth voltage is proportional to the error. In this, the position error is converted into a clock signal with frequency equal to that of the error. When the error becomes lower than a step, the frequency tends towards zero and the applied voltage is equivalent to that applied in the fine mode. Since the amplitude U is constant, the step is also constant and the positioning resolution is constant all along the displacement.

A technique based on the theory of dynamic hybrid systems has been used in [SED 03]. The mixture of the fine mode and the coarse mode actually constitutes a dynamic hybrid system. In the proposed technique, the hybrid system is first approximated by a continuous model by inserting a cascade with a hybrid controller. The approximation is called dehybridization. A PI-controller is then applied to the obtained continuous system.

In the following section, we propose a new controller scheme. In contrast to the dehybridization-based controller, the proposed scheme is very easy to implement because it does not require a hybrid controller. The proposed scheme always ensures the stability. The resolution that it provides is better than that of the basic algorithm. It will be shown that the controller is a globalization of three existing controllers: the bang-bang controller, the proportional controller and the frequency-proportional controller cited above.

1.6.1. Principle scheme of the proposed controller

The principle scheme of the controller is depicted in Figure 1.15. Basically, the principle is that the input signals (the amplitude and the frequency) are proportional to the error. This is why the proposed scheme is referred to as voltage/frequency (or U/f) proportional control. In Figure 1.15, the amplitude saturation limits any over-voltages that may destroy the piezoelectric microactuators. The frequency saturation limits the micropositioning system work inside the linear frequential zone. The controller parameters are the proportional gains $K_U > 0$ and $K_f > 0$.

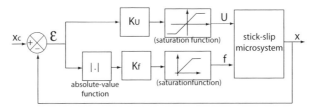

Figure 1.15. *Principle scheme of the U/f proportional control*

1.6.2. Analysis

Because of the presence of saturation in the controller scheme (Figure 1.15), different situations can occur [RAK 08] dependent upon the frequency and/or the amplitude being in the saturation zones. In this section, we analyze these situations.

Let U_s and f_s be the saturations used for the voltage and the frequency, respectively.

1.6.2.1. *Case a*

In the first case, we assume that both the amplitude and the frequency are saturated, i.e.

$$K_U \left| x_c - x \right| > U_s \text{ and } K_f \left| x_c - x \right| > f_s. \tag{1.23}$$

This can be intepreted in two ways: the present position of the device is different from the reference position or the chosen proportional gains are very high. The equation of the closed-loop system in this case is obtained using the principle scheme in Figure 1.15 and equation (1.18). We have:

$$\dot{x} = \alpha f_s \left(U_s - U_0 \right) \text{sgn} \left(x_c - x \right). \tag{1.24}$$

In such a case, the amplitude U is switched between U_s and $-U_s$ according to the sign of the error (Figure 1.16a). This case is therefore equivalent to a sign or bang-bang controller. With a sign control, there are oscillations. The frequency and the amplitude of these oscillations depend on the response time T_r of the process, on the refreshing time T_s of the controller and on the frequency saturation f_s (Figure 1.16b). To minimize the oscillations, the use of realtime feedback systems is recommended.

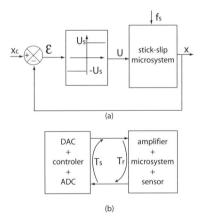

(a)

(b)

Figure 1.16. *Sign controller equivalence of the U/f controller*

1.6.2.2. *Case b*

If the amplitude U is lower than the threshold U_0 regardless of frequency, i.e. if

$$U_0 > K_U \left| x_c - x \right|, \forall f = K_f \left| x_c - x \right|, \tag{1.25}$$

the speed is null ($\dot{x} = 0$) and the static error is $x_c - x$.

1.6.2.3. *Case c*

In this case, the frequency is saturated while the amplitude is not. The condition corresponding to this case is:

$$U_s \geq K_U \left| x_c - x \right| \text{ and } K_f \left| x_c - x \right| > f_s. \tag{1.26}$$

In such a case, the system is controlled by a classical proportional controller with gain K_U (Figure 1.17).

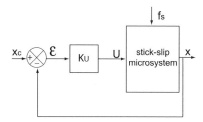

Figure 1.17. *Voltage proportional control*

The equation of the closed loop is easily obtained:

$$\dot{x} = \alpha f_s \left(K_U \left(x_c - x \right) - \text{sgn} \left(x_c - x \right) U_0 \right). \tag{1.27}$$

If we consider a positive reference position $x_c > 0$ and an initial value $x(t = 0)$ equal to zero, we obtain the Laplace transformation:

$$X = \frac{1}{1 + \frac{1}{\alpha f_s K_U} s} X_c - \frac{\frac{1}{K_U}}{1 + \frac{1}{\alpha f_s K_U} s} U_0. \tag{1.28}$$

According to equation (1.28), the closed-loop process is a first-order dynamic system with a static gain equal to unity and a disturbance U_0. The static error due to the disturbance U_0 is minimized when increasing the gain K_U. Because the order is equal to that of the closed-loop system, this case is always stable.

1.6.2.4. *Case d*

Here we consider that the amplitude is saturated while the frequency is not, i.e.

$$K_U \left| x_c - x \right| > U_s \text{ and } f_s \geq K_f \left| x_c - x \right|. \tag{1.29}$$

In such a case, the frequency of the sawtooth voltage is proportional to the error. The controller is therefore a frequency proportional controller (Figure 1.18). The

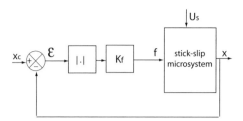

Figure 1.18. *Frequency proportional control*

difference between this case and the controller proposed in [BRE 98] is that, in the latter, the controller is digital and based on an 8-bit counter.

Using Figure 1.18 and model (1.18), we have the non-linear differential model:

$$\dot{x} = \alpha K_f \left| x_c - x \right| (U_s - U_0) \operatorname{sgn}(x_c - x) \tag{1.30}$$

where x_c is the input and x is the output. For $x_c > 0$ and an initial value $x(t = 0) = 0$, we deduce the transfer function from equation (1.30):

$$\frac{X}{X_c} = \frac{1}{1 + \frac{1}{\alpha K_f (U_s - U_0)} s}. \tag{1.31}$$

According to equation (1.31), the closed-loop process is a first-order system. Because the static gain is unity, there is no error static.

1.6.2.5. *Case e*

In this case, we consider that both the amplitude and the frequency are not saturated:

$$U_s \geq K_U \left| x_c - x \right| \text{ and } f_s \geq K_f \left| x_c - x \right|. \tag{1.32}$$

Using Figure 1.15 and equation (1.18), we have:

$$\dot{x} = \alpha K_f \left| x_c - x \right| (K_U (x_c - x) - \operatorname{sgn}(x_c - x) U_0). \tag{1.33}$$

The previous expression is equivalent to:

$$\begin{aligned}
\frac{dx}{dt} &= (\alpha K_f (U_0 - \alpha) K_f K_U \left| x_c - x \right|) x \\
&+ (-\alpha K_f (U_0 + \alpha) K_f K_U \left| x_c - x \right|) x_c.
\end{aligned} \tag{1.34}$$

Hence, the closed-loop system is equivalent to a first-order pseudo-linear system. Indeed, equation (1.34) has the form:

$$\frac{dx}{dt} = A\left(x_c, x\right) x + B\left(x_c, x\right) x_c. \tag{1.35}$$

1.6.3. Stability analysis

Here we analyze the stability of the closed-loop system. We note that all the cases stated above may appear during a displacement according to the values of K_U, K_f and the error $(x_c - x)$. To analyze the stability, we assume $x_c = 0$ and $x(t = 0) > 0$ without loss of generality. In addition, let us divide the whole displacement into two phases as depicted in Figure 1.19:

– Phase 1: concerns the amplitude and the frequency in saturation. This corresponds to the error $(x_c - x)$ being initially high (case a). The speed is then constant.

– Phase 2: the error becomes smaller and the speed is not yet constant (equivalent to the rest of the cases).

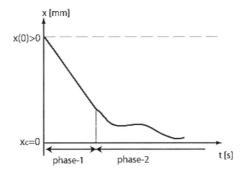

Figure 1.19. *Division of the displacement into two phases*

According to equation (1.18), the device works in a quasi-static manner. Hence, there is no acceleration and any one case does not influence the succeeding case. Conditions relative to initial speed are not necessary so we can analyze phase 2 independently of phase 1. In phase 2, there are two sub-phases:

– Phase 2.1: either the frequency is in saturation but not the amplitude (case c) or the amplitude is in saturation but not the frequency (case d).

– Phase 2.2: neither the frequency nor the amplitude are in saturation (case e).

Because phase 2.1 is stable and does not influence phase 2.2, we can analyze the stability using the latter. For that, equation (1.34) is used. Applying the conditions

$x_c = 0$ and $x(t = 0) > 0$, we have:

$$\frac{dx}{dt} = -\alpha K_f x \left(K_U x - U_0 \right). \tag{1.36}$$

To prove the stability, we use the direct method of Lyapunov. A system $dx/dt = f(x, t)$ is stable if there exists a Lyapunov function $V(x)$ that satisfies:

$$\begin{aligned} V(x = 0) &= 0 \\ V(x) > 0 \quad &\forall \quad x \neq 0 \\ \frac{dV(x)}{dt} \leq 0 \quad &\forall \quad x \neq 0. \end{aligned} \tag{1.37}$$

If we choose a quadratic form $V(x) = \gamma x^2$, where any $\gamma > 0$ is convenient, the two conditions in equation (1.37) are satisfied. In addition, taking the derivative of $V(x)$ and using equation (1.36), the third condition is also satisfied:

$$\frac{dV(x)}{dt} = -2\gamma \alpha K_f x^2 \left(K_U x - U_0 \right) < 0. \tag{1.38}$$

Phase 2.2 (which corresponds to case e) is therefore asymptotically stable. When the error still decreases and the condition becomes $(K_U x - U_0) < 0$, case b occurs and the device stops. The static error is therefore given by $K_U x$.

1.6.4. *Experiments*

According to the previous analysis, three existing controllers are merged to form the U/f proportional controller. These are the sign controller (case a), the classical proportional controller (case c) and the frequency proportional controller proposed in [BRE 98] (case d).

As for the classical proportional controller, the choice of K_U is a compromise. A low value of K_U leads to a high static error (case b) while a high value of K_U may generate oscillations (case a).

The first experiment concerns high values of K_u and K_f. They have been chosen such that phase 2 never occurs and only case a occurs. The controller was implemented using Labview software and the Windows-XP operating system. The refreshing time is not relatively high so oscillations appear in the experimental results (Figure 1.20).

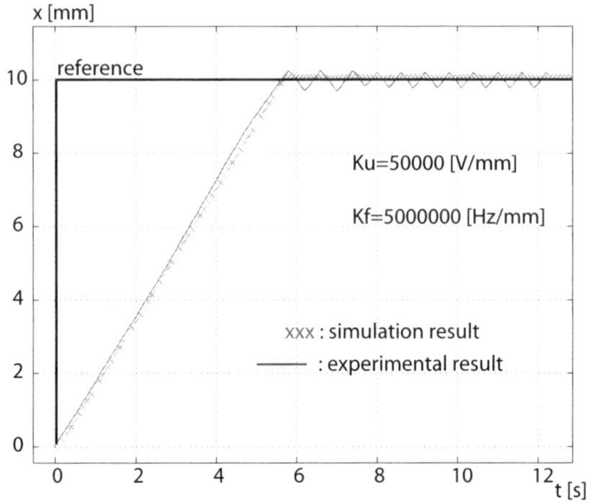

Figure 1.20. *High values of K_U and K_f: case a*

In the second experiment, we use a low K_U and a high K_f. The amplitude and the frequency are first saturated and the speed is constant (phase 1). When the error becomes lower than $x_{US} = U_s/K_U$, the amplitude becomes proportional to the error while the frequency is still saturated (case c). As the results in Figure 1.21 show, there is a static error. Its value can be computed using equation (1.28); we obtain

$$\varepsilon_s = \frac{U_0}{K_U}.$$

Concerning the use of a high K_U and a low K_f, phase 1 is left at $(x_c - x) = x_{fS} = f_s/K_f$ (Figure 1.21b). In this case, case d occurs and the controller becomes the frequency proportional controller. In such a case, there is no static error.

Finally, we use reasonable values of K_U and K_f. The simulation and experimental results are shown in Figure 1.22. First, the speed is constant (case a) because both the amplitude and the frequency are saturated. At $x_{fs} = f_s/K_f$, the frequency leaves the saturation but not the amplitude. This corresponds to the frequency proportional controller presented in case d. According to the values of K_U and K_f, the amplitude saturation may occur instead of the frequency saturation. From $x_{US} = U_s/K_U$, the voltage is no longer saturated and case e occurs. Hence, the static error is given by $\varepsilon_{\text{stat}} = U_0/K_U$.

1.7. Conclusion

In this chapter, the modeling and control of a stick-slip micropositioning device, developed at *Franche-Comté Electronique Mécanique Thermique et Optique - Science*

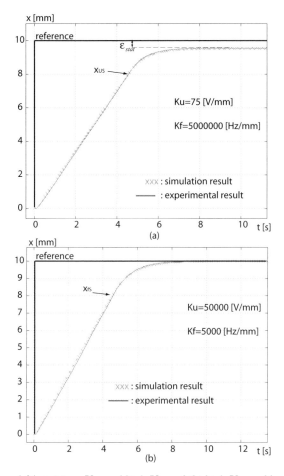

Figure 1.21. (a) Low K_U and high K_f and (b) high K_U and low K_f

et Technologie (FEMTO-ST) Institute in the AS2M department, has been discussed. Based on the use of piezoelectric actuators, this device can be operated either in coarse mode or in sub-step mode.

In the sub-step mode, the legs never slide and the obtained accuracy is 5 nm. This mode is suitable when the difference between the reference position and the current position is less than 1 step.

The coarse mode allows step-by-step displacements; long-range displacements can therefore be achieved. The voltage/frequency (U/F) proportional control presented in this chapter is easy to implement and demonstrates a good performance. The stability

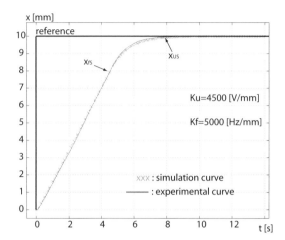

Figure 1.22. *Acceptable values of* K_U *and* K_f

of the controller has been proven. The performances of the coarse mode are given by the hardware performances. Combining the sub-step mode and the coarse mode is a solution for performing high-stroke/high-precision positioning tasks. The coarse mode will be used to drive the device close to the reference position and the sub-step mode will provide additional displacement details required to reach the reference. However, this approach requires the use of a long-range/high-accuracy position sensor, which is not easy to integrate. This will be an area of future research.

1.8. Bibliography

[ARM 94] ARMSTRONG-HÉLOUVRY B., DUPONT P., CANUDAS-DE-WIT C., "A survey of models, analysis tools and compensation methods for the control of machines with friction", *IFAC Automatica*, vol. 30, num. 7, p. 1083–1138, 1994.

[BER 03] BERGANDER A., DRIESEN W., VARIDEL T., BREGUET J. M., "Monolithic piezoelectric push-pull actuators for inertial drives", *IEEE International Symposium on Micromechatronics and Human Science*, p. 309–316, 2003.

[BER 04] BERGANDER A., DRIESEN W., VARIDEL T., MEIZOSO M., BREGUET J., "Mobile cm3-microrobots with tools for nanoscale imaging and micromanipulation", *Proceedings of IEEE International Symposium on Micromechatronics and Human Science (MHS)*, Nagoya, Japan, p. 309–316, 2004.

[BOU 06] BOURLÈS H., *Systèmes Linéaires: de la Modélisation à la Commande*, Hermès–Lavoisier, 2006.

[BRE 98] BREGUET J., CLAVEL R., "Stick and slip actuators: design, control, performances and applications", *IEEE International Symposium on Micromechatronics and Human Science*, p. 89–95, 1998.

[DRI 03] DRIESEN W., BERGANDER A., VARIDEL T., BREGUET J., "Energy consumption of piezoelectric actuators for inertial drives", *IEEE International Symposium on Micromechatronics and Human Science*, p. 51–58, 2003.

[DUP 02] DUPONT P., HAYWARD V., ARMSTRONG B., ALTPETER F., "Single state elastoplastic friction models", *IEEE Transactions on Automatic Control*, vol. 47, num. 5, p. 787–792, 2002.

[FAT 95] FATIKOW S., MAGNUSSEN B., REMBOLD U., "A piezoelectric mobile robot for handling of micro-objects", *Proceedings of the International Symposium on Microsystems, Intelligent Materials and Robots*, p. 189–192, 1995.

[GAR 00] GARTNER C., BLUMEL V., KRAPLIN A., POSSNER T., "Micro-assembly processes for beam transformation systems of high-power laser diode bars", *MST news I*, p. 23–24, 2000.

[RAK 06] RAKOTONDRABE M., Design, development and modular control of a microassembly station, PhD thesis, University of Franche-Comté, 2006.

[RAK 08] RAKOTONDRABE M., HADDAB Y., LUTZ P., "Voltage/frequency proportional control of stick-slip micropositioning systems", *IEEE Transactions on Control Systems Technology*, vol. 16, num. 6, p. 1316–1322, 2008.

[RAK 09] RAKOTONDRABE M., HADDAB Y., LUTZ P., "Development, sub-step modelling and control of a micro/nano positioning 2DoF stick-slip device", *IEEE/ASME Transactions on Mechatronics*, 2009, DOI 10.1109/TMECH.2009.2011134.

[SED 03] SEDGHI B., Control design of hybrid systems via dehybridization, PhD thesis, Ecole Polytechnique Fédérale de Lausanne, Switzerland, 2003.

Chapter 2

Microbeam Dynamic Shaping by Closed-loop Electrostatic Actuation using Modal Control

A contribution to flexible microstructure control is developed in this chapter using large arrays of nanotransducers. The distributed transduction scheme consists of two sets of N electrodes located on each side of the microstructure for electrostatic driving and capacitive detection. Since accurate point-to-point control requires a large number of controllers, modal control is proposed to limit integration complexity. This is carried out by projecting the measured displacements on the n ($<< N$) modes to be controlled before calculating the stresses that must be distributed throughout the beam. Although simple PID control can be used, fabrication tolerances, parameter variations and model simplifications require robust specifications ensured by sophisticated control laws. An example of the combination of the Loop Transfer Recovery (LTR) method with the Full State Feedback (FSF) control extended standard models is presented, showing high robust stability and performances.

2.1. Introduction

Smart materials and intelligent structures are a new rapidly growing technology embracing the fields of sensor and actuator systems, information processing and control. They are capable of sensing and reacting to their environment in a predictable and desired manner and are used to carry mechanical loads, alleviate vibration, reduce acoustic noise, monitor their own condition and environment, automatically perform precision alignments or change their shape or mechanical properties on command.

Chapter written by Chady KHARRAT, Eric COLINET and Alina VODA.

While active structural control may be described as seeking a distributed control actuation such that a desired spatial distribution of the structure displacement is reached, in dynamic shape control the desired shape has to be additionally prescribed as a function of time.

In astronomical sciences, adaptive optical elements such as deformable mirrors used to correct for atmospheric aberrations provide a good example of shape control structures [LIA 97, ROO 02]. As the high cost of piezoelectric actuated mirrors prevented the broader adoption of this technology, deformable mirrors based on microelectromechanical systems (MEMS) have recently emerged [KEN 07]. These micromirrors are less costly and have enabled many new applications in bio-imaging including retina imaging, optical coherence tomography and wide-field microscopy. They were first used by [DRE 89] for a membrane mirror with 13 actuators in a scanning laser ophthalmoscope. More recently, adaptive aberration correction was investigated using membrane mirrors having 37 actuators [FER 03], while retinal images were obtained by a 140-actuator micromachined mirror [DOB 02].

It is highly desirable to suppress residual vibrations introduced in the mechanical structures by high-speed scanning motion and flexure actuation [POP 04]. In this context, the zero-vibration derivative method introduced by Singer and Seering [SIN 89] is well known. Other input-shaping work using a model-matching technique [POP 03] makes it possible to enforce realistic input and state constraints. This time-domain model-matching method is also used in [POP 04] to address the inverse control problem without using sensors for feedback. Moreover, other performances are required such as minimizing overshoot or following a certain motion profile. In optical switching systems, for example, the point-to-point motion of micromirrors used for redirecting optical signals has to be controlled. Typical settling times are of the order of a few milliseconds [CHI 00].

In recent years, a new MEMS actuation-sensing paradigm has been applied to control microstructures, particularly in aerospace and the automotive industry where microactuators, multistable relays, microconnectors and micropropulsion systems are used. Since fabrication technologies and processes have been developed and implemented, MEMS microstructures must be integrated with signal processing and controlling ICs and controllers must be designed [JUD 97, HO 98, LYS 99]. Point-to-point actuation and sensing performed by microstructures are not sufficient in such advanced applications. The real-time intelligent coordinated motion of microstructure arrays, a very challenging problem, is required to guarantee the desired surface deflections and geometries [LYS 01].

The application of multiscalar digital signal processors (DSPs) allows us to design distributed control systems to control MEMS arrays. Distributed embedded control systems offer several advantages since affordable systems can be designed using low-cost high-performance MEMS nodes. Energy and control signals are transmitted within the microdevices (actuators–sensors) through power, communication and control channels. The complexity of distributed systems is therefore greater than the complexity of centralized control systems [LYS 02].

Actuation mechanisms for MEMS vary depending on the suitability to the particular application. The most common actuation mechanisms are electrostatic, pneumatic, thermal and piezoelectric; electrostatic actuation is one of the most common principles in the field of MEMS [ABD 05], from simple RF microswitches [PAR 01] to high-precision adaptive micromirrors [VDO 01]. This is due to its simplicity, since it requires few mechanical components, and small voltage levels for actuation.

The structural elements that are used in MEMS devices are typically simple elements such as beams, plates and membranes. However, the fact that the pressure–voltage and displacement–pressure relationships are non-linear makes such MEMS very difficult to design accurately: the mechanical part of the device is most often described by linear models or simple non-linear models [WAN 96, DUF 99]. Some approaches to the design of electrostatic microactuators include: [HIS 93] in which a micromirror is fabricated with a three-dimensional (3D) thickness profile and allows an optically ideal deformation; and [HUN 98] in which the shape of an electrode is changed to achieve a particular voltage–capacitance relationship.

In [COL 05], the authors describe a method for calculating the voltage distribution necessary to achieve a given shape. They solve the non-linear mechanical inverse problem to calculate the ideal pressure distribution and then solve the quadratic programming problem to find the voltages that give the best approximation to this ideal pressure distribution. At the same time, piezoelectric (PZT) actuators have long been used in lightweight adaptive optics.

In [LIU 93] and [HUO 97], PZT actuators were bonded in optical mirrors to achieve designed surface shapes. Recently, as dynamic shape tracking has gained attention as well as integrating structural shape control and motion control, dynamic displacement tracking of smart beams has been studied using distributed self-stress/strain sensors and actuators [KRO 07] or piezoelectric types [IRS 02, IRS 06]. A sequential linear least-squares algorithm (SLLS) for tracking the dynamic shapes of PZT smart structures is formulated in [LUO 06]. In [LUO 07], an efficient algorithm for dynamic shape tracking with optimum energy control is proposed. [KAD 03] present an implementation of distributed optimal control strategy that limits the required data to only adjacent sensors.

Being different from vibration suppression or attenuation, dynamic shape tracking of smart flexible structures controls their designated dynamic movements, including deformation, vibration or other motion states over a given time period. However, important computational time and algorithms as well as complex controller networks remain the main problems of distributed active MEMS control.

In this chapter, we describe an automatic mode-based control method applied to electrostatically driven microstructures in order to accurately track a dynamic shape reference with fast time response, high robustness against parameter uncertainty and measurement noise reduction. A modal analysis describes the structure displacement shape by a few modal components that are to be controlled instead of the point-to-point control. This technique allows the number of required controllers to be reduced, especially when many transducers are used. Control design is carried out using two approaches: proportional integral derivative (PID) control and full state feedback (FSF) control. The main advantage of the former lies in the simplicity of its design and implementation, while the latter is superior in terms of robustness properties.

2.2. System description

Smart structures used in the literature are of several types and geometrical shape. The most popular are cantilevers, clamped-clamped beams and membranes. Since electrostatic actuation has the merits of low power consumption, simple driving electronics and ease of fabrication and integration, it has become one of the most popular driving methods; it offers integrated detection without the need for an additional position sensing device. In the example discussed in this chapter, a continuous deformable microbeam clamped on both extremities is considered. Two sets of N nanoelectrodes are disposed on both sides of the microbeam forming distributed electrode-to-structure capacitors that act as electromechanical transducers, transferring the energy between the electrical and mechanical domains (actuation and detection means). A view of the system is depicted in Figure 2.1.

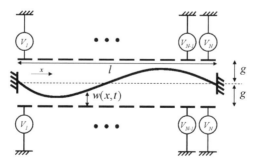

Figure 2.1. *Schematic view of the system*

When a voltage is applied to the electrode of position x_i along the beam, a local electrostatic force $f(x_i, t)$ is generated attracting the microbeam towards the electrode direction. For each position x_i, depending on the calculated control signal, the voltage is applied to one of the two electrodes on either side according to the sign of the required force. The commutation of the drive electrodes is accomplished by a multiplexing system as depicted in Figure 2.1. The first-order approximate relation expressing the electrostatic force on position x_i as a function of the electrode voltage V_i applied to the corresponding electrode is:

$$f(x_i, t) = \frac{\epsilon_0 S_e V_i^2}{2(g - w(x_i, t))^2} \tag{2.1}$$

where S_e is the area of the electrode, ϵ_0 is the permittivity in vacuum, g is the initial gap between the microbeam and the electrode and $w(x_i, t)$ is the transverse displacement of the microbeam at position x_i. The latter is measured by capacitive means which consists of detecting an output current, dependent upon the electrode-to-resonator capacitance, as a function of the microbeam displacement. The first-order approximate equation expressing this capacitance to the displacement is

$$C(x_i, t) = \frac{\epsilon_0 S_e}{2(g - w(x_i, t))}. \tag{2.2}$$

In previous research, actuation and capacitive sensing are implemented through separate physical structures [CHA 95, HOR 00, KUI 04] which increase the overall size of the device, modify its mechanical characteristics and add flexural structures that reduce the displacement range of the system. It is therefore more advantageous to use the same capacitive structure for both actuation and sensing purposes.

When tracking static deformations or low-frequency dynamical shapes, the capacitive detection becomes more problematic because no current flow is obtained for low or null frequencies. However, since the mechanical device behaves as a superposition of modal low-pass filters (as described in the next section), a low input signal with frequency orders of magnitude higher than the mechanical modal frequencies can be used as a sensing signal without evoking mechanical response. Electrically, this sensing signal experiences amplitude and phase modulation due to the capacitance change of the drive (function of the mechanical displacement). By monitoring it, a measure of the displacement is inferred [DON 08]. Figure 2.2 shows the displacement measurement scheme of simultaneous actuating/sensing capacitive drives.

One of the persistent problems is the noise added to the measured output signals due to the electric measurement circuitries and the ADC converters. The smaller the sensing electrode surfaces, the smaller the measured capacitances with the same electric noise, decreasing the signal-to-noise ratio. In the studied system, this results when a high number of electrodes are used to generate continuously distributed local forces and to detect continuous deformation along the microstructure, allowing more accurate reference tracking and improving the detection resolution. In addition, using

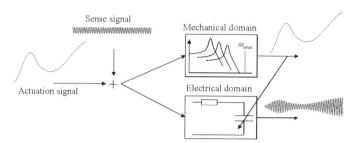

Figure 2.2. *Displacement measurement scheme on simultaneous actuating/detection capacitive drives*

many electrodes adds to the complexity of fabrication, miniaturization and control computation for the point-by-point classical control methods.

2.3. Modal analysis

The out-of-plane time-dependent transverse displacement $w(x, t)$ of the micro-beam at every position x is governed by the Euler–Bernoulli equation. By considering a beam of length l, thickness e and width h, we can describe its deformation behavior when subjected to an external distributed strength $f(x, t)$ by:

$$EI\frac{\partial^4 w(x,t)}{\partial x^4} + T(w(x,t))\frac{\partial^2 w(x,t)}{\partial x^2} + b\frac{\partial w(x,t)}{\partial t} + \rho S\frac{\partial^2 w(x,t)}{\partial t^2} = f(x,t) \quad (2.3)$$

where $S = he$ is the transversal section of the beam, E is Young's modulus, $I = e^3 h/12$ is the moment of inertia, ρ is density, b is the friction coefficient of interaction with the surrounding fluid and $T(w(x, t))$ is the stress associated with the beam elongation.

We associate boundary conditions of the structure with equation (2.3). Most often, in the MEMS field, the boundary conditions are defined by one of the two states:

– free edge: $w'' = w''' = 0$,

– clamped edge: $w = w' = 0$.

A schematic 3D representation of the clamped-clamped microbeam is shown in Figure 2.3.

A solution of equation (2.3) can be found by decomposing $w(x, t)$ on the eigenmodes of the operator $\partial^4/\partial x^4$, that is

$$w(x,t) = \sum_{k=1}^{n} a_k(t)w_k(x) \qquad (2.4)$$

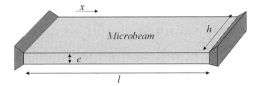

Figure 2.3. *Clamped-clamped microbeam illustrating the dimension variables l, e and h*

where

$$\frac{\partial^4 w(x)}{\partial x^4} = \lambda_k^4 w_k(x), \tag{2.5}$$

and where $w_k(x)$ are the n eigenvectors (also called mode shape vectors), λ_k^4 are the corresponding eigenvalues and $a_k(t)$ are the dynamic corresponding modal coefficients.

A solution of equation (2.5) is

$$w_k = A\cos(\lambda_k x) + B\sin(\lambda_k x) + C\cosh(\lambda_k x) + D\sinh(\lambda_k x) \tag{2.6}$$

where A, B, C and D are four constants that depend on the boundary conditions. Considering our clamped-clamped case, we have

$$\begin{cases} w_k(0) = 0 \\ w_k'(0) = 0 \\ w_k(l) = 0 \\ w_k'(l) = 0 \end{cases} \Leftrightarrow \begin{cases} A + C = 0 \\ B + D = 0 \\ A\cos(\lambda_k l) + B\sin(\lambda_k l) + C\cosh(\lambda_k l) + C\sinh(\lambda_k l) = 0 \\ -A\sin(\lambda_k l) + B\cos(\lambda_k l) + C\sinh(\lambda_k l) + C\cosh(\lambda_k l) = 0. \end{cases} \tag{2.7}$$

A non-trivial solution of this system of equations is obtained by solving the determinant of the system

$$\begin{vmatrix} \cos(\lambda_k l) - \sin(\lambda_k l) & \sin(\lambda_k l) - \sinh(\lambda_k l) \\ -\sin(\lambda_k l) - \sinh(\lambda_k l) & \cos(\lambda_k l) - \cosh(\lambda_k l) \end{vmatrix} = 0$$

$$\Rightarrow \cos(\lambda_k l)\cosh(\lambda_k l) = 1, \tag{2.8}$$

which gives

$$\lambda_k l = \begin{bmatrix} 4.73 & 7.85 & 10.99 & 14.13 & 17.27 & \dots \end{bmatrix}. \tag{2.9}$$

The eigenvectors $w_k(x)$ become

$$
w_k(x) = A_k \left[\cos(\lambda_k x) - \frac{\cos(\lambda_k l) - \cosh(\lambda_k l)}{\sin(\lambda_k l) - \sinh(\lambda_k l)} \sin(\lambda_k x) - \cosh(\lambda_k x) \right.
$$
$$
\left. + \frac{\cos(\lambda_k l) - \cosh(\lambda_k l)}{\sin(\lambda_k l) - \sinh(\lambda_k l)} \sinh(\lambda_k x) \right] = A_k \varphi_k(x)
$$
(2.10)

and form an orthogonal basis for the scalar product

$$
\langle u | v \rangle = \int_0^l u(x)v(x)\,dx.
$$
(2.11)

To obtain an orthormal basis, A_k is chosen such that

$$
A_k = \left(\int_0^l \varphi_k^2(x)dx \right)^{-1/2}.
$$
(2.12)

Considering equations (2.4) and (2.5), equation (2.3) can be written as

$$
\sum_{k=1}^{n} \left(EI a_k \lambda_k^4 w_k(x) + T(w)a_k \frac{\partial^2 w_k(x)}{\partial x^2} + b w_k(x)\dot{a}_k + \rho S w_k(x)\ddot{a}_k \right)
$$
$$
= \sum_{k=1}^{n} f_k w(x)
$$
(2.13)

where f_k are the components of the distributed force on each mode k. Note that the beam elongation $T(w)$ is independent of the position x.

Figure 2.4 shows the modal shapes of the five first modes of a clamped-clamped microbeam of length $l = 5\,\mu m$.

Projecting equation (2.13) on each eigenvector w_i ($i = 1 \rightarrow n$), taking into consideration the orthogonality of the basis, yields N equations of the form

$$
EI a_i \lambda_i^4 + T(w) \sum_{k=1}^{n} a_k \left\langle \frac{\partial^2 w_k}{\partial x^2} \middle| w_i \right\rangle + b\dot{a}_i + \rho S \ddot{a}_i = f_i.
$$
(2.14)

These n equations represent the equations of motion of the N modal coefficients a_i in relation to their corresponding force modal component f_i, and they can be written in a matrix form as

$$
KX + N(X) + B\dot{X} + M\ddot{X} = F
$$
(2.15)

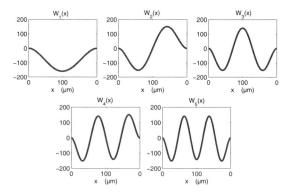

Figure 2.4. *First five modal shapes of the clamped-clamped microbeam*

where

$$
X = \begin{bmatrix} a_1(t) \\ a_2(t) \\ \vdots \\ a_n(t) \end{bmatrix}, \quad
F = \begin{bmatrix} f_1(t) \\ f_2(t) \\ \vdots \\ f_n(t) \end{bmatrix}, \quad
K = EI \begin{bmatrix} \lambda_1^4 & 0 & \cdots & 0 \\ 0 & \lambda_2^4 & & \vdots \\ \vdots & & \ddots & 0 \\ 0 & \cdots & 0 & \lambda_n^4 \end{bmatrix},
$$

$B = bI_n$ and $M = \rho S I_n$, where I_n is the identity matrix of size n. $N(X) = T(w)AX$, where

$$
A = \begin{bmatrix} \left\langle \frac{\partial^2 w_1}{\partial x^2} \middle| w_1 \right\rangle & \cdots & \left\langle \frac{\partial^2 w_n}{\partial x^2} \middle| w_1 \right\rangle \\ \vdots & \ddots & \vdots \\ \left\langle \frac{\partial^2 w_n}{\partial x^2} \middle| w_1 \right\rangle & \cdots & \left\langle \frac{\partial^2 w_n}{\partial x^2} \middle| w_n \right\rangle \end{bmatrix}.
$$

The stress due to the small elongation Δl of the microbeam is expressed as

$$
T(w) = ES \frac{\Delta l}{l} \tag{2.16}
$$

where

$$
\Delta l = \frac{1}{2} \int_0^l \left(\frac{\partial w(x,t)}{\partial x} \right)^2 dx. \tag{2.17}
$$

Equation (2.16) becomes

$$
T(w) = \frac{ES}{2l} \int_0^l \left(\sum_{k=1}^N a_k \frac{\partial w_k}{\partial x} \right)^2 dx \tag{2.18}
$$

which gives

$$T(w) = \frac{ES}{2l} \int_0^l \sum_{k=1}^{n} \sum_{l=1}^{n} a_k \frac{\partial w_k}{\partial x} \frac{\partial w_l}{\partial x} a_l \, dx. \tag{2.19}$$

Given that

$$\forall i, j \le n, \quad \int_0^l \frac{\partial w_i}{\partial x} \frac{\partial w_j}{\partial x} dx = - \int_0^l \frac{\partial^2 w_i}{\partial x^2} w_j dx,$$

the stress can be described in a matrix representation as

$$T(w) = \frac{-ES}{2l} X^T A X \tag{2.20}$$

leading to the non-linear term

$$N(X) = \frac{-ES}{2l} \left(X^T A X \right) AX. \tag{2.21}$$

2.4. Mode-based control

As mentioned in section 2.1, smart structures are usually used to track a reference shape or deformation which can be represented by a set of reference displacements along the microstructure surface. This reference can be static or dynamic (or null in the case of vibrations suppression).

For the microbeam example described in section 2.2, the reference shape is described by a 1D vector of N displacements on N positions along the microbeam length corresponding to the centers of the actuating/sensing electrodes. In the literature, many MEMS devices are typically driven in an open-loop fashion by applying simple input control signals. Modifying and improving the mechanical design of MEMS actuators have resulted in more suitable straightforward driving signals. Pre-shaped control is also adopted to achieve better dynamical performance when knowledge of system dynamics is available. However, the lack of accurate models, fabrication inconsistencies, parameter variation, external disturbances and dynamical behavior specifications call for the use of closed-loop control design.

The most critical problem of closed-loop approach is the complexity of the whole system and controllers integration issue. In the case of a point-to-point microstructure shape control, we might need a huge network of simple local controllers or one complicated controller difficult to implement in the case of centralized control. This problem becomes more obvious when increasing the number of actuating electrodes for better approximation of continuous deformation case.

One solution to this problem is to control only the dynamic modal coefficients instead of the direct displacements. The number of the required controllers will therefore be limited to a few modes independently of the actuators number. The number n of the controlled modes is fixed by the required reference shapes considered (in our case) as a linear combination of the five first modes, believed to comprise sufficient deformation shapes for one microbeam. When regulating all $a_k(t)$ to their reference values $\bar{a}_k(t)$ for $k = 1 \to n$, the shape deformation $w(x_i, t)$ tracks the reference $\bar{w}(x_i, t) = \sum_1^n \bar{a}_k(t) w_k(x_i)$.

The architecture of the closed-loop system using modal control is depicted in Figure 2.5.

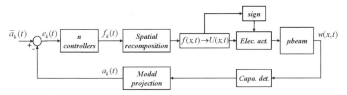

Figure 2.5. *Closed-loop system using modal control*

By using modal control, we will be dealing with the modal equations of motion represented in equation (2.15), avoiding the (equation (2.3)) non-linear coupled point-to-point displacements. These modal equations of motion are assumed to be linear for small displacements, neglecting the modes-coupling term resulting from elongation stresses. In this case, the equations in matrix equation (2.15) describe the behavior of n linear uncoupled second-order mass-spring-damping systems with known parameters of stiffness, mass and damping coefficient. Hence, shape tracking dynamics can be fixed by control.

Basically, two types of time-varying functions for smart structure deflections are considered: the triangular and the sinusoidal [LUO 06, LUO 07]. In this chapter, two methods of control design are adopted: PID control based on the tracking errors and FSF control based on all the states of a so-called 'standard model'. In both approaches, displacement measures are projected on the five modes to obtain the modal coefficients $a_k(t)$ and controller outputs are expressed by modal force coefficients $f_k(t)$, used to recompose the required distributed force to be applied to the microbeam:

$$f(x_i, t) = \sum_{k=1}^n f_k(t) w_k(x_i). \tag{2.22}$$

Considering small reference displacements relative to the gap g, the amplitudes of the control voltages to be distributed on the N electrodes are calculated as

$$u(x_i, t) = g\sqrt{\frac{2\,|f(x_i, t)|}{\epsilon_0 S_e}}. \tag{2.23}$$

Even though the generated force that depends on $w(x_i, t)$ is not exactly the same as the desired $f(x_i, t)$, this expression simplifies the computation of the control signal $u(x_i, t)$. The advantage to this is that the limitation of data communication within the controller and the decrease of the measurement noise affect the controlled system outputs.

2.4.1. *PID control*

PID control, attractive due to its simple design procedure as well as practical implementation, is directly applied to the tracking errors. Consider the modal tracking errors

$$e_k(t) = a_k(t) - \bar{a}_k(t). \tag{2.24}$$

Using a PID controller, the control force for each mode k is found from

$$f_k(t) = P_k\left(e_k(t) + \frac{\int e_k(t)dt}{I_k} + D_k\dot{e}_k(t)\right) \tag{2.25}$$

where P_k, I_k and D_k are the proportional, integral and derivative gain weighting, respectively. Thus, for each mode k, the controller's transfer function is described by

$$K_k(s) = P_k\left[1 + \frac{1}{I_k s} + D_k s\right]. \tag{2.26}$$

For reasons of feasibility, the pure derivative action $D_k s$ is replaced by a filter of the form $D_k s/(1 + D_k s/N)$. The transfer functions relating each dynamic modal coefficient a_k to f_k are extracted from the equations of motion in equation (2.15) and are represented by

$$G_k(s) = \frac{1}{ms^2 + bs + k_k} \tag{2.27}$$

where $k_k = EI\lambda_k^4$.

For modes tracking dynamics characterized by a damping coefficient ζ_d and a natural pulsation w_d, the desired closed-loop transfer functions relating the modal coefficients a_k to their references are expressed:

$$H_k(s) = \frac{w_d^2}{s^2 + 2\zeta_d w_d s + w_d^2}. \tag{2.28}$$

Hence, the PID parameters must be chosen such that

$$
\begin{cases}
P_k = \frac{\omega_d I_k k_k}{2\zeta_d} \\
I_k = b/k_k - \frac{1}{2\zeta_d \omega_d} \\
D_k = \frac{m/k_k}{I_k} - \frac{1}{2\zeta_d \omega_d} \\
\frac{D_k}{N_k} = \frac{1}{2\zeta_d \omega_d}.
\end{cases}
\tag{2.29}
$$

ω_d and ζ_d define the bandwidth of the closed-loop system (i.e. response time), the overshoot factor and the error oscillations. These specifications can be improved by choosing high ω_d and $\zeta_d = 1$. On the other hand, however, this amplifies the noise effect on the output displacements and on the input control voltages. A compromise must therefore be made. Since the controller design is based on desired tracking performance, disturbance rejection is not optimized.

Although PID control guarantees nominal stability and performances, some problems cannot be resolved unless sophisticated control design is used. In fact, due to fabrication tolerances of microscale structures, the designer is always confronted by modeling uncertainty and mechanical non-linearities are neglected. For this reason, robust control method becomes crucial. In the next section, a combination of a FSF control and loop-transfer-recovery (LTR) method is described, which guarantees robust performances and the stability of the closed-loop system.

2.4.2. FSF-LTR control

FSF control is well adapted for shape tracking of known reference types. It is applied to an extended so-called standard model which takes into consideration the exogenous states defined by the reference and the disturbance. This is carried out using the regulator problem with internal stability (RPIS) principle considered by Wonham [WON 85], which guarantees nominal performance and stability of the closed-loop system. Since this type of controller assumes knowledge of all the standard model states, estimators are needed. Performance and stability properties can therefore be lost when full state feedback is replaced by state estimate feedback.

One of the most popular ways of designing robust regulators (controller and observer) is to use the well-known LTR technique. This consists of choosing an appropriate parameterization of the compensator design, in order to recover a robust target loop [LAR 99].

The vibrating shape reference is described by a combination of modal dynamic coefficients sinusoidally varying in time with frequency $\bar{\omega}$. For each mode k, a state-space standard model is defined describing the system behavior as well as the behavior of the reference states. To take into consideration possible constant disturbance actions on the input force, the disturbance state d is also added to the standard model. This is written

$$
\begin{bmatrix} \dot{a}_k \\ \ddot{a}_k \\ \dot{d} \\ \dot{\bar{a}}_k \\ \ddot{\bar{a}}_k \end{bmatrix} = \begin{bmatrix} 0 & 1 & 0 & 0 & 0 \\ -k_k/m & -b/m & 1/m & 0 & 0 \\ 0 & 0 & 0 & 0 & 0 \\ 0 & 0 & 0 & 0 & 1 \\ 0 & 0 & 0 & -\omega^2 & 0 \end{bmatrix} \begin{bmatrix} a_k \\ \dot{a}_k \\ d \\ \bar{a}_k \\ \dot{\bar{a}}_k \end{bmatrix} + \begin{bmatrix} 0 \\ 1/m \\ 0 \\ 0 \\ 0 \end{bmatrix} f_k,
$$

$$
e_k = \begin{bmatrix} -1 & 0 & 0 & 1 & 0 \end{bmatrix} \begin{bmatrix} a_k \\ \dot{a}_k \\ d \\ \bar{a}_k \\ \dot{\bar{a}}_k \end{bmatrix} = \bar{a}_k - a_k, \tag{2.30}
$$

$$
y_k = \begin{bmatrix} 1 & 0 & 0 & 0 & 0 \\ 0 & 0 & 0 & 1 & 0 \end{bmatrix} \begin{bmatrix} a_k \\ \dot{a}_k \\ d \\ \bar{a}_k \\ \dot{\bar{a}}_k \end{bmatrix} = \begin{bmatrix} a_k \\ \bar{a}_k \end{bmatrix},
$$

where e_k are the tracking errors and y_k are the observed outputs which include the measured displacements and the references for each mode k.

More generally, this standard model is written

$$
\begin{bmatrix} \dot{x}_1 \\ \dot{x}_2 \end{bmatrix} = \begin{bmatrix} A_{11} & A_{12} \\ 0 & A_{22} \end{bmatrix} \begin{bmatrix} x_1 \\ x_2 \end{bmatrix} + \begin{bmatrix} B_1 \\ 0 \end{bmatrix} u,
$$

$$
e = \begin{bmatrix} C_{e_1} & C_{e_2} \end{bmatrix} \begin{bmatrix} x_1 \\ x_2 \end{bmatrix}, \tag{2.31}
$$

$$
y = \begin{bmatrix} C_{y_1} & C_{y_2} \end{bmatrix} \begin{bmatrix} x_1 \\ x_2 \end{bmatrix},
$$

where x_1 are the system states, x_2 are the exogenous states, u is the control signal, e the tracking errors and y the observed outputs. Finding a regulator that ensures e tends towards 0 for any initial conditions and guarantees the closed-loop stability is referred to as the regulator problem with internal stability (RPIS).

The following conditions must be satisfied:

$$
- \left(\begin{bmatrix} C_e \\ C_y \end{bmatrix}, \begin{bmatrix} A_{11} & A_{12} \\ 0 & A_{22} \end{bmatrix} \right) \text{ is observable;}
$$

$- (A_{11}, B_1)$ is stabilizable; and

– A_{22} is unstable.

It has been proven in [WON 85] that the FSF static controller, defined

$$F = \begin{bmatrix} F_1 & F_1 T_a + F_a \end{bmatrix}, \qquad (2.32)$$

guarantees the nominal stability of the closed-loop system as well as nominal reference tracking and disturbance rejection (nominal performances). F_1 is chosen such that $A_{11} + B_1 F_1$ is stable and $\left(F_a \in \Re^{1 \times 3}, T_a \in \Re^{2 \times 3} \right)$ are the solutions of the equations:

$$\begin{cases} -A_{11} T_a + T_a A_{22} + A_{12} = -B_1 F_a \\ \qquad -C_{e_1} T_a + C_{e_2} = 0. \end{cases} \qquad (2.33)$$

This leads to

$$T_a = \begin{bmatrix} 0 & -1 & 0 \\ 0 & 0 & 1 \end{bmatrix}$$

and

$$F_a = \begin{bmatrix} -1 & m\bar{\omega}^2 - k_k & b \end{bmatrix}.$$

As the number of reference and disturbance states included in the standard model is greater than the number of the measured outputs, robust performances are obtained. This is referred to as the 'sufficient duplication principle' in [LAR 00].

As the FSF assumes a complete knowledge of all the standard model states, an observer Q is required because displacement velocities and external disturbances are not measured. The global controller/observer structure is depicted in Figure 2.6 and is described:

$$\begin{cases} u = \begin{bmatrix} F_1 & F_1 T_a + F_a \end{bmatrix} \begin{bmatrix} \hat{x}_1 \\ \hat{x}_2 \end{bmatrix} \\ \begin{bmatrix} \dot{\hat{x}}_1 \\ \dot{\hat{x}}_2 \end{bmatrix} = \begin{bmatrix} A_{11} & A_{12} \\ 0 & A_{22} \end{bmatrix} \begin{bmatrix} \hat{x}_1 \\ \hat{x}_2 \end{bmatrix} + \begin{bmatrix} B_1 \\ 0 \end{bmatrix} u + \begin{bmatrix} Q_1 \\ Q_2 \end{bmatrix} (y - \hat{y}) \quad (2.34) \\ \hat{y} = \begin{bmatrix} C_{y_1} & C_{y_2} \end{bmatrix} \begin{bmatrix} \hat{x}_1 \\ \hat{x}_2 \end{bmatrix}, \end{cases}$$

where $\hat{x}$ and $\hat{y}$ are the estimated states and outputs, respectively.

Let

$$A = \begin{bmatrix} A_{11} & A_{12} \\ 0 & A_{22} \end{bmatrix},$$

$$B = \begin{bmatrix} B_1 \\ 0 \end{bmatrix},$$

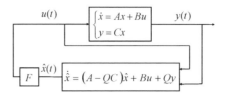

Figure 2.6. *Closed-loop control system*

$$C = \begin{bmatrix} C_{y_1} & C_{y_2} \end{bmatrix},$$

and

$$Q = \begin{bmatrix} Q_1 \\ Q_2 \end{bmatrix}.$$

We can guarantee that $\hat{e} = x - \hat{x} \to 0$ when choosing Q such that $A - QC$ is stable.

Although nominal stability of the closed loop is guaranteed, microstructure control always calls for robustness. In fact, parameter variation with environmental conditions, fabrication errors and neglect of mechanical non-linearities may cause stability loss if the transfer loop set by the observer-based control shows low phase and gain margins, even when robust specifications are considered in controller design. This is because additional observers used for full states estimation modify the loop transfer function $L(j\omega)$ on which the closed-loop stability depends, defined

$$L(j\omega) = -(G(s)K(s))_{11} \tag{2.35}$$

where $G(s) = C(sI - A)^{-1}B$ and $K(s) = F(sI - A - BF + QC)^{-1}Q$.

To overcome this problem, the LTR technique is used. Classically, the first step of the LTR design procedure consists of defining a target loop $L_{\text{tar}}(j\omega)$ which has desirable properties in terms of stability margins. The second step consists of minimizing the difference between the loop of the observer-based control system and the target loop [LAR 99].

In fact, the only regulator that exactly restores the target loop has a non-proper form (the numerator order is higher than the denominator order), presenting a derivative action that amplifies the output noise influence on the control signals. For this reason, asymptotic LTR is applied which consists of simply approaching $L_{\text{tar}}(j\omega)$ without reaching it. In the primal LTR approach, the controller design fixes $L_{\text{tar}}(j\omega)$ and the observer poles are chosen such that recovery is carried out. In the dual LTR approach, however, the observer design fixes the target loop and controller poles are chosen for recovery.

In our control design, the second approach is used. In addition, instead of one complete multivariable observer, two separate observers must be designed: one for the system plus disturbance states and one for the reference states, leading to two separate monovariable subsystems.

In this case, the target loop is defined

$$L_{\text{tar}}(j\omega) = C_{sd}\left(sI - A_{sd}\right)^{-1}Q_{sd} \tag{2.36}$$

where C_{sd}, A_{sd} and Q_{sd} are the parts of C, A and Q related to the system and the disturbance states.

To guarantee robustness specifications for the target loop, we must choose the i poles of the closed loop p_{c_i} such that $\forall i$ and $\forall \omega$, $|j\omega - p_{c_i}| \geq |j\omega - p_{o_i}|$, where p_{o_i} are the poles of the open-loop system. It follows that the target sensitivity of the closed-loop system $S_{\text{tar}}(j\omega)$ inevitably satisfies the inequality:

$$|S_{\text{tar}}(j\omega)| = \frac{\prod_i |j\omega - p_{o_i}|}{\prod_i |j\omega - p_{c_i}|} \leq 1, \; \forall \omega. \tag{2.37}$$

Thus, the loop transfer function $|L_{\text{tar}}(j\omega)|$ satisfies

$$|1 + L_{\text{tar}}(j\omega)| = \frac{1}{|S_{\text{tar}}(j\omega)|} \geq 1, \quad \forall \omega. \tag{2.38}$$

This means that $\forall \omega$, $L_{\text{tar}}(j\omega)$ is outside the circle of radius 1 and centered at -1 (see Figure 2.7), which guarantees the properties:

– gain margin ≥ 6 dB and

– phase margin $\geq 60°$.

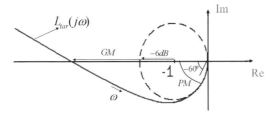

Figure 2.7. *Nyquist plot of a loop transfer with robust stability margins*

A robust poles placement strategy is proposed in [LAR 96] and defines a scaling parameter T_o which represents an image of the response time in a closed loop. The strategy is applied following three steps:

1) Place the unstable open-loop poles (real parts strictly positive) symmetrically with respect to the imaginary axis.

2) Project the open-loop poles, as well as those resulting from the first step, on the vertical axis fixed on $-1/T_o$ when these poles are placed on the right side of this axis.

3) For closed-loop poles, choose the open-loop poles unmodified placed on the left side of the axis $-1/T_o$, plus those resulting from steps (1) and (2).

Increasing T_o improves the stability margins but this leads to increased control signals and actuators solicitation. For smaller T_o, however, $p_{c_i} \rightarrow \infty$ creating faster dynamics. The poles placement strategy is illustrated in Figure 2.8. On the other hand, the poles of the reference states separate observer are chosen to be faster than the reference variation frequency $\bar{\omega}$ in order to guarantee an accurate reference estimation that does not affect the tracking dynamics. Once the target loop is fixed by the observer gains, the second step of the dual LTR consists of selecting the controller F_1 in such a way that the loop transfer function represented in equation (2.35) approaches $L_{\text{tar}}(j\omega)$.

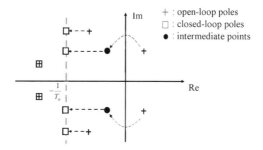

Figure 2.8. *Robust closed-loop poles placement strategy*

It has been proven by Saberi *et al.* [SAB 93] that this asymptotic recovery can be obtained when choosing the controller poles such that n_z poles tend towards the n_z zeroes of the open-loop system, and the rest towards infinity, when a scalar σ tends towards 0. A controller poles placement strategy based on the dual LTR rule is proposed in [LAR 96] and defines a scaling parameter T_c that represents an image of the recovery scalar coefficient σ.

The strategy is applied in four steps:

1) Place the unstable open-loop zeroes (real parts strictly positive) symmetrically with respect to the imaginary axis.

2) Project the open-loop zeroes as well as those resulting from step (1) on the vertical axis fixed at $-1/T_c$, when these poles are placed on the left side of this axis.

3) For controller poles, choose the open-loop zeroes unmodified placed on the right side of the axis $-1/T_c$ plus those resulting from steps (1) and (2).

4) Place the remaining controller poles on $-1/T_c$.

When $T_c \rightarrow 0$ and for minimum phase systems, exact recovery can be reached; at the same time, however, the output noise is dramatically amplified. The controller poles placement strategy is illustrated in Figure 2.9. The control scheme is applied to a microbeam with dimensions and mechanical characteristics listed in Table 2.1.

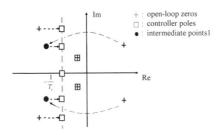

Figure 2.9. *Controller poles placement strategy*

System parameters	Values
l	$100\,\mu\text{m}$
h	$1\,\text{nm}$
e	$0.1\,\text{nm}$
g	$1\,\text{nm}$
m	$2.23 \times 10^{-14}\,\text{kg}\,\text{m}^{-1}$
b	$2.5 \times 10^{-7}\,\text{N}\,\text{m}^{-1}\,\text{s}$
k_1	$70\,\text{N}\,\text{m}^{-1}$
k_2	$535\,\text{N}\,\text{m}^{-1}$
k_3	$2058\,\text{N}\,\text{m}^{-1}$
k_4	$5625\,\text{N}\,\text{m}^{-1}$
k_5	$12,553\,\text{N}\,\text{m}^{-1}$
n	5
N	1000

Table 2.1. *System characteristics and dimensions*

The reference shape, depicted in Figure 2.10, is described by the first five modal coefficients which vary sinusoidally in time at a frequency $\bar{\omega}/2\pi = 0.1\,\text{MHz}$ with amplitudes $\bar{a}_1 = 3 \times 10^{-11}$, $\bar{a}_2 = 2.5 \times 10^{-11}$, $\bar{a}_3 = 2 \times 10^{-11}$, $\bar{a}_4 = 1.5 \times 10^{-11}$ and $\bar{a}_5 = 1 \times 10^{-11}$.

The reference observer poles are set at $-10^6 \pm j\bar{\omega}$. Note that achieving robust properties and high performance simultaneously is very difficult. We choose $T_o^{(k)} =$

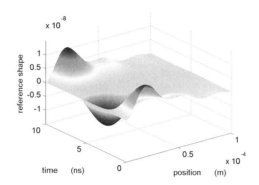

Figure 2.10. *Shape reference evolution in time (see color section)*

5×10^{-7} and $T_c^{(k)} = T_o^{(k)}/10$ in order to achieve the best compromise. The dynamical variation of the modal reference coefficients compared to the outputs is depicted in Figure 2.11, showing efficient reference tracking and accurate rejection of the modal disturbances d_k added to the input forces.

The distribution of the microbeam displacements and the control voltages on a fixed instant t are depicted in Figure 2.12. Robust performances and stability are depicted in Figure 2.13, considering a dispersion of 50% on modal stiffness values k_k.

Noise reduction is shown in Figure 2.14, where a capacitive white noise of power spectral density equal to 2.8×10^{-6} aF Hz$^{0.5}$ is considered on displacement output measures within a bandwidth of 0.1 GHz.

2.5. Conclusion

Modal control is an interesting method to address intelligent structures, especially when actuator/sensor arrays are used. It replaces the point-to-point control strategy by few modes control, reducing the complexity and the size of the controllers. Although modal control can be associated with almost all actuation/sensing schemes, electrostatic drive and capacitive detection remain the most common method of practical implementation on microsystem control schemes.

Since modal analysis allows the system to be described by a simple combination of linear modes models, well-known control theories can be applied to fix the closed-loop desired tracking dynamics as in shape tracking systems. Many issues must be taken into consideration in control design, such as parameter variation, modeling

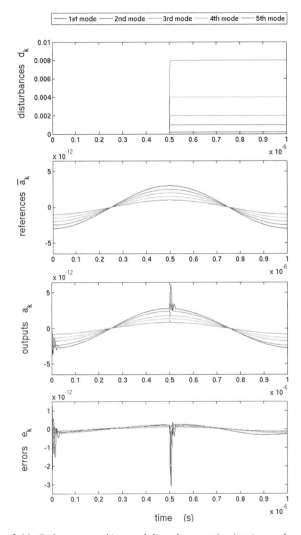

Figure 2.11. *Reference tracking and disturbance rejection (see color section)*

uncertainties, mechanical and electronics noise, eventual disturbances and response time. Even if simple PID controllers ensure desired tracking dynamics and nominal performances, the control approach fails when the system is slightly modified. The FSF control method using the RPIS principle and robust poles placement, followed by the LTR technique, demonstrates high robustness properties in both performance and stability.

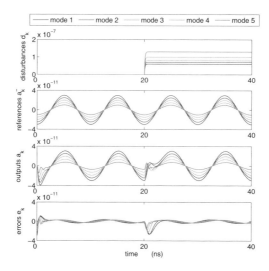

Figure 2.12. *Microbeam shape and control voltages on instant t (see color section)*

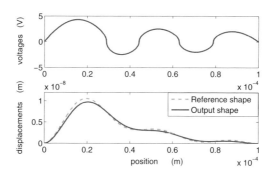

Figure 2.13. *Robust reference tracking and disturbance rejection with 50% dispersion on k_k*

Actuator and sensor arrays are used to control only one microstructure in this chapter. Nevertheless, based on the same analysis, modal control can be expanded to a coupled nanostructure array with separate transducers. This transition from MEMS to NEMS systems opens up the field to many new possibilities, such as parallel nanopositioning, nanometrology and high nanosensing resolution.

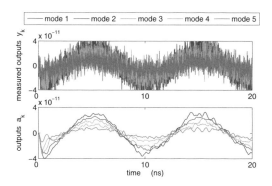

Figure 2.14. *Noise reduction on outputs (see color section)*

2.6. Bibliography

[ABD 05] ABDALLA M., REDDY C., FARIS W., GÜRDAL Z., "Optimal design of an electrostatically actuated microbeam for maximum pull-in voltage", *Computers & Structures*, vol. 83, num. 15–16, p. 1320–1329, 2005.

[CHA 95] CHAU K.-L., LEWIS S., ZHAO Y., HOWE R., BART S., MARCHESELLI R., "An integrated force-balanced capacitive accelerometer for low-G applications", *Proceedings of the 8th International Conference on Solid-State Sensors and Actuators and Eurosensors IX*, vol. 1, 25–29 June 1995, p. 593–596, 1995.

[CHI 00] CHIOU J.-C., LIN Y.-C., CHANG Y.-C., "Dynamic characteristics measurement system for optical scanning micromirror", *Society of Photo-Optical Instrumentation Engineers (SPIE) Conference Series, Micromachining and Microfabrication*, vol. 4230, 28–30 November 2000, p. 180–186, 2000.

[COL 05] COLINET E., JUILLARD J., "2D deformation of arbitrarily-shaped membranes by means of electrostatic actuation", *Proceedings of the Symposium on Design, Test, Integration and Packaging on MEMS/MOEMS*, 1–3 June 2005, p. 331–335, 2005.

[DOB 02] DOBLE N., YOON G., CHEN L., BIERDEN P., SINGER B., OLIVIER S., WILLIAMS D., "Use of a microelectromechanical mirror for adaptive optics in the human eye", *Optics Letters*, vol. 27, num. 17, p. 1537–1539, 2002.

[DON 08] DONG J., FERREIRA P., "Simultaneous actuation and displacement sensing for electrostatic drives", *J. Micromech. Microeng.*, vol. 18, num. 3, p. 1–10, 2008.

[DRE 89] DREHER A., BILLE J., WEINREB R., "Active optical depth resolution improvement of the laser tomographic scanner", *Applied Optics*, vol. 28, num. 4, p. 804–808, 1989.

[DUF 99] DUFFOUR I., SARRAUTE E., "Analytical modeling of beam behavior under different actuations: profile and stress expressions", *Journal of Modeling and Simulation of Microsystems*, vol. 1, p. 57–64, 1999.

[FER 03] FERNANDEZ E., ARTAL P., "Membrane deformable mirror for adaptive optics: performance limits in visual optics", *Optic Express*, vol. 11, num. 9, p. 1056–1069, 2003.

[HIS 93] HISANAGA M., KOUMURA T., HATTORI T., "Fabrication of 3-dimensionally shaped Si diaphragm dynamic focusing mirror", *Proceedings of the IEEE conference on Micro Electro Mechanical Systems (MEMS'93), An Investigation of Micro Structures, Sensors, Actuators, Machines and Systems*, 7-10 February 1993, p. 30–35, 1993.

[HO 98] HO C.-M., TAI Y.-C., "Micro-electro-mechanical-systems (MEMS) and fluid flows", *Annual Review of Fluid Mechanics*, vol. 30, num. 1, p. 579–612, 1998.

[HOR 00] HORENSTEIN M., PERREAULT J., BIFANO T., "Differential capacitive position sensor for planar MEMS structures with vertical motion", *Sensors and Actuators A: Physical*, vol. 80, num. 1, p. 53–61, 2000.

[HUN 98] HUNG E., SENTURIA S., "Tunable capacitors with programmable capacitance voltage characteristic", *Technical Digest of Solid State Sensor and Actuator Workshop*, 8 11 June 1998, p. 292–295, 1998.

[HUO 97] HUONKER M., WAIBEL G., GIESEN A., HUGEL H., "Fast and compact adaptive mirror", *Proceedings of SPIE: International Society of Optical Engineering*, vol. 3097, p. 310–319, 1997.

[IRS 02] IRSCHIK H., "A review on static and dynamic shape control of structures by piezoelectric actuation", *Engineering Structures*, vol. 24, num. 1, p. 5–11, 2002.

[IRS 06] IRSCHIK H., NADER M., ZEHETNER C., "Tracking of displacements in smart elastic beams subjected to rigid body motions", *III European Conference on Computational Mechanics Solids, Structures and Coupled Problems in Engineering*, 5–8 June 2006, 2006, page 571.

[JUD 97] JUDY J., MULLER R., "Magnetically actuated addressable microstructures", *Journal of Microelectromechanical Systems*, vol. 6, num. 3, p. 249–256, 1997.

[KAD 03] KADER M., LENCZNER M., MRCARICA Z., "Distributed optimal control of vibrations: a high frequency approximation approach", *Journal of Smart Materials and Structures*, vol. 12, p. 437–446, 2003.

[KEN 07] KENNEDY G., PATERSON C., "Correcting the ocular aberrations of a healthy adult population using microelectromechanical (MEMS) deformable mirrors", *Optics Communications*, vol. 271, num. 1, p. 278–284, 2007.

[KRO 07] KROMMER M., IRSCHIK H., "Sensor and actuator design for displacement control of continuous systems", *Proceedings of SPIE: International Society of Optical Engineering*, vol. 3, num. 2, p. 147–172, 2007.

[KUI 04] KUIJPERS A., WIEGERINK R., KRIJNEN G., LAMMERINK T., EL-WENSPOEK M., "Capacitive long-range position sensor for microactuators", *Proceedings of the 17th IEEE International Conference on Micro Electro Mechanical Systems (MEMS'04)*, 25–29 January 2004, p. 544–547, 2004.

[LAR 96] LARMINAT DE P., *Automatique: Commande des Systèmes Linéaires*, Hermes, 2nd edition, 1996.

[LAR 99] LARMINAT DE P., LEBRET G., PUREN S., "About some interconnection between LTR and RPIS", *Proceedings of the 7th Mediterranean Conference on Control and Automation (MED'99)*, 28–30 June 1999, p. 2169–2179, 1999.

[LAR 00] LARMINAT DE P., *Contrôle d'Etat Standard*, Hermes, Paris, France, 2000.

[LIA 97] LIANG J., WILLIAMS D., MILLER D., "Supernormal vision and high-resolution retinal imaging through adaptive optics", *Journal of the Optical Society of America A*, vol. 14, num. 11, p. 2884–2892, 1997.

[LIU 93] LIU C., HAGOOD N., "Adaptive lightweight mirrors for the correction of self-weight and thermal deformations", *ASME Adaptive Structures and Materials Systems*, vol. AD-35, p. 1AD–183, 1993.

[LUO 06] LUO Q., TONG L., "A sequential linear least square algorithm for tracking dynamic shapes of smart structures", *International Journal of Numerical Methods in Engineering*, vol. 67, p. 66–88, 2006.

[LUO 07] LUO Q., TONG L., "A segment based sequential least squares algorithm with optimum energy control for tracking the dynamic shapes of smart structures", *Journal of Smart Materials and Structures*, vol. 16, num. 5, p. 1517–1526, 2007.

[LYS 99] LYSHEVSKI S., "Integrated control of microactuators and integrated circuits: a new turning approach in MEMS technology", *Proceedings of the 38th IEEE Conference on Decision and Control*, vol. 3, 7–10 December 1999, p. 2611–2616, 1999.

[LYS 01] LYSHEVSKI S., "Distributed control of MEMS-based smart flight surfaces", *Proceedings of the American Control Conference*, vol. 3, 25–27 June 2001, p. 2351–2356, 2001.

[LYS 02] LYSHEVSKI S., "Smart flight control surfaces with microelectromechanical systems", *IEEE Transactions on Aerospace and Electronic Systems*, vol. 38, num. 2, p. 543–552, 2002.

[PAR 01] PARK J., KIM G., CHUNG K., BU J., "Monolithically integrated micromachined RF MEMS capacitive switches", *Sensors and Actuators A: Physical*, vol. 89, num. 1–2, p. 88–94, 2001.

[POP 03] POPA D., BYOUNG H., WEN J., STEPHANOU H., SKIDMORE G., GEISBERGER A., "Dynamic modeling and input shaping of thermal bimorph MEMS actuators", *Proceedings of the IEEE International Conference on Robotics and Automation*, vol. 1, 14–19 September 2003, p. 1470–1475, 2003.

[POP 04] POPA D., WEN J., STEPHANOU H., SKIDMORE G., ELLIS M., "Dynamic modeling and input shaping for MEMS", *Technical Proceedings of the NSTI Nanotechnology Conference and Trade Show (NANOTECH 2004)*, vol. 2, 7–11 March 2004, p. 315–318, 2004.

[ROO 02] ROORDA A., ROMERO F., DONNELLY III W., QUEENER H., HEBERT T., CAMPBELL M., "Adaptive optics scanning laser opht almoscopy", *Optics Express*, vol. 10, num. 9, p. 405–412, 2002.

[SAB 93] SABERI A., CHEN B., SANNUTI P., *Loop Transfer Recovery: Analysis and Design*, Springer Verlag, 1993.

[SIN 89] SINGER N., SEERING W., "Design and comparison of command shaping methods for controlling residual vibration", *Proceedings of the IEEE International Conference on Robotics and Automation*, vol. 2, 14–19 May 1989, p. 888–893, 1989.

[VDO 01] VDOVIN G., SARRO P., "Flexible mirror micromachined in silicon", *Applied Optics*, vol. 34, num. 16, p. 2968–2972, 2001.

[WAN 96] WANG P., HADAEGH F., "Computation of static shapes and voltages for micromachined deformable mirrors with nonlinear electrostatic actuators", *Journal of Microelectromechanical Systems*, vol. 5, num. 3, p. 205–220, 1996.

[WON 85] WONHAM M., *Linear Multivariable Control: A Geometric Approach*, Springer Verlag, 3rd edition, 1985.

PART II

Nanosystems and Nanoworld

Chapter 3

Observer-based Estimation of Weak Forces in a Nanosystem Measurement Device

The problem of force measurement at smaller and smaller scales has motivated the development of new measurement devices as well as various related operation modes [GAR 02]. From a system point of view, however, this force measurement problem amounts to a problem of *state observer*, as initially noted in [BES 04]. From this, an observer approach can yield measurement results in operation modes not easily addressed by classical methods [HRO 06], as well as interesting performances in terms of noise attenuation [BES 07]. The purpose of this chapter is first to briefly sketch such an observer approach in the mostly representative context of Atomic Force Microscope (AFM) measurement and then show its possible extension to push the limits of measurement accuracy, in particular by tackling the problem of *back action* [JOU 08]. This chapter is based on the first successful experimental results on the proposed observer approach presented in [BES 09], as well as simulations of [BES 07].

3.1. Introduction

The problem of weak force measurement typically arises when studying material properties at an atomic scale. The most-used tool for measurements at such very low scales is the so-called *Atomic Force Microscope* (AFM). Since the first apparatus designed by G. Binnig and H. Rohrer appeared in 1986 [BIN 86], numerous operation

Chapter written by Gildas BESANÇON, Alina VODA and Guillaume JOURDAN.

modes have been developed in order to image a sample and to extract various local physical properties using this *near-field* concept.

However, the heart of the device roughly remains the same: it consists of a microlever bearing a tip at its end, on which a force exerted by a sample is applied. Additional excitation forces can be implemented, through a bimorph for instance, to run a specific measurement (dynamic AFM). Microlever motion, generated by an external force, is acquired through various techniques (spot laser deflection, interferometer, piezo-resistive microlever, etc.) and determines the raw signal of an experiment. It is connected to the force through the microlever mechanical response: as a result, the measured signal can strongly differ from the applied force.

On the other hand, sample analysis in biology, chemistry and material physics requires more powerful tools for increasing amounts of data to be processed. For instance, biological processes such as DNA replication, protein synthesis or drug interaction are largely governed by intermolecular forces. As AFM has the ability to measure weak forces in the sub-nanoNewton range, this makes it possible to quantify the molecular interaction in biological systems such as a variety of important ligand-receptor interactions.

In addition to measuring binding forces, AFM can also probe the micromechanical properties of biological samples since it can observe the elasticity and the viscosity of samples such as live cells and membranes. In this context, force estimation requires efficient methods to improve sample analysis. Numerous trade-offs have to be made when selecting microlever model and scanning method and its relative parameters. In general, however, steady-state signals are used, resulting in methods limited in bandwidth.

From a system viewpoint, the problem of force measurement can be considered as a problem of internal information reconstruction or, in a state-space formalism, a problem of *state observation* [KWA 72]. An approach using *transient signals* may improve the analysis ability of an AFM device by reducing scanning time; it can also offer a more comprehensive control of the system. It can be further extended to other related fields, from manipulation of nano-objects to inertial sensors, as they arise in nanosciences.

The purpose of the present chapter is therefore to show how this problem of force measurement can be handled in that spirit of state observation. The presentation focuses on a very simple formulation for the sake of illustration, and proposes an appropriate experimental set-up with the purpose of illustrating and validating the implementation and performances of the proposed methodology.

We also demonstrate the possibility of using the approach in order to cope with the problem of *back action*, which is present in the highly sensitive measurement of small displacements.

The chapter is organized as follows. In section 3.2 the force measurement problem is first stated, the proposed observer approach is then described and its performances are finally illustrated with real data. In section 3.3 its possible extension to the context of back action is discussed and illustrated in simulation. The chapter ends with some conclusions in section 3.4.

3.2. Observer approach in an AFM measurement set-up

3.2.1. *Considered AFM model and force measurement problem*

The basic AFM principle is depicted in Figure 3.1. It basically consists of a cantilever bearing a tip which makes contact with a sample. Both the cantilever and the sample can be appropriately positioned via a couple of drivers. The deflection of the lever end, denoted z, is generated by forces appearing between the tip and the sample. Numerous operation modes have been implemented to run sample analysis. Most of them consist of keeping the mechanical state of the lever constant by appropriately changing tip sample distance while scanning sample surface. This operation makes it possible to derive surface topology. These mechanical states depend on tip sample distance and can be the deflection in case of contact AFM or amplitude deflection or resonance frequency in case of dynamic mode, as in so-called tapping or AM/FM AFM modes [ALB 91, GAR 02, GIE 03].

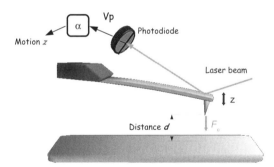

Figure 3.1. *Typical AFM set-up: the microlever is deflected under the effect of a force F and its motion z is picked up through a laser beam deflection system*

In addition, various physical properties can be determined from the interaction of the tip with the sample being analyzed: electrostatic, magnetic, thermal or mechanical properties. Lever motion resulting from the interaction of the tip with the sample provides the signal to be processed by the AFM operation mode. In this context, force estimation is generally not a prerequisite. The problem we consider is that of measuring the force between the sample and the tip via the measurement of deflection z.

A description of the system requires mechanical response modeling of the lever undergoing a force F at its end. Various noise sources are then added to account for signals experimentally acquired. Beginning from the Euler–Bernouilli theory of beams (e.g. as in [CLO 93, CLE 04]), it appears that the dynamical behavior of the whole lever can be represented by a set of harmonic vibration modes with different resonance frequencies. Reducing the lever motion to the first flexural vibration mode proved to be a convenient and relevant approximation when working at a low frequency below and around the first resonance frequency. The discrepancy resulting from not taking into account upper modes is estimated to be lower than a few percent, as will be shown in the system identification section. As a result, we obtain a model of the classical form:

$$m\ddot{z}(t) + f\dot{z}(t) + kz(t) = F(t, d) \tag{3.1}$$

where m, k and f respresent the effective mass of the cantilever and the first mode stiffness and friction coefficients, respectively, while F is the force between the tip and the sample. The observation method which is advocated here can actually include several modes in estimating the lever motion: this capability has to be used when working on higher frequency signal. However, the present chapter aims at presenting the method principle and is therefore based on a simpler model.

In addition to the classical representation equation (3.1), the coupling of the device with the environment depicted as a thermal bath at temperature $T = 300$ K results in a thermomechanical force noise which further affects the dynamics, denoted by f_n. It is related to the stochastic part of the Langevin force, which also includes the damping force $-f\dot{z}$ acting on the system.

Statistical physics requires force noise density S_f to be related to damping coefficient f, so that the elastic energy or kinetic energy of the first mode is equal to $(k_bT)/2$ (where k_b is the Boltzmann constant, 1.3806×10^{-23} J K^{-1}) [REI 65]. This is the equipartition theorem: it can be applied in thermal equilibrium on any system having degrees of freedom which appear quadratically in its energy. As a result the force noise density, which is assumed to be white, can be expressed as $S_{f_n} = 4k_bTf$. The mechanical response of the lever then acts as a resonant filter on the thermal mechanical force noise. In this context, the lever motion can be broken down into component z generated by force F and component z_n generated by force noise f_n, which corresponds to a stochastic motion with spectral density S_{z_n}:

$$S_{z_n} = H(j\omega)^2 S_{f_n} \tag{3.2}$$

where $H(j\omega)$ accounts for the mechanical susceptibility of the lever in the frequency domain (i.e. force to position transfer function).

The motion sensor and various electronic elements of the detection system incorporate some additional noise w on the lever position. Finally, the measurement y

can be expressed:

$$y = z + z_n + w. \tag{3.3}$$

Figure 3.2 illustrates typical force noise density that can be acquired with the AFM used in experiments presented in this chapter. It consists of detection noise w, which forms a background at a value around $1 \, \text{pm}^2 \, \text{Hz}^{-1}$, and thermomechanical noise z_n which has a dominant peak around the resonance frequency ω_r.

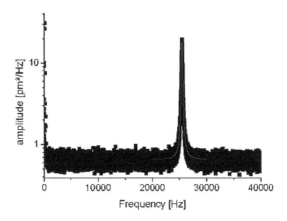

Figure 3.2. *Typical noise spectral density on an AFM at room temperature (here Asylum MFP 3D AFM)*

The main purpose in this context is to recover as closely as possible the interaction force F from direct measurement y.

3.2.2. *Proposed observer approach*

In view of the previous problem formulation, we aim to summarize how a solution can be obtained via observer techniques. This provides an alternative approach to the most common use of AFM devices.

Such an approach can already be found in recent references, either with the idea of reconstructing $z, \dot{z}$ and from this detecting F (as in [SAH 05] when dealing with tapping mode), or with the purpose of direct reconstruction of F together with z and $\dot{z}$ (as in [BES 04, BES 07]). We will focus on the latter approach in this chapter, and illustrate its performances on actual experiments.

As emphasized in [SAH 05] for instance, the strong interest in such an approach with respect to standard methods is to use transient signals rather than wait for steady-state signals. In addition, considering a direct reconstruction scheme as we propose here – rather than an observer-based detection scheme – makes it even simpler and independent of the considered AFM mode. In particular, experimental results will be presented here for the case of non-contact mode as in [BES 09], which (to our knowledge) has not yet been considered elsewhere with such techniques.

In short, the idea consists of extending the system description by including a force model to be estimated. The most simple model which can be considered is obtained by neglecting the force dynamics, which can be justified either because the considered force is indeed not varying or because its reconstruction will be fast enough. In both cases, this means that F can be assumed to satisfy $\dot{F} = 0$ (extensions to more complicated force models easily follow).

Variables $z + z_n, \dot{z} + \dot{z}_n$ and F from z, z_n, F of equations (3.1)–(3.3) can be considered as state variables of a vector x for a state-space representation only driven by thermomechanical noise f_n and detection noise w, as follows:

$$
\begin{aligned}
\dot{x} &= \begin{pmatrix} 0 & 1 & 0 \\ \frac{-k}{m} & -\frac{f}{m} & \frac{1}{m} \\ 0 & 0 & 0 \end{pmatrix} x + \begin{pmatrix} 0 \\ \frac{1}{m} \\ 0 \end{pmatrix} f_n := Ax + Df_n \\
y &= \begin{pmatrix} 1 & 0 & 0 \end{pmatrix} x + w := Cx + w.
\end{aligned}
\tag{3.4}
$$

From their definition in equation (3.4), matrices A and C clearly satisfy the observability condition (in the classical sense [KWA 72]). Consequently, a standard state observer can be designed in order to recover all state variables from only direct measurement of y, namely an observer of the form ($\hat{x}$ classically denoting the estimate for x):

$$
\dot{\hat{x}} = A\hat{x} - K(C\hat{x} - y)
\tag{3.5}
$$

where matrix K is to be chosen appropriately.

In a deterministic framework, this matrix can be chosen according to any pre-specified set of observer poles but with no guarantee with respect to the noises. Alternatively, in a stochastic framework the well-known *Kalman observer* provides an optimal choice for K, in the sense of minimizing the mathematical expectation $E[(\hat{x}(t) - x(t))^T (\hat{x}(t) - x(t))]$. This is possible provided that noise variances are known and used in the gain computation. However, it can be noted that an admissible constant gain can be obtained in this context only if (A, D) is stabilizable, which is not true in equation (3.4).

In practice, D can be changed into

$$\begin{pmatrix} 0 & 0 \\ \frac{1}{m} & 0 \\ 0 & \varepsilon \end{pmatrix}$$

for some ε to be chosen, assuming some additional possible fluctuations in the force profile. By adjusting the parameter ε, for instance, we can tune the observer convergence rate with respect to the noise attenuation.

This observer approach has been tested on an experimental set-up comprising a standard AFM specifically configured for this purpose of observer validation, as presented in the next section.

Note that in this set-up, the force to be reconstructed is created via an electrostatic action driven by a voltage which can be used as a reference. For this reason, the observer performance will be validated by voltage estimation, relying on a force model with respect to this voltage injected in model equation (3.4).

3.2.3. *Experimental application and validation*

In order to experimentally validate the proposed force measurement approach, the basic AFM scheme of Figure 3.1 has been slightly modified according to Figure 3.3. The AFM is an Asylum MFP-3D microscope. The microlever (Mikromash CSC37 Ti-Pt lever B) has a conductive coating on both sides. It is located at a distance $d \sim 1\,\mu\text{m}$ from the gold sample surface. A bias voltage is put on the tip with respect to the sample, thus generating an electrostatic force F_e. Microlever motion z is picked up through a laser beam deflection system.

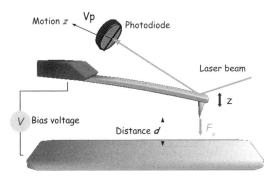

Figure 3.3. *Considered AFM set-up for experimental validation*

A controlled voltage V is introduced between the tip and the sample in order to produce an electrostatic force. In this way, the set-up described here makes it possible to monitor the non-contact force applied to the lever. The corresponding model (3.4) between the tip and the force has therefore been experimentally identified, and a corresponding observer defined by equation (3.5) has then been designed. The configurations corresponding to these two steps are summarized in Figure 3.4.

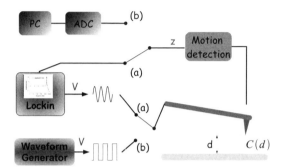

Figure 3.4. *Experimental configurations: (a) for mechanical response acquisition through the lock-in and (b) enables the measured deflection to be recorded and processed on a PC after AD conversion*

3.2.3.1. *Microlever model identification*

The experiment is carried out using an Asylum MFP-3D microscope. As shown in Figure 3.3, a microlever is brought within about 1 μm from a gold flat surface. It corresponds to model Mikromash CSC37 Ti-Pt lever B, and has been chosen for its low stiffness ($k = 0.4\,\mathrm{N\,m^{-1}}$) and for the conductive layer coating it.

The microlever and the surface form a capacitance $C(d)$ that depends on the distance d between them. When applying a bias voltage V, an electrostatic force F_e i.e. an attraction arises on the probe. It is described:

$$F_e = \frac{1}{2}C'V^2 \tag{3.6}$$

where C' is the capacitance derivative with respect to tip sample distance d. As a result, tuning the bias V makes it possible to easily monitor the force intensity. As explained in section 3.2.1, the probe is described as a harmonic oscillator with mass m, stiffness k and damping coefficient f. It should be noted that these parameters depend on how the force F_e is applied. Resonance frequency $\omega_r = \sqrt{k/m}$ and damping rate $\gamma = f/m$ nevertheless remain the same: they can be identified from the motion noise spectral density or the force tuning diagram.

In the frequency domain, the mechanical response is therefore defined:

$$H(s) = \frac{Z(s)}{\mathcal{F}(s)} = \frac{1/m}{s^2 + \gamma s + w_r{}^2} \tag{3.7}$$

where s represents the Laplace variable and $Z, \mathcal{F}$ represent Laplace transforms of $z(t), F(t)$, respectively.

Motion detection calibration is performed using a force–distance curve which consists of putting the tip into contact with the sample surface and extending the sample stage piezo-translator Z towards it. The microlever deflection is then equal to the piezo-translator extension. Sensitivity $\alpha = Z/V_p$ is estimated at $188 \, \text{nm V}^{-1}$ (in the range 100–$200 \, \text{nm V}^{-1}$ or the corresponding value), where V_p is the voltage delivered by the photodiode in Figure 3.3.

As mentioned, it appears more convenient in this experiment to directly reconstruct bias voltage V rather than external force F, so that its estimation ($\hat{V}$) can be directly compared to the 'reference' V.

From this, the response $G(s) = Z(s)/V_2(s)$ has to be identified, where $V_2(s)$ represents the Laplace transform of $V^2(t)$. From equations (3.6) and (3.7), we have

$$G(s) = \frac{C'/2m}{s^2 + \gamma s + w_r{}^2}. \tag{3.8}$$

Flowchart (a) of Figure 3.4 describes the corresponding experimental set-up. A sinusoidal shape voltage $V = V_0 \sin(wt)$ is applied between the tip and the sample, thus generating an electrostatic force F proportional to V^2 with

$$V^2 = V_0^2 \frac{1 - \cos(2wt)}{2}. \tag{3.9}$$

The $2w$ frequency component is scanned from 1–$100 \, \text{kHz}$ and demodulated by a lock-in amplifier. The mechanical response is finally plotted and compared to that obtained with model (3.8) in Figure 3.5.

The parameters of equation (3.8) are found to be: $w_r = 1.5215 \times 10^5 \, \text{rad s}^{-1}$; $\gamma = 1570 \, \text{rad s}^{-1}$; and $C'/2m = 1.27 \times 10^9 \, \text{nm s}^2 \, \text{V}^{-2}$.

The discrepancy between data and model is lower than 5%, and could be reduced by introducing a mechanical response background associated with higher vibration modes. As a result, this analysis validates the damped harmonic oscillator as the model that captures the microlever mechanical behavior well. The resulting model can then

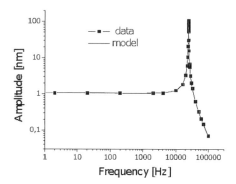

Figure 3.5. *Mechanical response of the lever on Asylum MFP 3D AFM, using a cantilever Mikromash CSC37 Ti-Pt lever B*

be rewritten as a state-space representation as in equation (3.4) and used for observer design.

The corresponding measurements are carried out following flowchart (b) of Figure 3.4. Rectangular shape voltages are applied to the tip, causing the lever to deflect as shown in Figure 3.6. An Analog Digital Converter (ADC) samples the microlever motion signal at 1 MHz. The deflection signal is therefore sampled here and in addition disturbed by noise, mechanical resonance phenomenon and various drift (mechanical or electrical). However, the latter are neglected here because the measurement time, the sampling effect and the sampling period are all small.

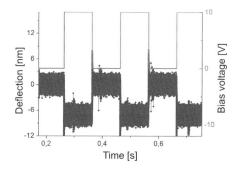

Figure 3.6. *Typical cantilever deflection (bottom) versus bias voltage (top) on Asylum MFP 3D AFM using a cantilever Mikromash CSC37 Ti-Pt lever B*

3.2.3.2. *Observer-based force reconstruction*

We now present some experimental observation results obtained in the context previously described. Two cases will be discussed in particular: a low-frequency problem and some higher frequency cases. The first experiment reported here corresponds to a single step change in the applied voltage, resulting in the transient response of the cantilever depicted in Figure 3.7.

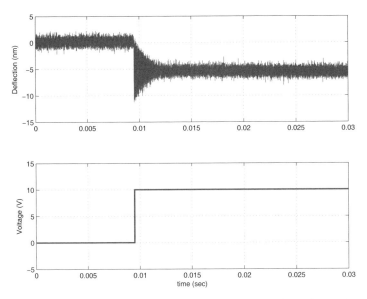

Figure 3.7. *Measured cantilever deflection (top) versus applied voltage (bottom): step case. Asylum MFP 3D AFM is used*

On this basis, an observer can be designed which achieves a very good noise filtering in a few milliseconds, as illustrated by the voltage reconstruction shown in Figure 3.8.

Note that this corresponds to the estimation of a force with a magnitude of a few nanoNewtons according to Figure 3.8, where the force is reconstructed from equation (3.6) and the estimated voltage.

In the case of faster force variations (here voltage variations), e.g. up to 1 kHz step variations (as considered for a second experiment presented in Figure 3.9), the observer will be limited.

A faster observer can be designed (with the same structure) and still achieve a fairly good voltage (and force) reconstruction as depicted in Figure 3.10. Recall

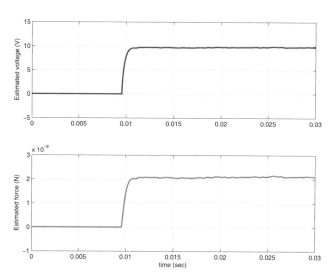

Figure 3.8. *Observer-based estimated voltage (top) and estimated force (bottom): step case. Asylum MFP 3D AFM is used*

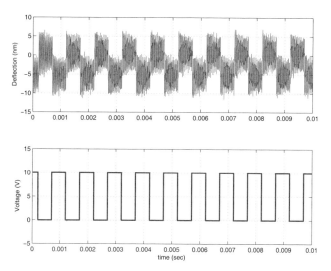

Figure 3.9. *Measured cantilever deflection (top) versus applied voltage (bottom): 1 kHz variation case*

that, in practice, the voltage estimation results from a force-based model. In view of equation (3.6), the force can only be positive which explains the lowest values limited to zero on the figure.

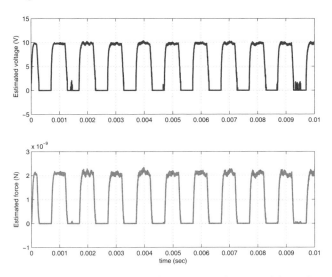

Figure 3.10. *Observer-based estimated voltage (top) and estimated force (bottom): 1 kHz variation case*

Finally, note that we can test the performances of the observer approach with respect to the force magnitude under consideration with the same experiments. As seen in Figures 3.8 or 3.10, the magnitude of the estimated force is a few nanoNewtons in those results. Assuming that a fraction of the applied voltage in the experimental set-up is known, we arrive at an estimation problem for even weaker forces.

For instance, assuming that 90% of the applied voltage is known, i.e. only the effect of 1 V variations is to be estimated, then the corresponding force magnitude to be estimated is about 20 picoNewtons.

Some estimation results for this case are depicted in Figure 3.11 where it can be checked that the observer performs well. It is a very promising approach for weak force measurement at room temperature.

3.3. Extension to back action evasion

3.3.1. *Back action problem and illustration*

In the problem formulation considered so far, only internal thermomechanical noise and external sensor noise have been taken into account. In addition to such

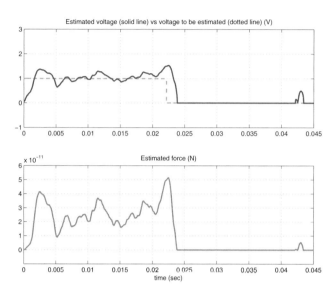

Figure 3.11. *Observer-based estimated voltage (top) and estimated force (bottom): 20 Hz small; variation case*

noises, the measurement accuracy can be limited by the noise generated by the measurement device itself, which can in turn affect the physical phenomenon being measured. This phenomenon is known as back action noise, and has been considered more specifically in the context of quantum physics. It has also been highlighted in the context of AFM [JOU 08]; we would like to highlight how such a phenomenon can also be tackled in an observer approach by including a back action model in the designed observer.

The purpose of this section is to illustrate this possibility. We still refer to the AFM measurement configuration as previously described. When the measurement is assumed to be given by some electrostatic detection scheme rather than an optical scheme, we follow the illustrative back action configuration studied in [BOC 96].

In this context, the second-order cantilever model can be extended with an electrostatic model as depicted in Figure 3.12.

The whole device takes the form of an electromechanical sensor comprising a capacitor with a mobile electrode of mass m, subject to the effect of a polarizing tension V_p through a resistance-inductance (RL) circuit on the one hand and an external force F_{ext} through a mass-spring configuration with damping f and stiffness k on the other hand. The mechanical part defines the probe, while the electrical part

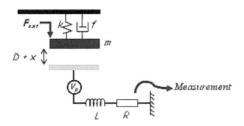

Figure 3.12. *AFM-like measurement with back action*

corresponds to the read-out circuit. The measurement problem is now to recover the applied external force from an electrical measurement.

3.3.2. *Observer-based approach*

The proposed observer-based approach still relies on an appropriate modeling of the considered device, extended with a force model.

If D, x, v, q, I represent the distance between the two electrodes at rest, the mass displacement, the mass velocity and the electrical charge and current in the circuit under the effects of V_p and F_{ext}, respectively, the system can be classically described by equations of the form:

$$
\begin{aligned}
\dot{x} &= v \\
\dot{v} &= -2\zeta_m w_m v - w_m^2 x + \tfrac{1}{m}(F_{\text{ext}} + F_c) \\
\dot{q} &= I \\
\dot{I} &= -2\zeta_e w_e I - w_e^2 q + \tfrac{1}{L}(V_p + V_c),
\end{aligned}
\tag{3.10}
$$

where $\zeta_m, \zeta_e, w_m, w_e$ denote the damping factors and the natural pulsations of the mechanical and electrical oscillators, respectively (depending on the above-listed parameters), while F_c and V_c represent the coupling force and voltage between them. If C_0 denotes the capacitance at rest, these forces can be classically expressed with respect to x and q as:

$$
F_c = -\frac{1}{2}\frac{q^2}{DC_0}, \quad V_c = -\frac{qx}{DC_0}.
\tag{3.11}
$$

Typically, the problem is that of estimating the mechanical force F_{ext} from the experimentally accessible electrical variables (I or q). The noise problem arises from the fact that, as before, the Brownian fluctuations in the mechanical damping can significantly affect the system. The system is also affected by its electrical counterpart (the so-called *Johnson noise*) in the electrical resistance. In practice, such noise is basically due to thermal fluctuations and can be modeled as white noise added to coupling terms F_c and V_c (denoted by ν_e and ν_m in the following).

Specific methods have been investigated in order to attenuate their effect and, in particular, the back action they induce. Research has been conducted on the basis of specific excitation and approximation-based analysis (e.g. [BRA 75, THO 78, ROC 92, CIN 93]).

The goal is to use tools from observer theory once more to obtain a guaranteed estimation of F_{ext} from electrical direct measurements, taking into account the back action effects as well as non-linear coupling terms in equation (3.10) and attenuating the effect of thermal noises. To that end, let us first assume (for the sake of simplicity as before) that dynamics of F_{ext} are negligible with respect to those of the system, namely $\dot{F}_{\text{ext}} \simeq 0$.

Then let us assume, as usual, that ν_e and ν_m are white noises, defining a vector

$$\nu = \begin{pmatrix} \nu_e \\ \nu_m \end{pmatrix}^T.$$

Finally, let us consider that among the accessible electrical variables, the electrical charge q is the measured output.

Equations (3.10) and (3.11) then yield a state-space representation which can be written as:

$$\begin{aligned} \dot{X} &= A(y)X + B(y, V_p) + G\nu \\ y &= CX \end{aligned} \tag{3.12}$$

with

$$X = \begin{pmatrix} x & v & q & I & F_{\text{ext}} \end{pmatrix}^T,$$

$$A(y) = \begin{pmatrix} 0 & 1 & 0 & 0 & 0 \\ -w_m^2 & -2\zeta_m w_m & 0 & 0 & \frac{1}{m} \\ 0 & 0 & 0 & 1 & 0 \\ -\frac{q}{LDC_0} & 0 & -w_e^2 & -2\zeta_e w_e & 0 \\ 0 & 0 & 0 & 0 & 0 \end{pmatrix},$$

$$B(y, V_p) = \begin{pmatrix} 0 \\ -\frac{y^2}{2mDC_0} \\ 0 \\ \frac{V_p}{L} \\ 0 \end{pmatrix},$$

$$G = \begin{pmatrix} 0 & \frac{1}{m} & 0 & 0 & 0 \\ 0 & 0 & 0 & \frac{1}{L} & 0 \end{pmatrix}^T,$$

and

$$C = \begin{pmatrix} 0 & 0 & 0 & 1 & 0 \end{pmatrix}.$$

On the basis of such a representation, an estimation of F_{ext} can be obtained via a state observer. In view of the structure of this system, various observer designs can be considered [BES 04].

Noting for instance that A and B depend on known time-varying signals, a classical (time-varying) Kalman observer (or a Kalman-like observer; [HAM 90, BES 96]) can be designed with a guaranteed exponential convergence under excitation V_p [BES 04]. This can in particular yield the 'optimal' state estimation under appropriate tuning of the observer, as discussed earlier [KWA 72]. However, in the present case this requires on-line heavy computations for the gain. For the high-frequency system requiring high precision considered here, a simpler implementation should be preferred.

Instead, in view of $(C, A(y))$, we can design an observer with a *constant* gain under some excitation V_p (possibly constant) of amplitude large enough to guarantee that $q(t)$ remains larger than some $q_0 > 0$. In this case, a so-called *high-gain* design can be achieved [GAU 94] (as in many available results e.g. [GAU 92, DEZ 93, DAB 99]), but generally presented for noise-free systems.

When taking disturbances into account and focusing on the estimation of a subset of state variables, an observer-like estimator can be designed on the same high-gain techniques [BES 03] which requires specific structure conditions on the system. The idea here is to relax those conditions and instead use the fact that the considered noise is white, together with the linear-like structure of equation (3.12), in order to modify the observer scheme towards noise attenuation [BES 07]. To summarize, assuming that the excitation V_p guarantees $q(t) \geq q_0 > 0$ for all t, we can design a gain K such that $\dot{z} = (A(y) - KC)z$ is asymptotically stable and use it as an observer gain to obtain an estimate $\hat{X}$ of X. Then, if $T = \begin{pmatrix} 0 & 0 & 0 & 0 & 1 \end{pmatrix}$, $T\hat{X}$ is an estimate of F_{ext} affected by some noise. We can then obtain a more accurate estimate of F_{ext} by filtering $T\hat{X}$ (using for instance some low-pass filter).

This can be formalized as follows.

Proposition 3.1. *Given a system*

$$\begin{aligned} \dot{z}(t) &= \mathcal{A}(u(t), y(t))z(t) + \mathcal{B}(u(t), y(t)) + G(t)w(t) \\ y(t) &= Cz(t) \\ z(t) &= (z_1(t) \cdots z_n(t))^T \end{aligned} \tag{3.13}$$

where w is some white noise of bounded intensity $W(t) = W^T(t) > 0$, the last lines of $\mathcal{A}$ and G are zero and there exists $K(t)$ such that $\dot{\zeta} = (\mathcal{A}(u,y) - KC)\zeta$ is asymptotically stable. Then for any $\lambda > 0$, observer (3.14) below yields estimates $\hat{z}$ for z and, more particularly, $\tilde{z}_n$ for z_n such that

$$\lim_{t \to \infty} E[\hat{z}(t) - z(t)] = 0, \quad \lim_{t \to \infty} E[\tilde{z}_n(t) - z_n(t)] = 0.$$

Moreover, for any $\varepsilon_v > 0$, there exist $\lambda > 0$ and $t_1 > 0$ such the estimate $\tilde{z}_n$ of z_n given by the corresponding observer (3.14) satisfies $E[(\tilde{z}_n(t) - z_n(t))(\tilde{z}_n(t) - z_n(t))^T] \leq \varepsilon_v \; \forall t \geq t_1$:

$$
\begin{aligned}
\dot{\hat{z}}(t) &= \mathcal{A}(u(t), y(t))\hat{z}(t) + \mathcal{B}(u(t), y(t)) - K(t)(C\hat{z}(t) - y(t)) \\
\dot{\tilde{z}}_n(t) &= -\lambda\tilde{z}_n(t) + \lambda T\hat{z}(t) + T\mathcal{B}(u, y)
\end{aligned}
\tag{3.14}
$$

where $T = (0, \dots, 1) \in \mathbb{R}^{1 \times n}$ and E denotes the mean of a stochastic variable.

The proof follows from stochastic properties of solutions of linear systems driven by white noise [BES 07].

This proposition basically means that we can filter out the noise on Tz as much as desired by decreasing λ (at the expense of an increasing estimation time). Such a design has been tested in simulation for system (3.12).

3.3.3. *Simulation results and comments*

3.3.3.1. *Simulated model data*

The purpose here is to illustrate the observer-based estimation with noise filtering presented in proposition 3.1. To that end, let us consider the electromechanical sensor of Figure 3.12, with numerical values of [BES 04, BES 07], corresponding to the case of a typical AFM (for instance as in [DIA 03]):

$$
\begin{aligned}
w_m &= w_e \simeq 2 \times 10^6 \, \mathrm{rad\,s^{-1}} \\
\zeta_m &= \zeta_e \simeq 2 \times 10^5 \\
m &\simeq 0.1 \, \mathrm{nkg} \\
D &\simeq 100 \, \mathrm{nm} \\
L &\simeq 0.2 \, \mathrm{H}.
\end{aligned}
$$

Here the quality factor is equal to 2.5×10^4, which is quite large. The excitation signal V_p is chosen to be constant, with an amplitude of $50 \, \mathrm{mV}$. Thermal noises ν are simulated as band-limited white noises. For realistic mechanical and electrical noises, the variances have first been chosen to be over $1.6 \times 10^{18} \, \mathrm{N^2}$ (respectively, $\mathrm{V^2}$), corresponding to a temperature of about 25°C according to the so-called fluctuation-dissipation theorem [REI 65]. This means that we consider an estimation at room temperature.

The corresponding time behavior of such noises is illustrated in Figure 3.13.

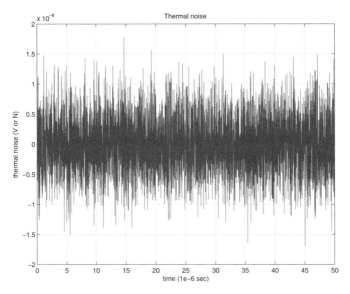

Figure 3.13. *Typical time behavior of simulated thermal noises (mechanical or electrical)*

The simulated external force to be estimated F_{ext} is chosen to be of amplitude 1 nN, i.e. comparable to that of the mechanical noise ν_m. It is set at time $t = 20\,\mu s$.

Note that all these values correspond to very low amplitudes of the state variables, as can be seen in Figure 3.14, showing the time evolution of all state variables in those conditions.

Note also that with this considered amount of noise, the back action effect on the mechanical motion is much lower than that of the direct thermomechanical noise. For this reason, in order to better illustrate the performances of the proposed observer approach in coping with back action, a second case has been considered. This has a much larger (even unrealistically) electrical noise (with a variance 1×10^6 times larger yielding voltage variations up to 0.01 mV), in order to have an effect on the mechanical motion comparable to that of the thermomechanical noise. Simulation results for both cases are presented in the next section.

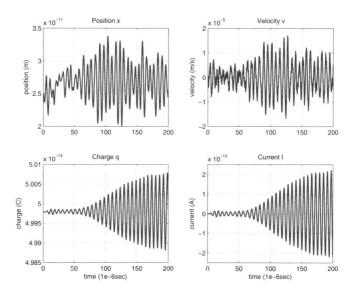

Figure 3.14. *State variable evolutions*

3.3.3.2. *Simulated force estimation*

For the first case of noise at room temperature, the successful estimation obtained with the proposed observer is illustrated in Figure 3.15. A constant gain K has been chosen on the basis of A, C and the parameter λ has been tuned in order to achieve an acceptable trade-off between the estimation time and the filtering performance.

Note that the effect of the additional filtering realized by λ can be seen by comparing Figure 3.15 with Figure 3.16, where the represented estimate is given by $T\hat{z}$ (omitting the additional filtering).

Also note that the same method can be applied when the measurement itself is significantly affected by noise. Assuming, for instance, that the measurement is corrupted by some additional white noise with an amplitude up to $1/1000$ of its nominal value, the force can still be estimated again with an appropriate observer tuning, as illustrated by Figure 3.17.

Finally, similar estimation results can be obtained in the case of a stronger back action noise, as illustrated in Figure 3.18 where electrical noise of amplitudes up to $0.01\,\mathrm{mV}$ was simulated.

Note also that the observer performance could be improved even further by appropriately tuning the *system excitation* in addition to the observer, as discussed in [BES 08]. This will be part of future developments.

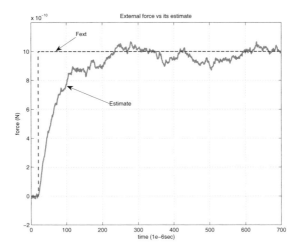

Figure 3.15. *External force estimation with observer (3.14)*

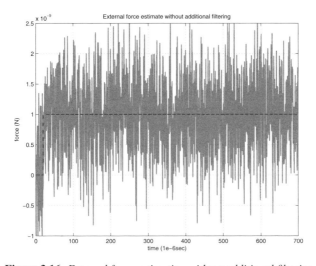

Figure 3.16. *External force estimation without additional filtering*

3.4. Conclusion

In this chapter, a full observer approach towards force reconstruction from indirect measurements at nanoscale has been proposed and illustrated both in simulation and

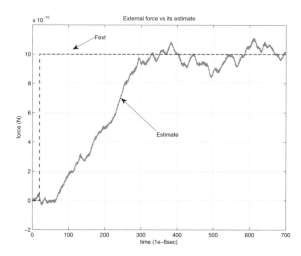

Figure 3.17. *External force estimation with noisy measurement and additional filtering*

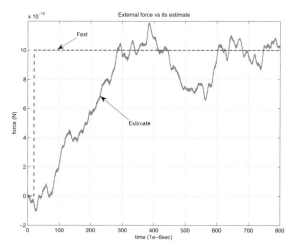

Figure 3.18. *External force estimation with 'strong' back action noise*

experimental contexts. In particular, the presentation was based on the emblematic example of AFM measurements, for which the obtained experimental results are very promising. In particular, the discussed possible extension to cope with the problem of back action can be a good solution to push the limits of measurement accuracy, and this will be part of future developments.

3.5. Acknowledgements

The authors would like to thank Professor J. Chevrier of UJF-Grenoble for helpful discussions on the topic of this chapter, as well as the ESRF staff in Grenoble for access to AFM facilities.

3.6. Bibliography

[ALB 91] ALBRECHT T., GRÜTTER P., HORNE D., RUGAR D., "Frequency modulation detection using high-Q cantilevers for enhanced force microscope sensitivity", *Journal of Applied Physics*, vol. 69, num. 2, p. 668–702, 1991.

[BES 96] BESANÇON G., BORNARD G., HAMMOURI H., "Observer synthesis for a class of nonlinear control systems", *European Journal of Control*, vol. 3, num. 1, p. 176–193, 1996.

[BES 03] BESANÇON G., "High gain observation with disturbance attenuation and application to robust fault detection", *Automatica*, vol. 39, num. 6, p. 1095–1102, 2003.

[BES 04] BESANÇON G., VODA A., CHEVRIER J., "Force estimation in fundamental physics: an observer application", *2nd Symposium on System Structure and Control*, 2004.

[BES 07] BESANÇON G., VODA A., CHEVRIER J., "An observer for nanoforce estimation with thermal noise attenuation", *Proceedings of Conference on Systems and Control*, Marrakech, Morocco, 2007.

[BES 08] BESANÇON G., VODA A., ALMA M., "On observer-based estimation enhancement by parametric amplification in a weak force measurement device", *Proceedings of IEEE Conf Decision and Control*, Cancún, Mexico, 2008.

[BES 09] BESANÇON G., VODA A., JOURDAN G., "Kalman observer approach towards force reconstruction from experimental AFM measurements", *Proceedings of 15th IFAC Symposium System Identification*, Saint-Malo, France, 2009.

[BIN 86] BINNIG G., QUATE C., GERBER C., "Atomic force microscopy", *Physics Review Letters*, vol. 56, p. 930–933, 1986.

[BOC 96] BOCKO M., ONOFRIO R., "On the measurement of a weak classical force coupled to a harmonic oscillator: experimental progress", *Review of Modern Physics*, vol. 68, num. 3, p. 755–799, 1996.

[BRA 75] BRAGINSKY V., VORONSTSOV Y., "Quantum mechanical limitations in macroscopic experiments and modern experimental techniques", *Sov. Phys. Usp*, vol. 17, p. 644–650, 1975.

[CIN 93] CINQUEGRANA C., MAJORANA E., RAPAGNANI P., RICCI F., "Back-action-evading transducing scheme for cryogenic gravitational wave antennas", *PhyS. Rev. D*, vol. 48, p. 448–465, 1993.

[CLE 04] CLELAND A., *Foundations of Nanomechanics*, Springer, 2004.

[CLO 93] CLOUGH R. W., PENZIEN J., *Dynamics of Structures*, McGraw-Hill, 1993.

[DAB 99] DABROOM A., KHALIL H., "Discrete-time implementation of high-gain observers for numerical differentiation", *International Journal of Control*, vol. 72, num. 17, p. 1523–1537, 1999.

[DEZ 93] DEZA F., BOSSANNE D., BUSVELLE E., GAUTHIER J., RAKOTOPARA D., "Exponential observers for nonlinear systems", *IEEE Transactions of Automatic Control*, vol. 38, num. 3, p. 482–484, 1993.

[DIA 03] DIANOUX R., MARTINS F., MARCHI F., ALANDI C., COMIN F., CHEVRIER J., "Detection of electrostatic forces with an AFM: analytical and experimental dynamic force curves in non-linear regime", *Phys. Rev. B (045403)*, vol. 68, p. 1–6, 2003.

[GAR 02] GARCÍA R., PÉREZ R., "Dynamic atomic force microscopy methods", *Surface Science Reports*, vol. 47, p. 197–301, 2002.

[GAU 92] GAUTHIER J., HAMMOURI H., OTHMAN S., "A simple observer for nonlinear systems: Application to bioreactors", *TAC*, vol. 37, p. 875–880, 1992.

[GAU 94] GAUTHIER J., KUPKA A., "Observability and observers for nonlinear systems", *SIAM Journal of Control and Optimization*, vol. 32, num. 4, p. 975–994, 1994.

[GIE 03] GIESSIBL F., "Advances in atomic force microscopy", *Reviews of Modern Physics*, vol. 75, p. 949–983, 2003.

[HAM 90] HAMMOURI H., MORALES J. D. L., "Observer synthesis for state-affine systems", *CDC90*, p. 784–785, 1990.

[HRO 06] HROUZEK M., BESANÇON G., VODA A., CHEVRIER J., "Observer-based position detection of a cantilever in atomic force microscopy", *4th IFAC Symposium on Mechatronic Systems*, Heidelberg, Germany, 2006.

[JOU 08] JOURDAN G., COMIN F., CHEVRIER J., "Mechanical mode dependence of bolometric back-action in an AFM microlever", *Physics Review Letters*, vol. 13, p. 1–4, 2008.

[KWA 72] KWAKERNAAK H., SIVAN R., *Linear Optimal Control Systems*, Wiley-Interscience, 1972.

[REI 65] REIF F., *Fundamentals of Thermal and Statistical Physics*, McGraw-Hill, New York, 1965.

[ROC 92] ROCH J., ROGER G., GRANGIER P., COURTY J., REYNAUD S., "Quantum non-demolition measurements in optics: a review and some recent experimental results", *Applied Physics*, vol. 55, num. 3, p. 291–297, 1992.

[SAH 05] SAHOO D., SEBASTIAN A., SALAPAKA M., "Harnessing the transient signals in atomic force microscopy", *International Journal of Robust Nonlinear Control*, vol. 15, p. 805–820, 2005.

[THO 78] THORNE K., DREVER R., CAVES C., ZIMMERMANN M., SANDBERG V., "Quantum nondemolition measurements of harmonic oscillators", *Physics Review Letters*, vol. 40, p. 667–671, 1978.

Chapter 4

Tunnel Current for a Robust, High-bandwidth and Ultra-precise Nanopositioning

This chapter proposes a control methodology to use a quantum phenomenon called tunnel current as a nanodisplacement sensor. To illustrate this, a control method is designed in order to control displacements of a microscopic cantilever. The proposed methodology has the advantage of damping the Brownian motion of the cantilever; it also rejects creep or thermal drifts which act as slowly varying disturbances on the cantilever position. The proposed control design is validated in a realistic simulation.

4.1. Introduction

In the last few decades, the demands for nanomanipulation techniques and stages have increased dramatically. Among the many applications that require high-precision manipulation, nanopositioning is one of the most important processes in nanotechnology. A nanopositioning system requires high accuracy, stability, no contacts, repeatability and a wide control bandwidth, i.e. a fast response.

Research has demonstrated that several transduction techniques can be employed in the framework of nanopositioning: magnetic actuation [GU 05, ZHA 07], electrostatic actuation [SUN 08, ZHA 06], thermal actuation [GOR 06, KUR 06] and piezoelectrical actuation [APH 07, LIA 08, WU 07].

Despite their non-linear behavior, piezoelectric and electrostatic actuation are the most used for manipulation purposes. They are both used for microscopy techniques

Chapter written by Sylvain BLANVILLAIN, Alina VODA and Gildas BESANÇON.

such as Scanning Tunneling Microscopy (STM) or Atomic Force Microscope (AFM) and allow molecules [DUW 08] or atoms [EIG 91, HEL 08] to be manipulated.

However, several challenges still require attention when manipulating at the nanoscale: surface forces (later referred to as proximity forces) can lead to the pull-in or sticking of manipulated objects [BLA 08, SAD 06]. Drifts are the major cause of spatial uncertainty. Some compensation techniques have been designed for this purpose [MOK 06], but can only estimate the drift in a short period of time. Non-linearities of actuators or sensors may be difficult to model [LEE 08], and can lead to complex control techniques [ZHU 07]. Moreover, the speed of manipulation (or control bandwidth) is often limited by the first resonance frequency of the system [ZHA 07]. Robustness of the control law is also an important solution to face with plant uncertainties [SUM 08, ZHU 07]. It is sometimes hard to find the trade-off between robustness and high bandwidth [SAL 02].

This chapter proposes solutions to these problems and suggests using the tunnel current as a nanopositioning sensor. Solutions provided by this chapter are not unique, but they offer the advantage of being simple and easily implementable. The choice of this sensor is mainly motivated by its small size (and hence can be embedded), very high accuracy (lower than the angstroms in STMs), very low power consumption (lower than the watt) and its extremely high bandwidth.

The tunnel current is a flow of electrons crossing an insulating layer from one electrode to another. This only happens if the electrodes are separated by a distance smaller than one nanometer. This principle was brought into application by Binnig and Rohrer [BIN 82] when they created the scanning tunneling microscope. Since then, tunnel current has been used in tunneling accelerometers to measure accelerations down to the nano-g [LIU 01, ROC 96].

The aim of this chapter is to propose a new application which uses tunnel current as a sub-nanometer positioning sensor. The potentialities of tunnel current as a position sensor have been discussed theoretically in a few papers, but experiments and a command point of view have never been presented.

In 1990, Bocko analyzed the problem focusing on the gain of this sensor ($\approx 10^8 \, \text{V m}^{-1}$) and on its low noise (limited by the thermal noise at ambient temperature or by the quantum limit due to the shot noise, around $1.8 \times 10^{-19} \, \text{N Hz}^{-0.5}$ under cryogenic conditions) [BOC 90]. In 1993, Bordoni *et al.* still focused on the thermal noise limitation but proposed a sampling strategy to overcome this limitation [BOR 93]. More recently, Ekinci wrote a short review, highlighting the unusual total noise of this sensor ($10^{-14} \, \text{A Hz}^{-0.5}$ at $0 \, \text{K}$ and in vacuum) and its very high bandwidth: greater than 1 GHz [EKI 05] (up to the THz range, according to [BOR 93]).

We aim to build on the research cited above. A new nanopositioning transducer using tunnel current sensing is presented and analyzed in sections 4.2 and 4.3. Challenges highlighted by this transducer are described in section 4.4 and two numerical tools are proposed in section 4.5 in order to deal with one of these challenges. Closed-loop requirements are presented in section 4.6 and the control strategy associated with the transducer in order to track a given position is described in section 4.7. Results are presented in section 4.8 by a practical and realistic simulation taking into account trends cited above. The presented transducer (patented) is under development at the Grenoble Image Parole Signal Automatic Laboratory (GIPSA-Lab).

4.2. System description

In order to sense displacements of a mass with tunnel current, a tunneling tip must approach the movable mass at one nanometer or less. To do so, the tip is piezoelectrically actuated as for STMs towards the mass. In order to be moved, an electrode electrostatically actuates the mass when a voltage difference V_a is set up between the mass and the electrode. The mass has been chosen to be an AFM cantilever layered with a thin gold film at the upper side. This coating prevents tunnel current fluctuations due to chemical reactions such as oxidation.

These parts are organized according to Figure 4.1. In this configuration, the mass is squeezed between two forces: an actuator force F_a pulling it downwards and 'proximity forces' F_{prox} generated by the tip pulling the cantilever upwards. In general, these forces are attractive and act both on the cantilever and on the tip. The effect of these forces on the tip is neglected here due to the high stiffness of the piezoelectric actuator compared to the cantilever's stiffness.

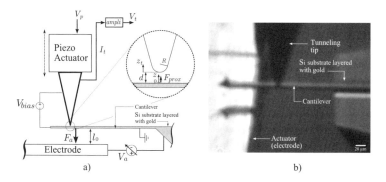

Figure 4.1. *Architecture of the system*

From a more external point of view, this system has two actuators and one sensor. A voltage amplifier is used before the piezoelectric actuator during the approach phase of the tip towards the cantilever. When the distance between the tip and the cantilever reaches 1 nm or less, tunnel current flows between these two parts. It is then amplified to a given voltage V_t and sent to the control hardware.

A first feedback loop is then switched on. The aim of this feedback loop is to keep the tunnel current at a constant value V_t by controlling the potential difference V_a between the tip and the cantilever. In this manner, this first loop keeps the distance d at a constant value. A second loop is then switched on in order to control the cantilever position and acts on the piezoelectric actuator. This latter loop works with small voltage variations and therefore does not need to pass through the amplifier.

4.2.1. *Forces between the tip and the beam*

Proximity forces acting between the tip and the beam are issued from a different nature: electrostatic [SEN 00], Van der Waals [HAM 37] and metallic adhesion forces [DUR 94]. Electrostatic and metallic adhesion forces are certain to be effective, and are attractive in our case. Van der Waals (or Casimir) forces, which are proportional to the radius of curvature of the tip in the case of sharp tips, may be neglected. The behavior of metallic adhesion forces is different from the predicted theory [CRO 98] and still needs to be studied. In order to simulate this type of force, the electrostatic force is taken into account and is added to a Van der Waals force:

$$
\begin{aligned}
F'_{\text{prox}} &= \frac{V^2_{\text{bias}}\pi\varepsilon_0 R}{d} + \frac{HR}{6d^2} \text{ if } d \geq 3.5\,\text{Å} \\
F_{\text{prox}} &= 20 \times 10^{-9} \text{ if } d < 3.5\,\text{Å}
\end{aligned}
\tag{4.1}
$$

in which V_{bias} is the voltage between the tip and the cantilever, ε_0 is the dielectric constant in vacuum, R is the radius of curvature of the tip apex and H is the Hamaker constant.

Even if the Van der Waals force has a low order of magnitude, accounting for its influence allows the estimation of proximity forces *in situ*. The behavior of this force, plotted in Figure 4.2, is compared with experimental results (defined by the area with circles) from [CRO 98]. These measurements have been carried out for an atomically defined tip apex. Because tip apexes are often not very sharp, proximity forces and their gradient presented in this section are overestimated. For realistic purposes, F_{prox} saturates at 20 nN for $d = 3.5\,\text{Å}$, according to equation (4.1).

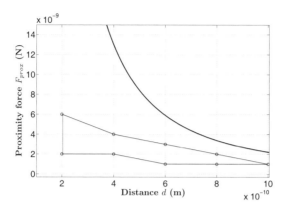

Figure 4.2. *Simulated proximity forces (bold curve) and measurements (area)*

4.3. System modeling

4.3.1. *Cantilever model*

Oscillatory parts are often modeled as a spring-mass-damper second-order linear system [LIU 01]. However, such a model does not take into account higher resonance modes of the mass, which become a drawback if some modes are close to the first mode. Moreover, these modes might exhibit a highest DC gain or damping factor than the first mode, and must therefore be taken into account.

In this section, a finite element method is carried out in order to identify the ten first modes of the cantilever. Its transfer function is made up of additive combinations of single degree-of-freedom systems as shown by equation (4.2). Each system has its numerator determined by the appropriate input/output eigenvector product, $z_{ki}z_{ji}$, where z_{ki} is the displacement of node number k when the input force F_a is applied and z_{ji} is the displacement of the tip's node [HAT 00]. As an example, a model including the ten first modes is:

$$H_{10} = \frac{z}{F_a} = \sum_{i=1}^{10} \frac{z_{ki}\, z_{ji}}{s^2 + 2\gamma_i\omega_i s + \omega_i^2} \; \text{m N}^{-1}. \tag{4.2}$$

Damping terms γ_i are estimated according to the literature [LI 07]. Natural frequencies ω_i (and modes shapes $\overrightarrow{\Phi_i}$) are obtained by solving the equation:

$$\mathbf{K}\overrightarrow{\Phi_i} = \omega_i^2 \mathbf{M}\overrightarrow{\Phi_i} \tag{4.3}$$

where the mass matrix $\mathbf{M}$ and the global stiffness matrix $\mathbf{K}$ are obtained by Finite Element Modeling (FEM) [ANS 05].

The cantilever model H_{10} contains three resonance modes with a very low DC gain, which can therefore be neglected. See Figure 4.3 for modal analysis results of a cantilever layered with a thin gold film (all modes are plotted with dot-dashed curves). The obtained model H_7 takes into account the dominant high-frequency dynamics of the cantilever and is used to simulate the open- and closed-loop behavior in section 4.3.5. On the other hand, the ten-modes model is of 20th order and is too high to be used for the controller synthesis. A model reduction is therefore performed accounting for the two dominant modes in term of DC gain and the DC gain contribution of truncated high-frequency modes. This model reduction results in a fourth-order model which is used to synthesize the controller of section 4.7.4. Figure 4.3 compares the Bode diagram of the complete and reduced model. A model has also been created using the Bernoulli method (thin curve on the same figure) to present the influence of the gold layer on the dynamical response of the cantilever.

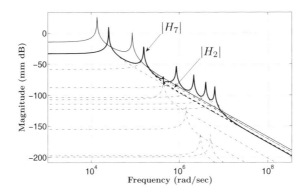

Figure 4.3. *The bold curve is the Bode diagram of the seven-modes model H_7 and the dashed curve is the Bode diagram of the reduced model H_2 (two modes); the thin curve is a fourth-order Euler–Bernoulli model of the cantilever without the gold film*

4.3.2. *System actuators*

Electrostatic actuators may be either charge or voltage controlled [SEN 00], taking into account fringing fields [ZHU 07] and inclination of plates [SEE 03] or not, depending on the geometry of the system.

In our case, the geometry is such that the common area of the capacitor plate does not include edges of the plate. In consequence, fringing field effects do not affect the actuator. In the same manner, the cantilever and the electrode remain almost parallel in the case of small displacements, such that the inclination effect of the cantilever can be neglected. Under these assumptions, if the cantilever deflection is controlled by a voltage difference V_a between itself and the electrode, the resulting force F_a is non-linear:

$$F_a = -\frac{A\varepsilon_0 V_A^2}{2(l_0 + z)^2},$$ (4.4)

where A is the common area of the electrode and the cantilever, ε_0 is the dielectric constant in vacuum and V_a and l_0 are the voltage and the gap between the electrode and the cantilever at rest, respectively.

Since this force appears immediately when a voltage V_a is applied, the bandwidth of this kind of actuator is almost infinite. The total bandwidth of the cantilever and the electrostatic actuator system is therefore limited by the cantilever bandwidth. In the scope of this chapter, the actuator is limited to small deflections and does not enter the pull-in area.

A piezoelectrical actuator is used to move the tip. Such actuators suffer two drawbacks: hysteresis and creep. Piezoelectrical actuators exhibit hysteresis in their dielectric large-signal behavior. For a given voltage, such actuators can be in several states depending on the previous states [DEV 07]. This behavior is mainly present if large-amplitude motions occur. The smaller the deflection, the smaller the uncertainty due to hysteresis. That explains why if the displacement of the actuator is limited to several nanometers, as for STMs, hysteresis can be neglected [BON 04, OLI 95].

Creep is a change in displacement with time without any accompanying change in the control voltage (due to the remnant polarization of the piezo). The rate of creep decreases logarithmically with time and can be described by the following equation:

$$\Delta_c z_t(t) \approx \Delta L_{t=0} \left[1 + \lambda \log \left(\frac{t}{0.1} \right) \right]$$ (4.5)

in which $\Delta L_{t=0}$ is the motion after the voltage change is complete (at $t = 0$) and λ is the creep factor (0.01–0.02). *In situ*, creep can add up to a few percent of the commanded motion.

Such actuators are therefore identified as a second-order mass-spring-damper model with an input voltage V_p:

$$\begin{pmatrix} \dot{z}_{t1} \\ \dot{z}_{t2} \end{pmatrix} = \begin{pmatrix} 0 & 1 \\ -k_p/m_p & -\lambda_p/m_p \end{pmatrix} \begin{pmatrix} z_{t1} \\ z_{t2} \end{pmatrix} + \begin{pmatrix} 0 \\ b_p \end{pmatrix} V_p,$$ (4.6)

where

$$z_t = (c_p\ 0) \begin{pmatrix} z_{t1} \\ z_{t2} \end{pmatrix} + \Delta_c z_t(t).$$ (4.7)

4.3.3. *Tunnel current*

The tunnel current is a flow of electrons which is able to cross an insulating layer if its thickness does not exceed 1 nm. The intensity of this very low current ($I_t \sim 1\,\text{nA}$) varies exponentially with the distance $d = z_t - z$ between the tip and the cantilever. This current can therefore be used as a distance sensor. According to the literature, the tunnel current is often modeled using different formulae as defined by equations (4.8) and (4.9) (illustrated in Figure 4.4).

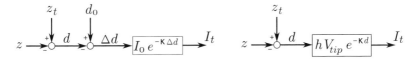

Figure 4.4. *Schema block of the tunnel current formula*

Equation (4.8) deals with the current fluctuation around a initial value I_0, and is written:

$$I_t = I_0\, e^{-\kappa \Delta d} \text{ if } 0 \le d \le 1\,\text{nm}$$
$$I_t = 0 \text{ if } d > 1\,\text{nm} \tag{4.8}$$

where I_0 is a given tunnel current at a given distance d_0 and $e^{-\kappa \Delta d}$ the current variation around I_0. This formula assumes that the distance d varies by Δd around an initial distance d_0, i.e. $\Delta d = d - d_0 = z_t - z - d_0$. Input parameters for equation (4.8) are z and z_t; d_0 can be seen as a constant perturbation.

The second formulation of the tunnel current deals with the absolute distance d [LIU 01]:

$$I_t = hV_{\text{tip}}\, e^{-\kappa d} \text{ if } 0 \le d \le 1\,\text{nm}$$
$$I_t = 0 \text{ if } d > 1\,\text{nm}. \tag{4.9}$$

This version has the advantage of being independent of the constant perturbation d_0, but the proportionality constant h is *a priori* unknown.

To summarize, equation (4.8) induces a constant unknown input perturbation d_0 at the sensor level, whereas equation (4.9) induces a constant unknown gain h at the output of the sensor.

Other formulations also involve the change of electrical resistance with d [KEM 07], and are very similar to equation (4.8). If the approximation of d is not accurate enough, I_t will be too far from a realistic value. On the other hand, an approximation of the gain h can be compensated by the robustness of a controller.

In order to be measured, tunnel current is amplified to a voltage V_t. This current amplifier has a gain of $G_{\mathrm{amp}} = 10^7\,\mathrm{V\,A^{-1}}$, an input noise of $n_{\mathrm{amp}} = 65 \times 10^{-12}\,\mathrm{A\,Hz^{-0.5}}$ and a cutoff frequency of $\omega_{\mathrm{amp}} = 400\,\mathrm{kHz}$ [FEM 05]. For such high gain, large bandwidth amplifiers can be built according to references [CHE 96, MUN 98]. Consequently, V_t can be written:

$$V_t = -\frac{\dot{V}_t}{\omega_{\mathrm{amp}}} + (G_{\mathrm{amp}} \times I_t).$$

4.3.4. *System model*

The components of the system illustrated in Figure 4.5 are first described and modeled. The dynamical behavior of the proposed system can then be presented. This system has two inputs:

– V_p, which controls the piezoelectric actuator vertically; and

– V_A, which drives the potential difference between the electrode and the cantilever and actuates the cantilever position z.

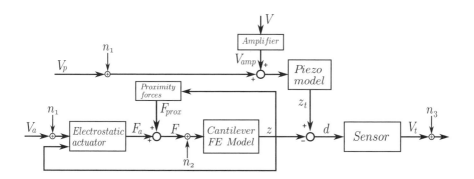

Figure 4.5. *Open-loop system*

Note that the dynamics of the cantilever and of the piezoelectric actuator are uncoupled (equation (4.10)), but the tip generates a proximity force F_{prox} on the cantilever. Equation (4.10) describes the simplified system equations:

$$
\begin{bmatrix} \dot{X}_{\text{cant}} \\ X_{\text{piezo}} \end{bmatrix} = \begin{bmatrix} A_{\text{cant}} & 0 \\ 0 & A_{\text{piezo}} \end{bmatrix} \begin{bmatrix} X_{\text{cant}} \\ X_{\text{piezo}} \end{bmatrix}
$$

$$
+ \begin{bmatrix} B_{\text{cant}} & 0 \\ 0 & B_{\text{piezo}} \end{bmatrix} \begin{bmatrix} F(V_A) \\ V_{\text{piezo}} \end{bmatrix}
$$

$$
V_{\text{out}} = \frac{\dot{V}_t}{\omega_{\text{amp}}} + G_{\text{amp}} h \exp\left[-\kappa\left(-C_{\text{cant}} X_{\text{cant}} + C_{\text{piezo}} X_{\text{piezo}}\right)\right].
$$

$$(4.10)$$

When $d = z_t - z$ is equal to or less than 1 nm, a tunnel current I_t appears and is amplified to an output voltage V_t according to:

$$
V_t = -\frac{\dot{V}_t}{\omega_{\text{amp}}} + G_{\text{amp}} \times hV_{\text{tip}} e^{-\kappa d} \text{ if } 0 \leq d \leq 1 \text{ nm}
$$

$$
V_t = 0 \text{ if } d > 1 \text{ nm}. \tag{4.11}
$$

It is also possible to use equation (4.8) to model the tunnel current, but $\Delta d = d - d_0$ must be used instead of d in the tunnel current formula. This results in the addition of an *a priori* unknown constant d_0 at the input of the sensor, instead of an *a priori* unknown gain h at the output of the tunnel current. The tunnel current formula and the amplifier together form the sensor block depicted by Figure 4.5.

Alternatively, dynamics of the system are uncoupled and the output V_{out} is a function of the difference between two states. The system is therefore unobservable. However, as the state-space matrix of the system is stable, the system is detectable. Consequently, states cannot be estimated dynamically, but can be reconstructed using a model of the system. This solution is sometimes called 'open-loop observer' because the reconstruction dynamic depends only on the poles of the system.

4.3.5. *System analysis*

As proximity forces F_{prox} behave according to the inverse of the distance d, they are susceptible to becoming very high when the distance d decreases. In this case, the cantilever irremediably crashes against the tip when a critical distance d_{PI} is reached. This behavior is comparable to the pull-in phenomenon arising in electrostatic actuators [MAI 05], but includes proximity forces. The critical distance can be computed using the Lyapunov indirect method.

A state-space model of the cantilever accounting for two resonance modes (or more) can be written in the frequency domain as a sum of two single-mode systems, as shown by equation (4.2). The denominator of the two-modes transfer function is the product of the denominators of each single-mode system. Hence, the two-modes system is stable if each single-mode system is stable. The model of the nth mode is of the form:

$$
\begin{bmatrix} \dot{x}_{ip} \\ \dot{x}_{iv} \end{bmatrix} = \begin{bmatrix} 0 & 1 \\ -\frac{k_i}{m} & -\frac{\gamma_i}{m} \end{bmatrix} \begin{bmatrix} x_{ip} \\ x_{iv} \end{bmatrix} + \begin{bmatrix} 0 \\ \frac{1}{m} \end{bmatrix} F,
\tag{4.12}
$$

where $F = F_{\text{prox}} + F_a$ and the output is $z = C_n\,x_{ip}$. If x_0 is an equilibrium position of the cantilever and we assume $z > -l_0$ and $z_s > z$, the state-space matrix describing this equilibrium is:

$$
A_{x_0} = \begin{bmatrix} 0 & 1 \\ -\frac{k_i}{m} + \frac{1}{m}\frac{\partial F}{\partial x_{ip}} & -\frac{\gamma_i}{m} \end{bmatrix}.
\tag{4.13}
$$

Then, x_0 is asymptotically stable if the real part of the eigenvalues of A_{x_0} are strictly negative, i.e. for a two-modes model:

$$
-k_1 + \frac{\partial F}{\partial z} < 0 \text{ and } -k_2 + \frac{\partial F}{\partial z} < 0.
\tag{4.14}
$$

On the other hand, pull-in occurs if the left member of equation (4.14) is positive or null. The lowest value of k_i corresponds to the first mode, so the pull-in criteria is

$$
-k_1 + \frac{\partial F}{\partial z} < 0.
\tag{4.15}
$$

This means that the gradient of the total forces acting on the cantilever must always be lower than the cantilever stiffness in order to guarantee stability.

When voltages of the system V_{tip}, V_a are fixed, the minimal distance at which the sensor can approach the cantilever apex without pull-in can be estimated by a minimization problem. The magnitude of V_a is limited to an operating range between 0 V and 20 V (for practical considerations), the bias voltage V_{tip} is assumed to have a maximum of 1 V, the displacement of the cantilever apex z is limited by the elastic regime of the cantilever (i.e. to small displacements) and the tip position z_t is limited to positive values. The minimization problem can therefore be defined:

$$\begin{cases} \min(z_t - z) \\ \text{With the constraints:} \\ 0 \le V_a \le 20 \\ 0 \le V_{\text{tip}} \le 1 \\ -100 \times 10^{-9} \le z \le 100 \times 10^{-9} \\ 0 \le z_t \\ \frac{\partial F}{\partial z} = k_1 \\ F = k_1 z. \end{cases} \qquad (4.16)$$

The minimum of $z_s - z$ is 5.8 Å and corresponds to the lowest values of V_{tip} and V_a, i.e. 0 V. Moreover, this problem proves that if a voltage V_a is initially applied to the electrode (the cantilever would be pre-stressed), the pull-in distance would be increased.

Since a bias voltage V_{tip} is needed in order to generate tunnel current, the simulation is carried out with $V_{\text{tip}} = 0.5$ V, which increases the pull-in distance to $d_{\text{PI}} = 5.9$ Å.

Figure 4.6 depicts a simulation of the tip approach (step by step) towards two cantilevers of different stiffnesses. If the stiffness is high enough, pull-in does not occur (continuous curve). However, if the stiffness decreases, the cantilever collapses on the tip (dashed curve).

Finally, the simplified system (4.10) highlights the fact that the system is non-observable and non-detectable.

States z, z_t or d cannot be dynamically estimated using the inputs and outputs. If the states are required, techniques other than estimation must be employed:

– Closed-loop piezoelectrical actuators use capacitive motion detection or strain gauges in order to control their deflexion. The best solution is to know the tip deflexion z_t, but accuracy is limited to a few nanometers (a strong drawback if tunnel current is required).

– Incorporation of an actuator or cantilever model in the feedback loop remains the best option, but the model must be sufficiently accurate. If the model is the piezoelectrical actuator, it is possible to reconstruct small changes of position z_t. It is difficult to approximate the dynamics of the actuator and to deal with creep, however.

A strategy based on a cantilever model is proposed in section 4.7 in order to reconstruct the cantilever position z, taking into account disturbances (proximity forces and creep) and noise.

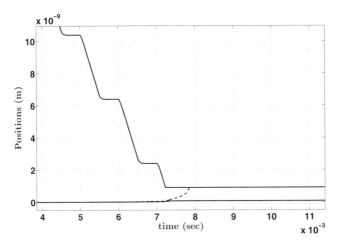

Figure 4.6. *Simulation of the open-loop behavior of two cantilevers with different stiffness*

4.4. Problem statement

Several challenges are adressed in this section; some are relative to the small-scale situation (noises and uncertainties) and others are more specific to the topic of nanopositioning (non-linearities).

4.4.1. *Robustness and non-linearities*

Small objects and signals may be difficult to characterize or identify with accuracy. Taking a cantilever as an example, data given by manufacturers are very approximate. Without specific measurement techniques, the model used in simulation is a strong approximation of the experimental model. On the other hand, the piezoelectric actuator's gain fluctuates with the temperature. Moreover, short distances such as l_0+z from the electrode to the cantilever can only be approximated (as can the area A). For all these reasons, the control law must be robust to approximations as listed in Table 4.1.

Another challenge is to take into account non-linearities of the tunnel current sensor and of the actuator in the control law. As an example, the electrostatic actuator cannot be linearized around an equilibrium: beginning with $V_a > 0$ would increase the sensitivity of the cantilever [KAI 93] and therefore the pull-in distance of the tip (section 4.3.5). Finally, the exponential behavior of the tunnel current must also be accounted for in the control law.

Variables	Uncertainties (%)
Cantilever DC gain ($z_{ki}\ z_{ji}$)	± 40
Cantilever resonance frequencies (ω_1, ω_2)	± 40
Cantilever damping (γ_1, γ_2)	± 50
Current amplifier bandwidth (ω_{amp})	± 50
Current amplifier gain (G_{amp})	± 40
Electrode area (A)	± 40
Electrode/cantilever distance ($l_0 + z$)	± 40
Piezo gain (G_p)	± 50
Piezo bandwidth (ω_p)	± 50

Table 4.1. *Robustness requirements*

4.4.2. *Experimental noise*

Noise represents a highly disturbing phenomenon in nanoscale manipulation and must not be forgotten in the simulation design. Noise can be classified into two categories: input and output noise.

4.4.2.1. *Input noise*

Input noise acts at the input of the cantilever and can be of different types:

– *Thermal noise* is generated by thermally excited particles hitting the mass. Their impacts on the cantilever generate a random force (n_2 in Figure 4.5) called the Langevin force which has the spectrum $S_{F_T} = 4k_B T \gamma_1$ [KIT 58], where $k_B = 1.38 \times 10^{-23}$ is the Boltzmann constant, T the temperature in Kelvin and γ_1 the damping of the first vibration mode of the cantilever. The mean-square displacement $\langle z^2 \rangle$ of an oscillator resulting from thermal noise is called the Brownian motion [RAS 00]:

$$\frac{1}{2}k_B T = \frac{1}{2}k_1 \langle z^2 \rangle \Leftrightarrow \langle z^2 \rangle = \frac{k_B T}{k_1}. \tag{4.17}$$

– *Back action* forces, which stochastically drive the cantilever, result from the random impact and momentum transfer of the discrete particles used by the measuring device (photons in the case of an optical interferometer; electrons in the case of a tunneling junction) [NAI 06]. This mechanical momentum (n_2 in Figure 4.5) imparted to the cantilever is thought to provide the ultimate limit to the position and force sensitivity (known as the standard quantum limit). In time δt, due to the RMS fluctuation $\sqrt{N \delta t}$ in the number of particles, the total change in momentum to the cantilever is [BOR 93]:

$$\Delta p = \sqrt{(N \delta t)} m_e v_e \tag{4.18}$$

where m_e and v_e are the mass and the velocity of the particles hitting the cantilever, respectively.

– *Actuation noise* is due to the last significant part of the electronic hardware used to generate command signals V_a and V_p. In the case of Digital/Analog (or vice versa) and 16-bit output cards, given a voltage amplitude of Amp $= \pm 10$ V, the output voltage has a resolution of the order of $\text{Amp}/2^{16} = 1.5 \times 10^{-4}$ V Hz$^{-0.5}$. This noise n_1 acts at the output of the controller.

4.4.2.2. *Output noise*

Output noise acts at the output of the cantilever model:

– $1/f$ *noise* occurs in almost all electronic devices. This is a fluctuation in the conductivity with a power spectral density proportional to $f^{-\rho}$, where $\rho = 1 \pm 0.2$ in a low frequency range, usually measured from 1 Hz to a maximum of a few kiloHertz (maximum). At some higher frequencies the slope must be steeper than -1. It has never been observed, however, for the reason that at higher frequencies the $1/f$ noise disappears within the white thermal noise that is always present. Its origin is still open to debate, but it is admitted that $1/f$ noise is a bulk effect and is not generated by the current [HOO 94]. In the case of a voltage V affected by $1/f$ noise, its spectral density is often modeled as [HOO 69]:

$$S_{V(f)} = \frac{\alpha V_{\text{DC}}^2}{N f^\rho} \tag{4.19}$$

where α is a constant and N is the number of charge carriers. The shape of its spectral density is approximated by equation (4.19) with $\alpha/N = 1 \times 10^{-5}$ and $\rho = 1.5$ ($V \sim 30$ mV). The variance of the simulated $1/f$ noise is $v_{1/f} \sim 3 \times 10^{-10}$ V^2 and its corner frequency is at 350 Hz.

– *Shot noise* is generated by the time-dependent fluctuations in the electrical current due to the discreteness of the electronic charges e. Its amplitude is negligible and, in the case of a current I subjected to shot noise, its power density is defined:

$$S_I = 2eI_{\text{av}} \tag{4.20}$$

where I_{av} is the average current.

– *Acquisition noise* appears when a device is used to record a signal. As for actuation noise, its amplitude is determined by the last significant bit of the hardware. This noise may be important due to the amplitude of the signal (see section 4.7.2). For the following simulation, this noise is assumed to be an output white noise with an amplitude of 1 mV (n_3 in Figure 4.5), corresponding to a signal-to-noise ratio of 10%.

– *Creep and thermal drift* may be seen as output noise acting on z_t and z, respectively. They are very low-frequency noise (a few Hertz). Thermal drift is due to the dilatation of materials when the temperature fluctuates by some milliKelvin. It can be modeled as a very low-frequency stochastic noise on z with an amplitude of some nanometers. Creep has already been defined in section 4.3.2, and acts on z_t.

Output noise is more delicate to deal with, as it cannot be attenuated at all frequencies. On the contrary, it are amplified at some frequencies if a closed loop is used. Two control strategies are therefore proposed in order to deal with output and input noise.

4.5. Tools to deal with noise

4.5.1. *Kalman filter*

The Kalman filter is a recursive algorithm which estimates states of a dynamical system corrupted by output noise. From a state-space representation of a system:

$$x_i = A_{\text{ss}} x_{i-1} + B_{\text{ss}} u_{i-1} + \psi_{i-1}$$
$$z_i = H_{\text{ss}} x_i + \nu_i,$$

the Kalman filter computes a prediction $\hat{x}_i^-$ of the state to be estimated and corrects it with an actual measurement z_i. Given an initial estimation of $\hat{x}_{i-1}^-$ and of its error covariance P_{i-1}, $\hat{x}_i^-$ can be predicted from:

$$\hat{x}_i^- = A_{\text{ss}} \hat{x}_{i-1} + B_{\text{ss}} u_{i-1} \tag{4.21}$$

which enables the projection of the prediction error covariance $E\left[e_i^- \; e_i^{-T}\right]$:

$$E\left[e_i^- \; e_i^{-T}\right] = A_{\text{ss}} \, E\left[e_{i-1}^- \; e_{i-1}^{-T}\right] A_{\text{ss}}^T + Q \tag{4.22}$$

where $e_i^- = x_i - \hat{x}_i^-$ is the error of the predicted state. A second correction step updates the state estimation using the prediction $\hat{x}_i^-$ and the measurement z_i:

$$\hat{x}_i = \hat{x}_i^- + K_i(z_i - H_{\text{ss}} \hat{x}_i^-) \tag{4.23}$$

where $K_i = P_i^- H_{\text{ss}}^T (H P_i^- H_{\text{ss}}^T + R)^{-1}$ is the Kalman gain. The error covariance is also updated during the correction step ($P_i = (I - K_i H_{\text{ss}}) P_i^-$). More details can be found in [WEL 01]. The Kalman filter offers the advantage of estimating signals dynamically. This tool is used in section 4.7.3 in order to reduce the noise of a constant output.

4.5.2. *Minimum variance controller*

The influence of noise (input noise as well as output noise) can be minimized by an appropriate placement of the closed-loop poles. A linear system can be modeled by an autoregressive moving average with external inputs (ARMAX) model as shown in Figure 4.7, where r is the system delay and $A(z^{-1}), B(z^{-1})$ and $C(z^{-1})$ are polynomials in z^{-1}. Any system with a nominal model $B_1(z^{-1})/A_1(z^{-1})$ and a perturbation model $C_2(z^{-1})/A_2(z^{-1})$ can be modeled in the form depicted by Figure 4.7 by choosing $A(z^{-1}) = A_1(z^{-1})A_2(z^{-1})$, $B(z^{-1}) = B_1(z^{-1})A_2(z^{-1})$ and $C(z^{-1}) = C_2(z^{-1})A_1(z^{-1})$. If the output noise is modeled as a white noise, $C_2(z^{-1}) = A_2(z^{-1}) = 1$ and $C(z^{-1}) = A_1(z^{-1})$.

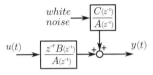

Figure 4.7. *Example of an ARMAX model*

In the case of RST controllers (where R, S and T are polynomials), it has been demonstrated [LAN 90] that minimizing the output variance around a reference trajectory is equivalent to minimizing the criteria

$$E\left([y(t+r+1) - y^\star(t+r+1)]^2\right) \tag{4.24}$$

$$= E\left(\left[\frac{R(z^{-1})}{C(z^{-1})}y(t) + \frac{S(z^{-1})}{C(z^{-1})}u(t) - y^\star(t+r+1)\right]^2\right)$$

$$+ E\left([S'(z^{-1})e(t+r+1)]^2\right)$$

$$+ 2E\left(\left[\frac{R(z^{-1})}{C(z^{-1})}y(t) + \frac{S(z^{-1})}{C(z^{-1})}u(t) - y^\star(t+r+1)\right]\left[S'(z^{-1})e(t+r+1)\right]\right)$$

in which $e(t)$ is the error signal and $y^\star$ is a reference trajectory. $B^\star(z^{-1})$ is defined by $B(z^{-1}) = z^{-1}B^\star(z^{-1})$ which allows $S'(z^{-1}) = S(z^{-1})/B^\star(z^{-1})$ to be computed. The criteria defined by equation (4.24) can be minimized when choosing the control law:

$$u(t) = \frac{T(z^{-1})\,t^\star(t+r+1) + R(z^{-1})\,y(t)}{S(z^{-1})} \tag{4.25}$$

in which $T(z^{-1})$ is chosen to be equal to $C(z^{-1})$, i.e. to the poles $A(z^{-1})$ of the system if the output noise is white. From a practical point of view, the influence of an output white noise on $y(t)$ (defined in Figure 4.7) is minimized if the frequency of the closed-loop poles is chosen to be equal to the first resonance frequency of the open-loop system.

4.6. Closed-loop requirements

This section discusses the conditions that a linear controller must fulfill in order to be robust and to reject disturbances encountered at a nanoscale. These requirements serve as a reference for the controllers' synthesis in sections 4.7.4 and 4.7.6.

4.6.1. Sensitivity functions

Stability and performance requirements can be expressed by means of constraints on the closed-loop sensitivity functions [LAN 97]. These constraints will be used for the controller design and performance analysis. In the case of an RST controller and, when the open-loop plant G is defined as $G(s) = B(s)/A(s)$, sensitivity functions are usually defined by the relationships:

$$\mathbf{S}(s) = A(s) \times S(s)/(A(s) \times S(s) + B(s) \times R(s)) \tag{4.26}$$

$$\mathbf{SG}(s) = G(s) \times \mathbf{S}(s) \tag{4.27}$$

$$\mathbf{KS}(s) = (R(s)/S(s)) \times \mathbf{S}(s) \tag{4.28}$$

$$\mathbf{T}(s) = B(s) \times T(s)/(A(s) \times S(s) + B(s) \times R(s)). \tag{4.29}$$

The output sensitivity function $\mathbf{S}$ characterizes the influence on the closed-loop measured output $V_{out}(t)$ of an output disturbance. The complementary sensitivity function $\mathbf{T}$ is the transfer from the reference signal r to the closed-loop system output V_{out}. $\mathbf{KS}$ is the input sensitivity function and characterizes the influence of an output disturbance on the control signal $u(t)$. $\mathbf{SG}$ is the output sensitivity function with respect to an input disturbance. Bold letters are used for sensitivity functions and are not to be confused with the controller polynomials R, S and T.

4.6.2. Robustness margins

Two robustness margins, namely the modulus margin and the delay margin, are important for designing robust digital controllers.

4.6.2.1. The modulus margin

The modulus margin (ΔM) is defined as the radius of the circle centered on $[-1, j_0]$ and tangent to the Nyquist plot of the open-loop transfer function $G(z^{-1})$. The modulus margin is linked to the output sensitivity function by [LAN 90]:

$$\Delta M = (\|\mathbf{S}\|_\infty)^{-1}. \tag{4.30}$$

As a consequence, the reduction (or minimization) of $|\mathbf{S}(s)|_{\max}$ will imply an increase (or maximization) of the modulus margin ΔM. This margin is very important because it gives a bound for the characteristics of the non-linearities and time-varying elements tolerated by the closed-loop system (it corresponds to the circle criterion for the stability of non-linear systems).

4.6.2.2. *The delay margin*

The delay margin $(\Delta\tau)$ is the additional delay which will make the closed-loop system unstable. If the Nyquist plot intersects the unit circle at several frequencies ω_{cr}^i, characterized by the corresponding phase margin $\Delta\phi_i$, the delay margin is defined:

$$\Delta\tau = \min_i \frac{\Delta\phi_i}{\omega_{cr}^i}. \tag{4.31}$$

4.6.2.3. *Typical values of robustness margins*

Typical values of these robustness margins for a robust controller design are:
- modulus margin: $\Delta M \geq 0.5 - 6\,\mathrm{dB}$ and
- delay margin: $\Delta\tau \geq T_s$.

Note that a modulus margin $\Delta M \geq 0.5$ implies that the gain margin $\Delta G \geq 2$ and the phase margin $\Delta\phi > 29°$. The converse is not generally true. More details about robustness of controllers can be found in [DOY 92, LAN 90].

4.6.3. *Templates of the sensibility functions*

4.6.3.1. *Template of* S

Using the small gain theorem and various representations of the open-loop system uncertainties, the modulus margin and the delay margin can be converted into robust stability conditions. For a delay margin of one sampling period, the robust stability condition is expressed [LAN 90]:

$$1 - |1 - z^{-1}|^{-1} < \mathbf{S}(z^{-1}) < 1 + |1 - z^{-1}|^{-1} \qquad z = e^{\omega j}, \tag{4.32}$$

where $0 \leq \omega \leq \pi$.

To ensure the delay margin $\Delta\tau = T_s$, it is required that the modulus of $\mathbf{S}(z^{-1})$ lies inside a 'tube' defined by a lower template $|W^{-1}|_{\inf} = 1 - |1 - z^{-1}|^{-1}$ and an upper template $|W^{-1}|_{\sup} = 1 - |1 + z^{-1}|^{-1}$. The chosen modulus margin will induce the maximum value of the upper template and the chosen delay margin will define an upper and a lower template, starting at around 0.15 times the sampling frequency (for $\Delta\tau = T_s$).

The nominal performance aims to reject low-frequency output disturbances such as creep (or thermal drift), $1/f$ noise and displacements of the tip z_t. An attenuation band for the output sensitivity function is required at frequencies of these disturbances, which are in general very low compared to the system dynamics. In the framework of this chapter, the closed-loop frequency is chosen to attenuate output disturbances at frequencies before the first resonant mode of the open-loop system and the first mode itself. Hence, the first resonance mode will be completely cancelled by the command.

4.6.3.2. Template of SG

The input sensibility function is responsible for the amplification or attenuation of input disturbances, but also illustrates the robustness towards parametric coefficients. The most dominant input noise is the actuation noise (from the hardware) and the Langevin force, whose spectral density is close that of a white noise. In order to minimize their influence on the closed-loop system, the H-infinity norm of **SG** in a closed loop must be inferior to the H-infinity norm of **SG** in an open loop, i.e. $\|\mathbf{SG}\|_\infty^{\mathrm{CL}} < \|\mathbf{SG}\|_\infty^{\mathrm{OL}}$.

The input sensibility function also allows the robustess towards uncertain parameters, such as damping ratios, to be characterized. Its dispersion can be modeled as a feedback uncertainty around the nominal transfer function $G_i(i = 1, 2)$ of each of the harmonic modes [DOY 92]:

$$\tilde{G}_i(s) = G_i(s)/(1 + \Delta W_i(s)G_i(s)) \tag{4.33}$$

$$W_i(s) = \frac{\delta\gamma_i\, s}{a_i}, \quad -1 \le \Delta \le 1, \tag{4.34}$$

where $W_i(s)$ provides an uncertainty profile (for each mode), $\delta\gamma_i$ is the damping coefficient variation around the nominal value and a_i is the gain of each harmonic mode times the sensor gain (see equation (4.38)).

The stability robustness condition for such an uncertainty model is:

$$\|W_i(s)\,\mathbf{GS}(s)\|_\infty \le 1 \iff |GS(s)| \le |1/W_i(s)|, \; \forall f. \tag{4.35}$$

The most restrictive constraint is obtained for $i = 2$, i.e. the uncertainty on the damping γ_2 of the second mode.

4.6.3.3. Template of KS

The frequency regions, where the modulus of the sensitivity function **KS** is high, correspond to regions where rejection of disturbances will lead to very strong input signals. The maximum of **KS** should therefore not cross a threshold value (generally fixed at 15 dB) in these frequency regions.

4.7. Control strategy

The goal of this section is to propose a robust control law in order to control the position z of the tip in the presence of noise, accounting for non-linearities and pull-in instability.

The control strategy which is exposed here is based on two feedback loops acting simultaneously. The first is designed to be fast and to control the distance d between the tip and the cantilever. It uses the signal $y(t)$ (Figure 4.8) as output. The second is slower and acts as a disturbance on the first feedback loop. It uses a reconstruction of the beam position z to track a given reference z_{ref}. Its command signal is $V_p(t)$ (Figure 4.8).

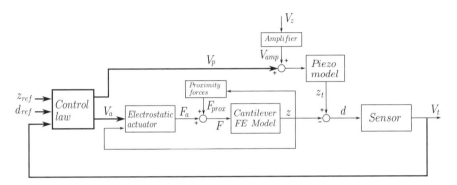

Figure 4.8. *Closed-loop system*

To design the first RST$_1$ controller, a feedback linearization of the electrostatic actuator is applied such that the signal $u(t)$ leaving the controller fulfills the condition $u(t) = F_a(t)$ (see equation (4.37) and Figure 4.8). A simplified linear model of the sensor is then computed under the assumption that the bandwidth of the amplifier is higher than the closed-loop model (see section 4.7.2). Since the model of the system is linear, a robust controller synthesis based on poles placement/sensitivity function shaping is applied to generate the controller RST$_1$. This synthesis is carried out using a simplified model of the cantilever (a fourth-order model).

Since $u(t) = F_a(t)$, this reconstruction is sent to a model of the cantilever to deduce its deflexion $\hat{z}(t)$ under $F_a(t)$. $\hat{z}(t)$ is in turn used as the output of the second closed loop which controls the piezoelectric actuator (thus the tip position z_t).

Finally, it must be noted that there are two ways to deal with position control: a relative position Δz, i.e. start from the rest position $z_{t=0}$ of the cantilever and control its deflexion, or the positioning can be absolute, i.e. the position z from a fixed reference is controlled. The only difference between these two methods is to sense, in real time, a distance from a fixed reference to the cantilever with an accuracy at least equal to the tunnel sensor (less than 1 Å). Until recently, sensors greater than the tunnel current have been very hard to find.

4.7.1. Actuator linearization

The force $F_a(t)$ acting on the cantilever is a function of the inverse of the squared distance $(l_0 + z)^2$ and of the square of $V_a(t)$. This force is limited to pulling the mass. Two control strategies can therefore be applied: a tangent linearization or a linearizing feedback.

The tangent linearization is valid if the cantilever position z maintains an equilibrium position where its behavior can be approximated as linear. Moreover, this strategy requires that the amplitude of the voltage generated by the command must be almost negligible in comparison to the equilibrium voltage [WAN 02]. As the cantilever is controlled from its rest position (see section 4.3.5), the solution is invalid. On the other hand, a linearizing feedback consists of using a law derived from the actuator law inside the feedback loop in order to cancel the non-linearity [BLA 08]. The control law must linearize the actuator, i.e.

$$F_a(t) = u(t) = \frac{A\varepsilon_0 V_a(t)^2}{2(l_0 + z(t))^2}. \tag{4.36}$$

Hence, writing $V_a(t)$ as a function of $u(t)$ yields the control law:

$$
\begin{aligned}
V_a(t) &= \sqrt{\frac{2\,(z(t) + l_0)^2}{\varepsilon_0 A}} \times u(t) \text{ if } u(t) \geq 0 \\
V_a(t) &= 0 \text{ if } u(t) < 0
\end{aligned}
\tag{4.37}
$$

where $u(t)$ is the control signal generated by an RST_1 controller (see section 4.7.4). The non-linearity due to the electrostatic actuator is therefore compensated for.

4.7.2. Sensor approximation

A logarithmic operation is always used in STMs in order to linearize the exponential behavior of the tunnel current $I_t(t)$ into a given voltage $y(t)$. However, when the amplification is made before the logarithmic conversion, the behavior from d to y is non-linear. This behavior can be approximated as linear if the bandwidth of the amplifier is fast enough regarding the bandwidth of the closed loop. Under this assumption, the amplifier can be simplified as its gain G_{amp} and the behavior from d to y becomes linear:

$$y = \log_{10} V_t = \log_{10}(G_{amp} h V_{tip}) - \kappa \log_{10}(e)d. \tag{4.38}$$

It is evident that, if the logarithmic operator is used, tunnel current formulae (equations (4.8) and (4.9)) yield the same tunnel current linear model for the controller design. This method offers the advantage of isolating G_{amp}, V_{tip} and h from the controller synthesis, since only the gain $-\kappa \log_{10}(e)d$ is used in the controller synthesis.

On the other hand, the presence of the $\log_{10}$ operator is very important if the hardware noise is not negligible (1 mV, for example). If a logarithmic amplifier is used between the tunnel current and the acquisition hardware, the hardware noise will affect the logarithmic amplification of the tunnel current. If the tunnel current is of amplitude 1 nA, the logarithmic amplification is then of the order –2. This configuration (used in STMs) results in a small signal-to-noise ratio.

On the contrary, if the logarithm is part of the control strategy (inside the hardware), the hardware noise will affect the linear amplification of the tunnel current, resulting in a signal-to-noise ratio two hundred times larger. These two configurations are illustrated in Figures 4.9 and 4.10.

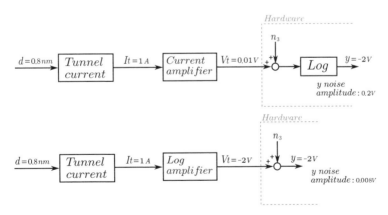

Figure 4.9. *Influence of the log operator*

Although we encourage the reader to use the first configuration, the second is also presented here in order to demonstrate the efficiency of control strategies regarding noise attenuation.

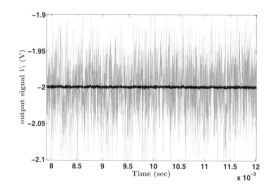

Figure 4.10. *Illustration of the noise of the system output y dependent on the place of the log operator*

4.7.3. *Kalman filtering*

As the sensor is corrupted by an output noise with an amplitude $n_3 = 1$ and with a root mean square value $< V_t >= 10$ mV, the output $y(t)$ has a non-negligible signal-to-noise ratio of 10%. If this output is used for regulation purposes, its noise may affect the stability of the closed loop. In order to tackle this problem, a Kalman filter is used to produce an estimate $\hat{y}$ of $y(t)$. As $\hat{y}(t)$ is used for regulation purposes during z_{ref} tracking, $\hat{y}(t)$ remains constant (in the absence of disturbances). A Kalman filter of an integrator form can then be used in order to estimate this constant. The pole of this filter must be approximately ten times faster than the closed-loop poles, but low enough to attenuate the variance of the estimated output $\hat{y}(t)$. The state-space model of the constant, corrupted by a noise n_{out}, can be written as:

$$\dot{x} = 0x + n_{\text{state}}; \ \hat{y} = x + n_{\text{out}} \tag{4.39}$$

where n_{state} is the state noise. Poles of this Kalman filter are adjusted after choosing the closed-loop poles.

4.7.4. *RST$_1$ synthesis*

The controller synthesis is carried out according to the poles placement/sensitivity functions shaping proposed by [LAN 90]. It is an iterative method which provides an instantaneous view of the sensitivity functions, tools to shape them and, furthermore, results for a low controller order (compare to other H_∞-like methods).

The first step is to choose the dominant closed-loop poles and to compute the resulting RST$_1$ controller. In our case, the desired dominant poles of the closed loop (P_D) are chosen as a second-order polynomial with the same natural frequency as the first vibration mode of the nominal plant ($f_0 = 4\,\text{kHz}$; see minimum variance controller in section 4.5.2), but with a damping factor equal to $\xi = 0.9$. In order to reject a steady-state error, an integrator is required in the denominator of the controller: a fixed part $H_s(z^{-1}) = 1 - z^{-1}$ is imposed on the polynomial $S(z^{-1})$. The Bezout equation:

$$AH_s S' + BR = P_D \tag{4.40}$$

is then solved for S' and R in order to compute the polynomials $R, S = S' \times H_S$ and T.

The corresponding sensitivity functions are plotted in Figure 4.11 (dots). The obtained output sensitivity function has a large value ($\|\mathbf{S}\|_\infty \approx 10\,\text{dB}$) between the two resonance modes. To further reduce the maximum of the output sensitivity function in this frequency range, a second filter H_{S2} such that $H_S = (1 - z^{-l})H_{S2}$ is imposed at $11.14\,\text{kHz}$, with a damping factor of $\xi = 0.4$ (resulting in the dashed curves in Figure 4.11). Finally, four auxiliary high-frequency poles $P_F(z^{-1}) = (1-0.5z^{-1})^4$ are added to P_D in order to decrease the maximum of $\mathbf{S}$ in high frequencies (dashed sensitivity functions in Figure 4.11). This fulfills the design requirements given in section 4.6.2: $\|\mathbf{S}\|_\infty = 5.3\,\text{dB}$, the gain margin is equal to $6.8\,\text{dB}$ and the phase margin to $42.5\,\text{dB}$.

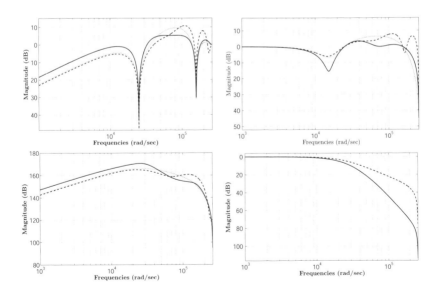

Figure 4.11. *Evolution of the sensitivity functions*

4.7.5. *z reconstruction*

The aim of this section is to propose a strategy to reconstruct the cantilever position z. It has already been mentioned that the system is not observable. The remaining method is to use a model of an actuator in order to reconstruct $\hat{z}$ from a signal. Since creep acts as an output disturbance of the piezoelectric actuator, a model of this in the control scheme would result in the non-rejection of creep. On the other hand, the linearizing feedback has been set such that $u(t) = F_a(t)$. Using this signal, it is then possible to reconstruct the deflexion $\hat{z}$ of the cantilever from a model.

In order to minimize the noise on $\hat{z}$, the model of the cantilever is used in closed loop: an RST_2 controller is designed with closed-loop poles located at the first resonance frequency of the model and without integrator. This latter choice is motivated by better disturbance rejections than in the presence of an integrator. In this manner, oscillations due to the noise of $u(t) = \hat{F}_a(t)$ are attenuated over all frequencies, as shown in Figure 4.12. Finally, $u(t) = \hat{F}_a(t)$ is considered in order to ensure that the static gain from $u(t) = \hat{F}_a(t)$ to $\hat{z}$ is equal to that of the open-loop model of the cantilever. Finally, the estimated cantilever position $\hat{z}$ can be used as output from the second closed loop.

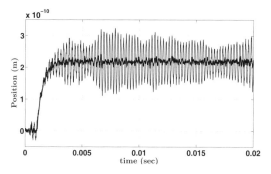

Figure 4.12. *Open-loop cantilever versus minimum variance controlled cantilever*

4.7.6. *RST₂ synthesis*

A second controller RST_2 is designed in order to control the position of the tip z_t with the piezoelectric actuator and using $\hat{z}$ as output (as illustrated in Figure 4.13). The system to control is the piezoelectric actuator (see section 4.3.2), which makes the design of the RST_2 straightforward. It will therefore not be detailed. The only specific requirement for this design is that the closed loop must be at least ten times slower than the first closed loop. The synthesis results in an PID-like RST_2 controller with very high robustness margins (modulus margin > 0.9). Consequently, it is more interesting to test the robustness performance of the first closed loop (see section 4.8.3).

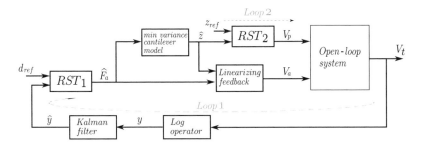

Figure 4.13. *Complete scheme of the control law*

4.8. Results

This section presents the simulation of the entire closed-loop system. We first recall challenges incurred by manipulation at the nanoscale and corresponding solutions. The behavior of the proposed control scheme is then presented in three sections: the first two sections demonstrate the tracking and regulation behavior and the third section illustrates robustness properties of the controller.

From a practical point of view, one of the most interesting challenges is to avoid the pull-in of the cantilever against the tip. Pull-in is a consequence of proximity forces. As these forces are considered as input disturbances, they (and therefore pull-in) can be rejected by an integrator inside the control law. The other challenging task is to work in a noisy environment. Many noises in the entire frequency range are present: low-frequency noise such as creep or *1/f* noise or white noise such as thermal noise. Characteristics of these noises used in the simulation were described in section 4.4.2. In order to deal with these noises, two control techniques have been proposed: minimum variance controllers and Kalman filters.

The control law must take into account non-linearities of the system: the non-linearity of the actuator has been cancelled by a linearizing feedback and that of the sensor is linearized using a simple log operator (under the assumption that the amplifier bandwidth is high enough compared to the closed-loop bandwidth). The control law must also be robust to variations and uncertainties in parameters. Robustness of controllers was described in sections 4.7.4 and 4.7.6, and is tested in section 4.8.3.

4.8.1. *Position control*

Once the tunneling tip is close enough to the cantilever to allow tunnel current to flow, the first loop is closed at $16\,\mathrm{ms}$ in order to regulate the distance d. The second loop is then closed at $20\,\mathrm{ms}$ in order to track a reference position z_{ref} of the cantilever. Figure 4.14 illustrates the performance of the Kalman filter and of the minimal variance cantilever model in a real-time simulation: both techniques strongly attenuate the variance of noise. Without these, noise variance would affect the stability of the system.

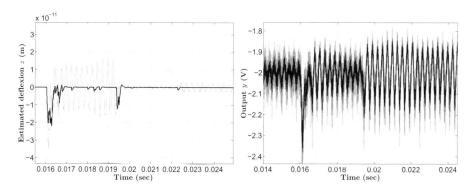

Figure 4.14. *Benefits of noise attenuation tools: closed-loop cantilever model (left) and Kalman filter (right)*

Figure 4.15 shows tracking performances when z_{ref} is changed to $-2\,\mathrm{nm}$ at $25\,\mathrm{ms}$, and then to $+1\,\mathrm{nm}$ at $175\,\mathrm{ms}$ once the second loop is in action. These two steps demonstrate the feasibility of controlling the cantilever in both directions, using the electrostatic actuator to pull it downwards and its stiffness for upwards positioning. The strategy presented in this section shows that the tunnel current can be used as a position or motion sensor for displacements of more than one nanometer.

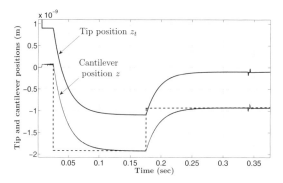

Figure 4.15. *Tracking and output disturbances rejection simulation*

In addition, Figure 4.15 also illustrates regulation performances towards output step disturbances of 1 Å (at 340 ms). Note that the cantilever position z must be well isolated from external disturbances (e.g. vibrations). If z moves downwards by several angstroms, the distance d between the tip and the cantilever may increase to more than 1 nm, stopping the tunnel current. In the present simulation, the distance d is kept constant at $d = 8.3$ Å. A perturbation opposite to the tip direction and resulting in a 1.7 Å displacement of the cantilever would stop the closed loop.

Figure 4.16 shows regulation performance when creep (or thermal drifts) is added to the simulation after a step of –4 nm. This low-frequency perturbation acts on the tip position z_t once the tip position reaches a constant value (at 180 ms). The dashed line of Figure 4.16 illustrates the behavior of the tip position if the second loop is open. If the second loop is closed, creep is rejected and the tip position remains at a controlled value.

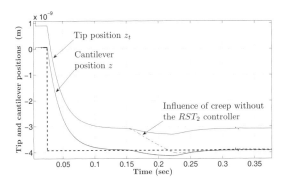

Figure 4.16. *Closed-loop simulation with creep and input disturbances added*

This kind of disturbance is of primary importance in nanopositioning: it is often a source of misunderstanding and spatial uncertainties when microscopes or other nanomanipulators must be used with high accuracy. This result proves that the problem of creep (or thermal drift) can be tackled by a proper control strategy. Figure 4.16 also illustrates input disturbance rejection performances: two steps of amplitude 3 nN are applied around 320 ms. Physically, these disturbances correspond to a doubling of the magnitude of proximity forces. As they are rejected with low overshoot, the control law demonstrates highly satisfactory performance in regulation.

4.8.2. *Distance d control*

Due to the very high gain of the tunnel current, it is possible to control very small variations of the distance d. Hence, by changing the reference y_{ref} of the first loop, it is possible to change the distance between the tip and the cantilever below the pull-in distance. This possibility is illustrated in Figure 4.17: from 150 ms, three steps of 1 Å are applied, bringing the cantilever closer to the tip of 3 Å. In this case, displacement control can be applied with an accuracy as high as in scanning tunneling microscopes, i.e. with an accuracy of < 1 Å.

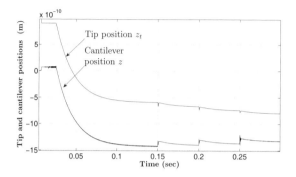

Figure 4.17. *Distance d control*

4.8.3. *Robustness*

Uncertainties which we are concerned with are listed in section 4.4.1. Figure 4.18 illustrates the influence of uncertainties on cantilever and amplifier models. On these figures, dotted lines show nominal models and continuous curves show the influence of parametric variations. The resonance peaks of the cantilever decreases by 40% and its DC gain changes by 5 dB. The bandwidth of the current amplifier varies by 50% as well as its DC gain.

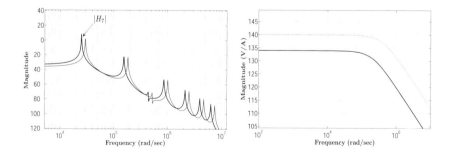

Figure 4.18. *Perturbed models of the cantilever and of the current amplifier*

Figure 4.19 shows numerical results of models plotted in Figure 4.18, with 40% variation of the electrostatic actuator parameters A and l. As shown by Figure 4.19, the control law remains stable even if the cantilever, the amplifier and the actuator parameters are approximated.

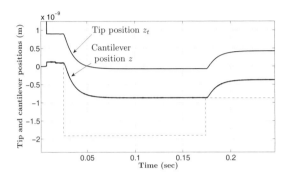

Figure 4.19. *Simulation with perturbed models*

The only drawback of this strategy is that the DC gain of the cantilever and the actuator must be known: if there is a difference in gain between the cantilever and its model used to compute $\hat{z}$, the displacement $\hat{z}$ resulting from $u(t) = F_a(t)$ will differ from the displacement z resulting in the force F_a. However, the identification of the DC gain of the cantilever is not a high constraint and appears to be easily achievable in practice.

4.9. Conclusion

The concept of tunnel current as a nanopositioning sensor has been explored in this chapter. Both practical and theoretical aspects have been taken into account in order to propose a complete and realistic objective simulation. The main drawbacks of nanoscale positioning have been defined and discussed. Control strategies have been proposed to either minimize or cancel these phenomenon: non-linearities (electrostatic actuator, tunnel current), robustness (towards parametric dispersions), noisy environment (10% signal-to-noise ratio) and creep (or thermal drift) of actuators.

The proposed control strategy is not unique, as the cantilever position z can be reconstructed using a sensor and a piezoelectric actuator model. However, this strategy would not reject output disturbances of the piezoelectrical actuator, i.e. creep. Results show satisfactory tracking and regulation behavior if the gain of the system electrostatic actuation and of the manipulated object is identified.

One of the main contributions of this chapter is to demonstrate, for the first time, that tunnel current can be used in order to sense displacements of amplitude > 1 nm. This can be achieved with a high resolution and speed, taking advantage of the tunnel current characteristics. In this way, a fast and precise sub-nanometric positioning without contact becomes possible.

4.10. Bibliography

[ANS 05] ANSYS, *User Manual on Theory Reference*, ANSYS Inc., 2005.

[APH 07] APHALE S., FLEMING A., MOHEIMANI S., "High speed nano-scale positioning using a piezoelectric tube actuator with active shunt control", *Micro & Nano Letters, IET*, vol. 2, num. 1, p. 9–12, March 2007.

[BIN 82] BINNIG G., ROHRER H., GERBER C., WEIBEL E., "Surface studies by scanning tunneling microscopy", *Phys. Rev. Lett. American Physical Society*, vol. 49, num. 1, p. 57–61, July 1982.

[BLA 08] BLANVILLAIN S., VODA A., BESANÇON G., "Pull-in control during nanometric positioning by near field position sensing", *47th IEEE Conference on Decision and Control*, Cancun, Mexico, 2008.

[BOC 90] BOCKO M., "The scanning tunneling microscope as a high-gain, low-noise displacement sensor", *Review of Scientific Instruments*, vol. 61, num. 12, p. 3763–3768, 1990.

[BON 04] BONNAIL N., TONNEAU D., JANDARD F., CAPOLINO G., DALLAPORTA H., "Variable structure control of a piezoelectric actuator for a scanning tunneling microscope", *IEEE Transactions on Industrial Electronics*, vol. 51, num. 2, p. 354–363, April 2004.

[BOR 93] BORDONI F., KARIM M., "Fundamental noise, electromechanical transduction and their role in resonant gravitational-wave detectors", *International Symposium on Experimental Gravitation*, vol. 11(6A), p. 61–72, 1993.

[CHE 96] CHEN Y., COX A., HAGMANN M., SMITH H., "Electrometer preamplifier for scanning tunneling microscopy", *Review of Scientific Instruments*, vol. 67, num. 7, p. 2652–2653, 1996.

[CRO 98] CROSS G., SCHIRMEISEN A., STALDER A., GRUTTER P., TSCHUDY M., DURIG U., "Adhesion interaction between atomically defined tip and sample", *Phys. Rev. Lett. American Physical Society*, vol. 80, num. 21, p. 4685–4688, May 1998.

[DEV 07] DEVASIA S., ELEFTHERIOU E., MOHEIMANI S., "A survey of control issues in nanopositioning", *IEEE Transactions on Control Systems Technology*, vol. 15, num. 5, p. 802–823, September 2007.

[DOY 92] DOYLE J., FRANCIS B., TANNENBAUM A., *Feedback Control Theory*, MacMillan, 1992.

[DUR 94] DURIG U., "Atomic-scale metal adhesion investigated by scanning tunneling microscopy", *IBM Journal of Research and Development*, vol. 4, p. 347–356, 1994.

[DUW 08] DUWEZ A.-S., "Nanomanipulation: Molecular cranes swing into action", *Nature Nanotechnology*, vol. 3, p. 188–189, 2008.

[EIG 91] EIGLER D., LUTZ C., RUDGE W., "An atomic switch realized with the scanning tunnelling microscope", *Nature*, vol. 352, p. 600–603, August 1991.

[EKI 05] EKINCI K., "Electromechanical transducers at the nanoscale: actuation and sensing of motion in nanoelectromechanical systems (NEMS)", *Small*, vol. 1, num. 8–9, p. 786–797, August 2005.

[FEM 05] FEMTO GROUP, *Femto Amplifier Overview (Amplifier LCA-400K-10M)*, FEMTO Messtechnik GmbH, 2005.

[GOR 06] GORMAN J., KIM Y., DAGALAKIS N., "Control of MEMS nanopositioners with nano-scale resolution", *Proceedings of the ASME International Mechanical Engineering Conference*, Chicago, Illinois USA, November 2006.

[GU 05] GU J., JONG-KIM W., VERMA S., "Nanoscale motion control with a compact minimum-actuator magnetic levitator", *Journal of Dynamic Systems, Measurement, and Control*, vol. 127, num. 3, p. 433–442, 2005.

[HAM 37] HAMAKER H., "The London–van der Waals attraction between spherical particules", *Physica*, vol. 4, p. 1058–1072, 1937.

[HAT 00] HATCH M., *Vibration Simulation Using MATLAB and ANSYS*, Chapman and Hall, 2000.

[HEL 08] HELLER E., "Electron wrangling in quantum corrals", *Nature Physics*, vol. 4, p. 443–444, 2008.

[HOO 69] HOOGE F., "$1/f$ noise is no surface effect", *Physics Letters A*, vol. 29, num. 3, p. 139–140, 1969.

[HOO 94] HOOGE F., "$1/f$ noise is no surface effect", *IEEE Transactions on Electron Devices*, vol. 41, num. 11, p. 1926–1935, November 1994.

[KAI 93] KAISER W., KENNY T., REYNOLDS J., ZANDT T., WALTMAN S., *Methods and Apparatus for Improving Sensor Performance*, United States Patent, California Institute of Technology, Pasadena, California, 1993.

[KEM 07] KEMIKTARAK U., NDUKUM T., SCHWAB K., EKINCI K., "Radio-frequency scanning tunnelling microscopy", *Nature*, vol. 450, p. 85–89, 2007.

[KIT 58] KITTEL C., *Elementary Statistical Physics*, Dover Publications, Mineola, New York, 1958.

[KUR 06] KURITA M., SHIRAMATSU T., MIYAKE K., KATO A., SOGA M., TANAKA H., SAEGUSA S., SUK M., "Active flying-height control slider using MEMS thermal actuator", *Microsyst. Technol.*, vol. 12, num. 4, p. 369–375, 2006.

[LAN 90] LANDAU I., *System Identification and Control Design*, Englewood Cliffs, 1990.

[LAN 97] LANDAU I., LOZANO R., M'SAAD R., *Adaptative Control*, Springer, 1997.

[LEE 08] LEE S., KIM J., MOON W., CHOI J., PARK I., BAE D., "A multibody-based dynamic simulation method for electrostatic actuators", *Nonlinear Dynamics*, vol. 54, num. 1–2, p. 53–68, October 2008.

[LI 07] LI P., HU R., FANG Y., "A new model for squeeze-film damping of electrically actuated microbeams under the effect of a static deflection", *Journal of Micromechanics and Microengineering*, vol. 17, num. 7, p. 1242–1251, 2007.

[LIA 08] LIAW H., SHIRINZADEH B., SMITH J., "Sliding-mode enhanced adaptive motion tracking control of piezoelectric actuation systems for micro/nano manipulation", *IEEE Transactions on Control Systems Technology*, vol. 16, num. 4, p. 826–833, July 2008.

[LIU 01] LIU C., KENNY T., "A high-precision, wide-bandwidth micromachined tunneling accelerometer", *Journal of Microelectromechanical Systems*, vol. 10, num. 3, p. 425–433, September 2001.

[MAI 05] MAITHRIPALA D., BERG J., DAYAWANSA W., "Control of an electrostatic microelectromechanical system using static and dynamic output feedback", *Journal of Dynamic Systems, Measurement, and Control*, vol. 127, num. 3, p. 443–450, 2005.

[MOK 06] MOKABERI B., REQUICHA A., "Drift compensation for automatic nanomanipulation with scanning probe microscopes", *IEEE Transactions on Automation Science and Engineering*, vol. 3, num. 3, p. 199–207, July 2006.

[MUN 98] MUNOZ R., VILLAGRA P., KREMER G., MORAGA L., "Control circuit for a scanning tunneling microscope", *Review of Scientific Instruments*, vol. 69, num. 9, p. 3259–3267, 1998.

[NAI 06] NAIK A., BUU O., LAHAYE M., ARMOUR A., CLERK A., BLENCOWE M., SCHWAB K., "Cooling a nanomechanical resonator with quantum back-action", *Nature*, vol. 443, p. 193–196, June 2006.

[OLI 95] OLIVA A., ANGUIANO E., DENISENKO N., AGUILAR M., "Analysis of scanning tunneling microscopy feedback system", *Review of Scientific Instruments*, vol. 66, num. 5, p. 3196–3203, 1995.

[RAS 00] RAST S., WATTINGER C., GYSIN U., MEYER E., "The noise of cantilevers", *Nanotechnology*, vol. 11, num. 3, p. 169–172, 2000.

[ROC 96] ROCKSTAD H., TANG T., REYNOLDS J., KENNY T., KAISER W., GABRIELSON T., "A miniature, high-sensitivity, electron tunneling accelerometer", *Sensors and Actuators*, vol. 53, p. 227–231, 1996.

[SAD 06] SADEWASSER S., ABADAL G., BARNIOL N., DOHN S., BOISEN A., FONSECA L., "Integrated tunneling sensor for nanoelectromechanical systems", *Applied Physics Letters*, vol. 89, num. 17, 2006, page 173101.

[SAL 02] SALAPAKA S., SEBASTIAN A., CLEVELAND J., SALAPAKA M., "High bandwidth nano-positioner: A robust control approach", *Review of Scientific Instruments*, vol. 73, num. 9, p. 3232–3241, 2002.

[SEE 03] SEEGER J., BOSER B., "Charge control of parallel-plate, electrostatic actuators and the tip-in instability", *Journal of Microelectromechanical Systems*, vol. 12, num. 5, p. 656–671, October 2003.

[SEN 00] SENTURIA S., *Microsystems Design*, Kluwer Academic, Boston, 2000.

[SUM 08] SUMEET S., MOHEIMANI S., "High-bandwidth control of a piezoelectric nanopositioning stage in the presence of plant uncertainties", *Nanotechnology*, vol. 19, num. 12, p. 125503–125512, 2008.

[SUN 08] SUN L., WANG J., RONG W., LI X., BAO H., "A silicon integrated micro nano-positioning XY-stage for nano-manipulation", *Journal of Micromechanics and Microengineering*, vol. 18, num. 12, p. 125004–125013, 2008.

[WAN 02] WANG J., ZHAO Y., CUI T., VARAHRAMYAN K., "Synthesis of the modeling and control systems of a tunneling accelerometer using the MatLab simulation", *J. Micromech. Microeng.*, vol. 12, p. 730–735, 2002.

[WEL 01] WELCH G., BISHOP G., *An Introduction to the Kalman Filter*, Association for Computing Machinery, 2001.

[WU 07] WU Y., ZOU Q., "Iterative control approach to compensate for both the hysteresis and the dynamics effects of piezo actuators", *IEEE Transactions on Control Systems Technology*, vol. 15, num. 5, p. 936–944, September 2007.

[ZHA 06] ZHAO Y., TAY F., ZHOU G., CHAU F., "Fast and precise positioning of electrostatically actuated dual-axis micromirror by multi-loop digital control", *Sensors and Actuators A: Physical*, vol. 132, num. 2, p. 421–428, 2006.

[ZHA 07] ZHANG Z., MENQ C., "Six-axis magnetic levitation and motion control", *IEEE Transactions on Robotics*, vol. 23, num. 2, p. 196–205, April 2007.

[ZHU 07] ZHU G., PENET J., SAYDY L., "Modeling and control of electrostatically actuated MEMS in the presence of parasitics and parametric uncertainties", *Journal of Dynamic Systems, Measurement, and Control*, vol. 129, p. 786–794, November 2007.

Chapter 5

Controller Design and Analysis for High-performance STM

This chapter is devoted to the control system design for the high-performance scanning tunneling microscope (STM). A common approach by the scanning probe community is to use conventional proportional integral (PI) control design to control the vertical movement of the STM tip (z direction). In this chapter, a modern H_∞ control design is analyzed in order to obtain the dual purpose of ultra-high positioning accuracy with high bandwidth; these are the greatest challenges in the fields of nanopositioning and scanning systems. The desired performances in the vertical z direction of the scanner are imposed on the closed-loop sensitivity functions using appropriate weighting functions; a mixed-sensitivity H_∞ controller is then designed. The results are compared to the conventional PI control design, highlighting the improvements obtained in terms of high precision with high bandwidth. A performance and robustness analysis is finally performed to test robust stability and performance of STM.

5.1. Introduction

In the early 1980s, Gerd Binnig and Heinrich Rohrer experienced the phenomenon of tunnel current between a metallic electrically charged tip and a conductive sample surface when the tip approached at the vicinity of the surface (distance between tip apex and sample surface in the range $0.1-1 \times 10^{-9}$ m). This phenomenon, combined with the ability to scan the tip against the sample surface, gave rise to the scanning

---

Chapter written by Irfan AHMAD, Alina VODA and Gildas BESANÇON.

tunneling microscope (STM) [BIN 86]. It was the first member of the family of scanning probe microscopes (SPM) that could characterize surface morphology with atomic resolution. Today, the STM has vast applications in different domains and the ultra-high positioning accuracy with high bandwidths are the greatest challenges. This chapter presents the controller design enabling a closed-loop STM to deal with such challenges.

As the distance between the STM tip apex and surface is $< 1 \times 10^{-9}$ m to achieve the tunneling effect, electronic control is critical in order to obtain good image quality of the surface in the presence of external disturbances. Presently, in most commercial STM equipment, only simple types of controllers (proportional-integral (PI) or proportional-integral with derivative (PID) control) are implemented to control the movement of the STM tip in the vertical z-direction where parameters of such controllers are fixed manually by the operator.

In such operation modes, the imaging process is not optimum and the image does not necessarily correspond to reality [ANG 98]. The feedback loop of STM in the vertical z-direction with some stability conditions has been presented in [MAT 05, OLI 95]. Such analysis is carried out by simple classical PI (PID) control techniques with a simplified version of the system model. This work also omits a discussion about noise. A step variation in sample surface is studied in [BON 01, BON 04]. A variable structure control (VSC) design methodology in the presence of PI control is proposed in order to avoid STM tip collision with the sample surface.

There is still a need for STM performance analysis and improvements in terms of positioning accuracy with high bandwidth and its trade-off with loop stability and robustness, in view of using it for a sample surface with fast variations (continuous).

A control design methodology based on pole placement with sensitivity function shaping using second-order digital notch filter is proposed in [AHM 08] for the feedback control system of STM. The general description of this control design methodology is given in [LAN 98, LAN 06, PRO 03]. The desired performance and stability requirements are expressed in terms of constraints on the shape of closed-loop sensitivity functions. Proper tuning of the control parameters in order to follow these constraints can be a difficult task for STM operators, however. The performance of STM in the vertical z-direction with modern H_∞ control design framework has not yet been analyzed, although it has been discussed in the case of atomic force microscope (AFM) control [SAL 02]. The control of AFM for vertical z-direction is discussed in [ABR 07, SCH 07] with classical PI (PID) control technique also.

This chapter illustrates the ineffectiveness of the traditional PI or PID architecture, used predominantly by the scanning probe community, in order to meet the dual goal of high positioning accuracy and high bandwidth. Such requirements can be achieved by the modern robust control techniques. The aim of the present work is therefore to propose an H_∞ control design for the vertical z-movement of the STM tip in order to improve performance in terms of positioning accuracy and closed-loop bandwidth. The desired performance and robustness requirements are therefore imposed on the closed-loop sensitivity functions using appropriate weighting functions which become part of the generalized plant. The mixed-sensitivity H_∞ control design methodology [SKO 96] is adopted to fulfill the requirements. The obtained results are compared to the traditional control design approach (PI/PID) to demonstrate the improvements in terms of high positioning accuracy with high bandwidth.

Further, the STM system is analyzed by an uncertainty model designed by considering variations in all parameters of STM nominal model. Robust stability and performance are then analyzed, in addition to nominal stability and performance of the system which can be critical depending on the range of parametric variations. The presence of noise, non-linearities and physical limitations in the control loop are always the limiting factors to be considered in order to achieve desired performance.

A complete system overview with corresponding simulation model is given in section 5.2. The control design model, together with its open-loop analysis and control problem formulation with desired performance, is presented in section 5.3. Section 5.4 then presents the H_∞ control algorithm, mixed-sensitivity H_∞ controller synthesis, the design of weighting functions and the obtained performance. In section 5.5, robust stability and robust performance are analyzed under parametric uncertainties of the system model. Simulation results to validate the controller and also its comparison with conventional PI control technique are presented in section 5.6. Finally, section 5.7 draws some conclusions.

5.2. General description of STM

In this section, the working principle of the STM and also the elements involved in the complete feedback loop will be briefly described. An illustrative simulation model will also be established for the STM feedback loop, on which the proposed control strategy will be validated (in the simulation results section).

5.2.1. *STM operation modes*

The sample topography can be obtained by operating the STM in different modes. There are mainly two modes of operation for STM. The 'constant height' mode keeps the position of the STM tip constant while scanning the surface; the variation of tunneling current then reflects the small atomic corrugation of the surface. However, the tip could crash if the surface corrugation is large. To avoid such problems another approach, referred to as 'constant current' mode, is generally used in STM imaging. This mode of operation is safe to use on rough surfaces since the distance between the tip and sample is adjusted and kept constant by a closed feedback circuit of STM. The analysis in this chapter is based on this second operation mode.

5.2.2. *Principle*

The STM works by scanning a very sharp metal wire tip over a surface (see Figure 5.1). By bringing the tip very close to the surface (less than 1×10^{-9} m) and by applying an electrical voltage v_b (bias voltage) to the tip or sample, the surface can be imaged at a very small scale, down to the resolution of individual atoms.

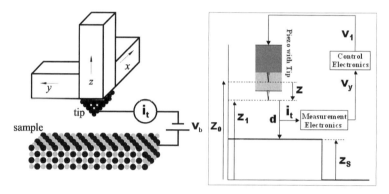

Figure 5.1. *General STM operation principle*

The principle of the STM is based on several theories. One is the quantum mechanical effect of tunneling which allows us to observe the surface. Another principle is the piezoelectric effect which allows us to precisely scan the tip with angstrom-level control. Lastly, a feedback control loop is required which monitors the tunneling current and tries to keep it constant while scanning the surface.

5.2.2.1. *Tunneling effect*

Tunneling is a quantum mechanical effect. In classical mechanics, a particle (electron) cannot pass through a potential barrier if $E < U(z)$ where E is the energy and $U(z)$ is the potential. In quantum mechanics, however, an electron is described by a wave function which can have a non-zero probability of tunneling through a potential barrier [LAN 77]. When an electron moves through the barrier in this fashion, it is referred to as the *tunneling effect*. If the barrier is thin enough (about a nanometer) then there is always a probability of observing an electron on the other side of the region.

The tunneling current in STM is based on the tunneling effect which falls exponentially with the barrier thickness. The barrier is the gap (air, vacuum or liquid) between the STM tip and surface. The tunneling is bidirectional which means the electrons in the sample can tunnel into the STM tip or vice versa, depending on the experimental set-up. By monitoring this tunnel current through the gap, the information on the tip–sample distance d can be obtained. The tunnel current can be expressed as:

$$i_t = \sigma_0 v_b e^{-1.025\sqrt{\Phi}d} \tag{5.1}$$

where i_t is tunnel current, σ_0 is the proportionality constant, v_b is the bias voltage and Φ is the work function. Refer to [CHE 08] for further details of the tunneling phenomenon. This principle was brought into application by Binnig and Rohrer [BIN 86] when they created the scanning tunneling microscope (STM).

5.2.2.2. Piezoelectric effect

The piezoelectric effect was discovered by Pierre Curie in 1880. The effect is created by squeezing the sides of certain crystals (quartz or barium titanate) and the result is the creation of opposite electrical charges on the sides. The effect can also be reversed: by applying a voltage across a piezoelectric crystal, it will elongate or compress. These materials are used to scan the tip over the surface in STM and in many other scanning probe techniques. A typical piezoelectric material used in STM is lead zirconium titanate (PZT). See [KAT 03] for details of the piezoelectric effect.

Piezoelectric actuators are now widely used for high positioning accuracy at nanometer and sub-nanometer resolution with high bandwidths [OHA 95, SCH 04, TAY 93]. One of the advantages of using piezoelectric actuators is that, under certain experimental conditions, their dynamics can be approximated by linear models [BHI 07]. This is why a second-order linear model can be used for the piezoelectric actuator:

$$G_a(s) = \frac{\gamma_0}{\left(\frac{1}{\omega_0^2}\right)s^2 + \left(\frac{1}{Q\omega_0}\right)s + 1} \tag{5.2}$$

where γ_0 is sensitivity, ω_0 is the resonance frequency and Q is the quality factor of piezoelectric actuator model.

5.2.2.3. Feedback loop

A feedback loop constantly monitors the tunneling current (i_t) and makes adjustments to the tip to maintain it at a constant value. Controlling this tunnel current by keeping the distance d constant in the presence of external disturbances (sensor noise n, sample surface variations (z_s), etc.) is the main objective of the feedback control system of STM. A complete overview of the closed-loop control scheme considered in this chapter is depicted in Figure 5.2.

The tunnel current (i_t) occurring in STM is very small, typically from 0.01×10^{-9} to 10×10^{-9} A. The current amplifier (pre-amplifier or I-V converter) is therefore an

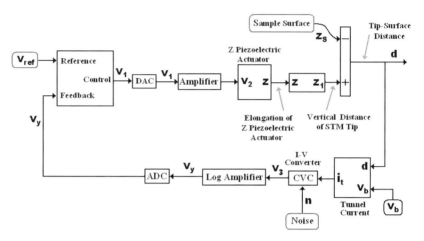

Figure 5.2. *Complete simulation model for STM closed-loop system*

essential element of STM, which converts the small tunneling current into a voltage v_3. This pre-amplifier has a finite bandwidth of 600 kHz and is usually the most important source of noise n.

Equation (5.1) between the tunneling characteristics (i_t) and the distance d is non-linear. To make the entire electronic response (approximately) linear with respect to the distance d, a logarithmic amplifier is added to the pre-amplifier output. The output of the logarithmic amplifier v_y is given by the non-linear relation:

$$v_y = K_L \log_{10}\left(\frac{|v_3|}{E_L}\right) \tag{5.3}$$

where K_L is the conversion factor of log amplifier and E_L is its sensitivity. This logarithmic amplifier has a finite bandwidth of 60 kHz and its output can be between $0 - 10$ V. These functionalities are performed by measurement electronics in the feedback loop, as can be seen in Figure 5.2.

The output voltage v_y of the logarithmic amplifier is one of the inputs of the control electronics which sends a required voltage (v_1) to an amplifier (gain $= 19$) and then to the z-piezoelectric actuator. This voltage (v_1) can be between ± 10 V. The tip of STM which is connected to the piezoelectric actuator will start moving towards the required position according to the applied voltage (v_2) in order to keep the distance d constant $(0.8 \times 10^{-9}$ m) in the presence of external disturbances (variation in sample surface (z_s), noise n).

Non-linear phenomena such as hysteresis are not expected for the piezoelectric actuator as the amplitude of input voltage v_2 is very small for the vertical movement of the STM tip. The output of the piezoelectric actuator z is used to determine the distance d between the STM tip and sample surface z_s from $d = z_0 - z - z_s$ (Figure 5.1), where z_0 is the equilibrium position of the STM tip when no voltage is applied to the piezo.

5.3. Control design model

In this section, the complete simulation model (Figure 5.2) is transformed into an appropriate linear design model (Figure 5.3) which is required before designing the linear controller for the STM feedback control system. The final simulation with actual non-linearities and sensor noise n in a closed loop will validate the linear controller and will help to observe the results close to the real system of STM.

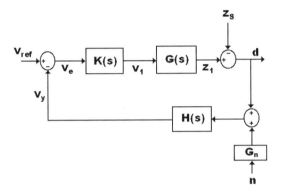

Figure 5.3. *Design model for closed-loop system of STM*

5.3.1. *Linear approximation approach*

In the previous analysis of the closed-loop STM, the effect of two non-linearities (exponential equation (5.1) and logarithmic equation (5.3)) are linearized for the linear control design model by coupling them directly through a constant gain $(1 \times 10^9 \Omega)$ of pre-amplifier. Such analysis neglected the dynamics of the two amplifiers (pre-amplifier and logarithmic amplifier) and the presence of noise n between these two non-linearities. Instead, here we have chosen to rely on a computed first-order linear approximation of the overall equations to linearize both non-linearities (equations (5.1) and (5.3)) independently around their equilibrium points (d_0 and v_{30}) without neglecting the dynamics of the two amplifiers and the presence of noise n.

The linearized equations corresponding to equations (5.1) and (5.3) are:

$$i_t = c_1 + c_3 - (c_2 \times d) \tag{5.4}$$

and

$$v_y = c_4 - c_6 + (c_5 \times v_3) \tag{5.5}$$

respectively, where $c_1, c_2, \ldots, c_6$ are constants which depend on the parameters of equations (5.1) and (5.3) and are defined:

$$\begin{cases} c_1 & = \sigma_0 v_b e^{-1.025\sqrt{\Phi} d_0} \\ c_2 & = 1.025\sqrt{\Phi} c_1 \\ c_3 & = d_0 c_2 \\ c_4 & = K_L \log_{10}\left(\frac{v_{30}}{E_L}\right) \\ c_5 & = \frac{K_L}{v_{30}\ln(10)} \\ c_6 & = \frac{K_L}{\ln(10)} \end{cases} \tag{5.6}$$

where σ_0, v_b, Φ, d_0, K_L, E_L and v_{30} are STM design parameters defined in Table 5.1 (values taken from [MAT 05]).

Symbols	Description	Value
σ_0	Proportionality constant	$0.5\Omega^{-1}$
v_b	Bias voltage	0.1 V
Φ	Work function	4 eV
K_L	Log amplifier conversion factor	2.5 V
E_L	Log amplifier sensitivity	0.001 V
R	Resistance for I-V conversion	$1 \times 10^9\Omega$
Q	Piezo quality factor	4.5
γ_0	Piezo sensitivity	$40\,\text{Å V}^{-1}$
ω_0	Piezo resonance frequency	40 kHz
z_0	STM tip initial position	12 Å
d_0	Exponential non-linearity equilibrium point	8 Å
v_{30}	Logarithmic non-linearity equilibrium point	3.77 V
ω_1	Pre-amplifier bandwidth	600 kHz
ω_2	Log amplifier bandwidth	60 kHz
ω_3	Piezo pre-amplifier bandwidth	100 kHz

Table 5.1. *System parameters with values used for simulation*

The feedback dynamics (Figure 5.2) where tunnel current (i_t) is converted into a voltage v_y can be represented by a second-order linear model $H(s)$, defined:

$$H(s) = \frac{c\omega_1\omega_2}{s^2 + (\omega_1 + \omega_2)\,s + \omega_1\omega_2} \tag{5.7}$$

where c is a constant term depending on the parameters of equations (5.4) and (5.5) and ω_1 and ω_2 are two bandwidths of the pre-amplifier and logarithmic amplifier, respectively, defined in Table 5.1.

The equivalent linear control design model after linearization is depicted in Figure 5.3, where $G(s)$ represents the third-order linear model including piezo pre-amplifier and piezoelectric actuator model and G_n is a constant term which represents the noise n transfer.

5.3.2. Open-loop analysis

The plant to be controlled is defined as the system between the controller output v_1 and the output of the logarithmic amplifier v_y. This system has five poles and no zero and all poles are located on the stable region of root locus plot (Figure 5.4). The three real poles represent the dynamics of the three amplifiers (pre-amplifier, logarithmic amplifier and piezo pre-amplifier) and two dominant imaginary poles are of the second-order linear piezo model (5.2).

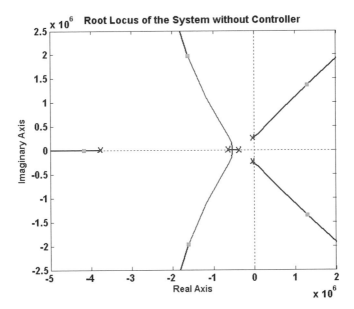

Figure 5.4. *System analysis without controller (squares and crosses represent the closed-loop and open-loop poles, respectively)*

The two dominant imaginary poles are located close to the unstable region of the root locus plot which causes the roots of closed-loop system to travel easily over an unstable region (Figure 5.4). The controller design is therefore critical because of the location of these two dominant imaginary poles of the piezo.

The state-space representation of the whole system with actual non-linearities can be described by the parameters:

$$
\left\{
\begin{aligned}
\dot{x}_1 &= (-w_1 - w_2)x_1 - (w_1 w_2)x_2 + n \\
&\quad + R\sigma_0 v_b \, \exp[-1.025\sqrt{\Phi} \left(z_0 - z_S - Aw_3\gamma_0 w_0^2\right) x_5] \\[6pt]
\dot{x}_2 &= x_1 \\[6pt]
\dot{x}_3 &= -\left(w_3 + \frac{w_0}{Q}\right)x_3 - \left(w_0^2 + \frac{w_3 w_0}{Q}\right)x_4 - \left(w_3 w_0^2\right)x_5 + v_1 \\[6pt]
\dot{x}_4 &= x_3 \\[6pt]
\dot{x}_5 &= x_4 \\[6pt]
v_Y &= K_L \log_{10}\left(\frac{w_1 w_2}{E_L}x_2\right).
\end{aligned}
\right.
\tag{5.8}
$$

The same representation of the system after first-order linear approximation approach is:

$$
\left\{
\begin{aligned}
\dot{x}_1 &= (-w_1 - w_2)x_1 - (w_1 w_2)x_2 - \left(Rc_2 Aw_3\gamma_0 w_0^2\right)x_5 \\
&\quad + n + R(c_1 + c_3 + c_2 \left(z_0 - z_S\right)) \\[6pt]
\dot{x}_2 &= x_1 \\[6pt]
\dot{x}_3 &= -\left(w_3 + \frac{w_0}{Q}\right)x_3 - \left(w_0^2 + \frac{w_3 w_0}{Q}\right)x_4 - \left(w_3 w_0^2\right)x_5 + v_1 \\[6pt]
\dot{x}_4 &= x_3 \\[6pt]
\dot{x}_5 &= x_4 \\[6pt]
v_Y &= (c_5 w_1 w_2)\, x_2 + c_4 - c_6
\end{aligned}
\right.
\tag{5.9}
$$

where all parameters used in equations (5.8) and (5.9) are defined in Table 5.1 and also in equation (5.6).

5.3.3. *Control problem formulation and desired performance for STM*

Before discussing the synthesis of the controller, the control problem and the desired closed-loop performance in the case of the STM feedback loop must be explained.

For a feedback control of the STM, the control problem can be formulated as a tracking problem where the STM tip tracks the unknown sample surface z_s by keeping the distance d constant between the STM tip and sample surface. It can also be formulated as a disturbance rejection problem. Variations in the sample surface z_s and the noise n are considered as external disturbances. The former can be considered as a slow-varying disturbance while the latter is fast-varying. These disturbances are rejected by moving the STM tip in the appropriate direction so that the distance d always remains constant at its desired value (0.8×10^{-9} m).

The main objective of the control system is to achieve better performance of STM in terms of high positioning accuracy $\pm 8 \times 10^{-12}$ m with high closed-loop bandwidth, in the presence of good robustness margin ($\|S\|_\infty \leq 6$ dB and $\|T\|_\infty \leq 3.5$ dB, where S and T represent sensitivity function and complementary sensitivity function, respectively) and stability margins (gain margin > 6 dB and phase margin $> 30°$). Such positioning accuracy is required with the maximum continuous surface variations of frequency 1×10^4 rad s^{-1} having amplitude 8×10^{-10} m in the presence of sensor (pre-amplifier) noise n of 45 mV Hz$^{-0.5}$.

The reference input voltage v_{ref} corresponds to the desired distance d between the STM tip and sample surface, hence the feedback voltage v_y always tries to follow the reference input voltage v_{ref} in the presence of the above-mentioned disturbances to keep the distance d constant at the desired value (0.8×10^{-9} m).

5.4. H_∞ controller design

In this section, a short description about standard H_∞ control design methodology is first presented (see [SKO 96] for details). This methodology will then be applied to the control design model of the STM feedback loop in order to achieve the desired performance in terms of high positioning accuracy with high bandwidth.

5.4.1. *General control problem formulation*

The general H_∞ problem is formulated using the general control configuration in Figure 5.5 where P(s) is the generalized plant model comprising the plant and the performance weighting functions, w is the exogenous input vector (such as external disturbances and reference signal), u is the control input vector, y is the controlled

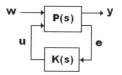

Figure 5.5. *Generalized plant with controller*

output vector and e is the measurement vector or so-called error signals which are to be minimized in some sense to meet the control objectives.

The system of Figure 5.5 is described by:

$$\begin{pmatrix} y \\ e \end{pmatrix} = P(s) \begin{pmatrix} w \\ u \end{pmatrix} = \begin{pmatrix} P_{11}(s) & P_{12}(s) \\ P_{21}(s) & P_{22}(s) \end{pmatrix} \begin{pmatrix} w \\ u \end{pmatrix} \qquad (5.10)$$

where $u = K(s)e$ and a state-space realization of generalized plant P is given by:

$$P = \begin{pmatrix} A & B_1 & B_2 \\ C_1 & D_{11} & D_{12} \\ C_2 & D_{21} & D_{22} \end{pmatrix}. \qquad (5.11)$$

The system closed-loop transfer function from w to y is given by the linear fractional transformation:

$$y = F_l(P, K)w \qquad (5.12)$$

where

$$F_l(P, K) = P_{11} + P_{12}K(I - P_{22}K)^{-1}P_{21}. \qquad (5.13)$$

The H_∞ control involves the minimization of the H_∞ norms of $F_l(P, K)$. The following assumptions are typically made in H_∞ problems [SKO 96]:

A1 (A, B_2, C_2) is stabilizable and detectable;

A2 D_{12} and D_{21} have full rank;

A3

$$\begin{pmatrix} A - j\omega I & B_2 \\ C_1 & D_{12} \end{pmatrix}$$

has full column rank for all ω;

A4

$$\left(\begin{array}{cc} A - j\omega I & B_1 \\ & \\ C_2 & D_{21} \end{array} \right)$$

has full row rank for all ω;

A5 $D_{11} = 0$ and $D_{22} = 0$; and

A6 $D_{12} = \left(\begin{array}{c} 0 \\ I \end{array} \right)$ and $D_{21} = \left(\begin{array}{cc} 0 & I \end{array} \right)$.

Assumption (A1) is required for the existence of a stabilizing controller K and assumption (A2) is sufficient to ensure the controllers are proper and hence realizable. Assumptions (A3) and (A4) ensure that the optimal controller does not try to cancel poles or zeroes on the imaginary axis, which would result in closed-loop instability. Assumption (A5) significantly simplifies the H_∞ algorithm formulae. For simplicity, it is also sometimes assumed that D_{12} and D_{21} are given by assumption (A6).

5.4.2. *General H_∞ algorithm*

The standard H_∞ optimal control problem is to find all stabilizing controllers K which minimize the quantity:

$$\|F_l(P, K)\|_\infty = \max_\omega \overline{\sigma}(F_l(P, K)(j\omega)). \tag{5.14}$$

In practice, it is not usually necessary to obtain an optimal controller for the H_∞ problem. It is simpler to design a sub-optimal model which is close to the optimal controller, in the sense of the H_∞ norm. Let $\gamma_{\min}$ be the minimum value of $\|F_l(P, K)\|_\infty$ over all stabilizing controllers K. Then the H_∞ sub-optimal control problem consists of finding all stabilizing controllers K, given a $\gamma > \gamma_{\min}$, such that:

$$\|F_l(P, K)\|_\infty < \gamma. \tag{5.15}$$

For the general control configuration of Figure 5.5 described by equation (5.13) with assumptions (A1)–(A6) listed above, there exists a stabilizing controller $K(s)$ such that $\|F_l(P, K)\|_\infty < \gamma$ if and only if:

1) $X_\infty \geq 0$ is a solution to the algebraic Riccati equation:

$$A^T X_\infty + X_\infty A + C_1^T C_1 + X_\infty(\gamma^{-2} B_1 B_1^T - B_2 B_2^T) X_\infty = 0 \tag{5.16}$$

such that $Re\lambda_i[A + (\gamma^{-2} B_1 B_1^T - B_2 B_2^T) X_\infty] < 0, \forall i$;

2) $Y_\infty \geq 0$ is a solution to the algebraic Riccati equation:

$$AY_\infty + Y_\infty A^T + B_1 B_1^T + Y_\infty(\gamma^{-2} C_1^T C_1 - C_2^T C_2) Y_\infty = 0 \tag{5.17}$$

such that $Re \, \lambda_i[A + Y_\infty(\gamma^{-2} C_1^T C_1 - C_2^T C_2)] < 0, \forall i$; and

3) $\rho(X_\infty Y_\infty) < \gamma^2$.

The family of all admissible controllers is given by $K = F_l(K_c, Q)$, where:

$$K_c = \begin{pmatrix} A_\infty & -Z_\infty L_\infty & Z_\infty B_2 \\ F_\infty & 0 & I \\ -C_2 & I & 0 \end{pmatrix}, \tag{5.18}$$

$$F_\infty = -B_2^T X_\infty, \quad L_\infty = -Y_\infty C_2^T, \quad Z_\infty = (I - \gamma^{-2} Y_\infty X_\infty)^{-1}, \tag{5.19}$$

$$A_\infty = A + \gamma^{-2} B_1 B_1^T X_\infty + B_2 F_\infty + Z_\infty L_\infty C_2 \tag{5.20}$$

and $Q(s)$ is any stable proper transfer function such that $\|Q\|_\infty < \gamma$. For $Q(s) = 0$, we have:

$$K(s) = -Z_\infty L_\infty (sI - A_\infty)^{-1} F_\infty. \tag{5.21}$$

$K(s)$ is called the central controller and has the same number of states as the generalized plant $P(s)$.

5.4.3. *Mixed-sensitivity H_∞ control*

Some weights are usually considered on the controlled outputs which represent the performance specifications in the frequency domain. The generalized plant P therefore includes the plant model and the considered weights (W_1, W_2 and W_3) as shown in Figures 5.6 and 5.7. The H_∞ control problem is then referred to as a mixed-sensitivity problem, W_1, W_2 and W_3 appearing in equation (5.13) as weights on the sensitivity functions.

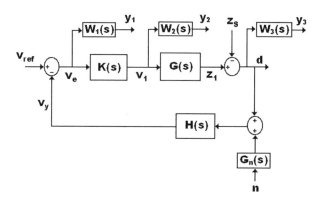

Figure 5.6. *Design model with weighting functions for closed-loop system of STM*

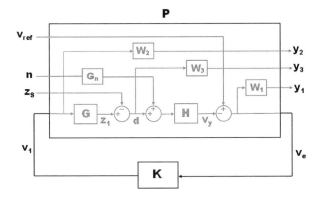

Figure 5.7. *Generalized design model for closed-loop system of STM*

Mixed-sensitivity is the name given to transfer function shaping problems in which sensitivity function S is shaped together with one or more other closed-loop transfer functions such as KS or the complementary sensitivity function $T = 1 - S$ (equation (5.22)). The transfer function shaping approach uses H_∞ optimization to shape the singular values of specified closed-loop transfer functions over the frequency. The maximum singular values are easy to shape by forcing them to lie below user-defined bounds, thereby ensuring desirable bandwidths and roll-off rates. For these reasons, we have chosen to use the loop-shaping approach by mixed-sensitivity H_∞ control for the STM case in order to achieve the desired performance in terms of high positioning accuracy with high bandwidth.

5.4.4. *Controller synthesis for the scanning tunneling microscope*

The closed-loop sensitivity functions are classically given by the relations:

$$\begin{cases} S(s) = 1/(1 + K(s)G(s)H(s)) \\ KS(s) = K(s)S(s) \\ T(s) = \frac{K(s)G(s)H(s)}{(1+K(s)G(s)H(s))}. \end{cases} \quad (5.22)$$

The desired performances are imposed on the closed-loop sensitivity functions using appropriate weighting functions and then the mixed-sensitivity H_∞ control design methodology is adopted to fulfill the requirements. The functions W_1, W_2 and W_3 weight the controlled outputs y_1, y_2 and y_3, respectively (Figure 5.6) and should be chosen according to the performance specifications.

The generalized plant P (Figure 5.7) (i.e. the interconnection of the plant and the weighting functions) is given by:

$$
\begin{pmatrix} y_1 \\ y_2 \\ y_3 \\ v_e \end{pmatrix} = \underbrace{\begin{pmatrix} W_1 & W_1H & -W_1HG_n & -W_1HG \\ 0 & 0 & 0 & W_2 \\ 0 & -W_3 & 0 & W_3G \\ I & H & -HG_n & -HG \end{pmatrix}}_{P} \begin{pmatrix} v_{\text{ref}} \\ z_s \\ n \\ v_1 \end{pmatrix}.
$$

Thus, the H_∞ control problem is to find a stabilizing controller $K(s)$ which minimizes γ such that:

$$
\left\| \begin{pmatrix} W_1S & W_1HS & -W_1HG_nS \\ W_2KS & W_2HKS & W_2HG_nKS \\ W_3GKS & -W_3S & -W_3G_nT \end{pmatrix} \right\|_\infty < \gamma. \tag{5.23}
$$

The obtained controller $K(s)$ has the same number of state variables as P. The choice of the weighting functions is therefore an important issue in the H_∞ control problem. The chosen weighting functions are:

1) W_1 is used to impose the desired performance specifications on closed-loop sensitivity function S, that is:

$$
W_1(s) = \frac{(1/M_s)\, s + \omega_s}{s + \omega_s \epsilon_s} \tag{5.24}
$$

where $M_s = 2.0$ for a good robustness margin (i.e. $\|S\|_\infty \leq 6\,\text{dB}$ for the entire frequency range), $\omega_s = 4 \times 10^5\,\text{rad s}^{-1}$ for a good attenuation of disturbances from low frequencies up to ω_s and $\epsilon_s = 0.012$ to reduce the steady-state error in the presence of maximum allowed variations in the sample surface (8×10^{-10} m).

2) W_2 is designed to meet the actuator limitations for STM. It is chosen as:

$$
W_2(s) = \frac{s + (\omega_u/M_u)}{\epsilon_u s + \omega_u} \tag{5.25}
$$

where $M_u = 3.2$ to impose a limitation on the maximum value of controller output up to the frequency ω_u, where $\omega_u = 1 \times 10^7\,\text{rad s}^{-1}$ and $\epsilon_u = 1$ to limit the effect of measurement noise n at high frequencies.

3) W_3 is designed to impose limitations on the complementary sensitivity function (T) and is defined:

$$
W_3(s) = \frac{s + (\omega_t/M_t)}{\epsilon_t s + \omega_t} \tag{5.26}
$$

where $M_t = 1.5$ for a good robustness margin (i.e. $\|T\|_\infty \leq 3.5\,\text{dB}$ for the entire frequency range) and $\omega_t = 1 \times 10^7\,\text{rad s}^{-1}$ to attenuate the noise n at high frequencies with $\epsilon_t = 1$.

Finally, a controller with an eighth-order transfer function is obtained. After computation, the minimal cost achieved for the STM feedback control system was $\gamma = 1.42$, meaning that the obtained sensitivity functions almost match the desired loop shaping. The obtained sensitivity functions with the desired loop shaping in terms of weighting filters are depicted in Figures 5.8–5.10.

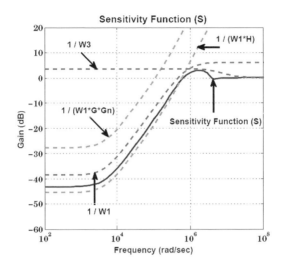

Figure 5.8. *Closed-loop sensitivity function (S) with* H_∞ *control and the associated templates (see color section)*

5.4.5. *Control loop performance analysis*

The weighting functions $(W_1, W_2$ and $W_3)$ were designed by considering the requirement of high positioning accuracy $\pm 8 \times 10^{-12}$ m with high bandwidth and good robustness. The proposed control technique achieves all the requirements as the obtained sensitivity functions match the desired loop shaping (Figures 5.8–5.10).

From a robustness point of view, we obtained a good modulus margin as $\|S\|_\infty = 2.4$ dB and $\|T\|_\infty = 0.08$ dB and good stability margins (gain margin = 14.7 dB and phase margin = 66.1°). The obtained closed-loop bandwidth is 6.1×10^5 rad s^{-1} which ensures the required good performance with fast variations 1×10^4 rad s^{-1} in the sample surface z_S. Similarly, all the other constraints in terms of better noise n rejection and to avoid actuator saturations are fully met with the proposed control technique.

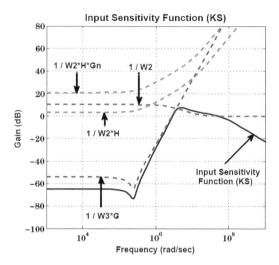

Figure 5.9. *Closed-loop sensitivity function (KS) with H_∞ control and the associated templates (see color section)*

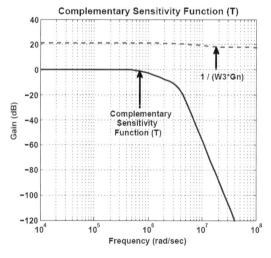

Figure 5.10. *Closed-loop sensitivity function (T) with H_∞ control and the associated template*

For the purposes of comparison, a standard PI controller is designed which can be represented as:

$$K(s) = K_P \left(1 + \frac{1}{sT_i}\right) \tag{5.27}$$

where K_P and T_i represent the proportional and integral action, respectively.

These two parameters are tuned according to the pole placement technique. With this classical PI control technique, the obtained closed-loop bandwidth is 4.1×10^4 rad s^{-1} which is much less than the bandwidth obtained with the H_∞ control technique. The gain margin obtained with the PI control technique is 5.5 dB which will not allow us to further increase the controller gains or the closed-loop bandwidth. This means that fast variations in sample surface z_S with a positioning accuracy of $\pm 8 \times 10^{-12}$ m is not possible with classical PI control technique (Figure 5.11), also evident in simulation results.

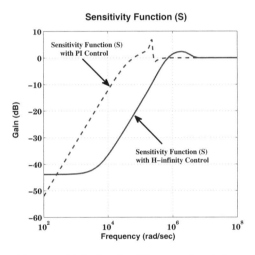

Figure 5.11. *Closed-loop sensitivity function (S) comparison between H_∞ and PI control*

5.5. Analysis with system parametric uncertainties

In this section the aim is to show how to represent system uncertainty by real perturbations, and to analyze robust stability (RS) and robust performance (RP) of the scanning tunneling microscope control system.

Usually, a control system is considered to be robust if it is insensitive to differences between the actual system and the model which has been used to design the controller. These differences are referred to as *model uncertainties*. To allow an accurate and non-conservative representation of the actual system, a simple frequency domain model of real parametric uncertainty is computed using real norm-bounded perturbations.

5.5.1. *Uncertainty modeling*

To account for model uncertainty it is assumed that the dynamic behavior of the plant is no longer described by a single linear time-invariant model $G(s)$, but by a set Π of possible linear time-invariant models $G_\Delta(s) \in \Pi$ described as an 'uncertainty set'. From the nominal plant model $G_0(s)$, the set Π of possible linear time-invariant models $G_\Delta(s)$ can be built by varying the model parameters inside a given range of values. We have considered variations in the parameters of the piezoelectric actuator model, being the sensitive element of the closed loop. The nominal values of the actuator physical parameters, together with their percentage variation, are listed in Table 5.2.

Parameter	Value	Variation (%)
ω_0 (kHz)	40 ± 2	5
Q	4.5 ± 0.225	5
γ_0 (mV^{-1})	$40 \times 10^{-10} \pm 2 \times 10^{-10}$	5

Table 5.2. *Values of the piezoelectric actuator physical parameters together with their percentage variation*

In order to check the robust stability (RS) and robust performance (RP) conditions, we have chosen a multiplicative uncertainty model for our system of STM (see Figure 5.12). In fact, multiplicative weights are usually preferred because their numerical value is more informative, giving an upper bound on the complementary sensitivity function T [SKO 96]. The multiplicative uncertainty model $G_\Delta(s)$ can be described by:

$$G_\Delta(s) = G_0(s)(1 + W_I(s)\Delta_I(s)) \tag{5.28}$$

where $|\Delta(j\omega)| \leq 1, \forall \omega$ represents the normalized real perturbations and $W_I(j\omega)$ is the uncertainty weight.

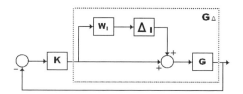

Figure 5.12. *System with multiplicative uncertainty*

In case of multiplicative uncertainty model, the relative error function can be computed as:

$$l_I(\omega) = \max_{G_\Delta \in \Pi} \left| \frac{G_\Delta(j\omega) - G_0(j\omega)}{G_0(j\omega)} \right| \tag{5.29}$$

and rational weight $W_I(j\omega)$ is chosen as:

$$|W_I(j\omega)| \geq l_I(\omega), \ \forall\omega. \tag{5.30}$$

Relative errors $l_I(j\omega)$, together with the rational weight $W_I(j\omega)$, are plotted in Figure 5.13.

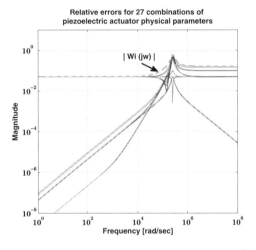

Figure 5.13. *Relative plant errors $l_I(j\omega)$ and rational weight $W_I(j\omega)$ for 27 possible combinations of the actuator physical parameters*

The weighting function $W_I(j\omega)$ is chosen to be equal to a third-order transfer function in such a way that it includes the set of all possible plant models:

$$W_I(s) = \frac{((1/\omega_B)s + A)(s^2 + 2\zeta_1\omega_n + \omega_n^2)}{((1/(\omega_B M))s + 1)(s^2 + 2\zeta_2\omega_n + \omega_n^2)}. \tag{5.31}$$

The values considered for all parameters of $W_I(s)$ are listed in Table 5.3.

5.5.2. *Robust stability and performance analysis*

In addition to nominal stability and performance, the objectives of a robust control system include:

A	M	ζ_1	ζ_2	ω_n	ω_B
0.052	0.165	0.7	0.17	2.55×10^5	1×10^6

Table 5.3. *Parameters for the rational weight $W_I(s)$ (the values of the frequencies are expressed in rad s^{-1})*

– RS: The system is stable for all perturbed plants around the nominal model up to the worst-case model uncertainty.

– RP: The system satisfies the nominal stability (NS) and the nominal performance (NP) conditions. It also guarantees that performance specifications are met for all perturbed plants up to the worst-case model uncertainty.

Using the small gain theorem, the condition for RS is [SKO 96]:

$$RS \Longleftrightarrow |T| < \frac{1}{|W_I|}, \quad \forall \omega. \tag{5.32}$$

Considering the performance specifications in terms of the sensitivity function, the condition for RP is obtained as [SKO 96]:

$$RP \Longleftrightarrow \max_{\omega}(|W_1 S| + |W_I T|) < 1, \quad \forall \omega. \tag{5.33}$$

For a single-input-single-output (SISO) system, the above two conditions represent the direct application of μ conditions for RS and RP.

5.6. Simulation results

The performance of the STM control design can be validated with a simulation model aiming to represent a real system as closely as possible. For this purpose, the controller is validated with the simulation model (Figure 5.2) having actual non-linearities, presence of noise n and physical limitations. It will then be compared to the classical PI control technique.

Figure 5.14 shows the first simulation result with the proposed H_∞ control technique in the presence of surface variations z_S with a frequency of 1×10^4 rad s^{-1} and an amplitude of 8×10^{-10} m, in the presence of sensor noise n (in the pre-amplifier) of 45 mV Hz$^{-0.5}$. The dotted lines represent the positioning accuracy (acceptable bounds) of $\pm 8 \times 10^{-12}$ m. It can be observed that the movement of the STM tip remains within the desired limits.

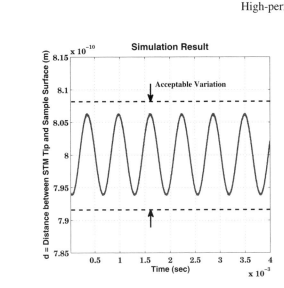

Figure 5.14. *Simulation result with H_∞ control having surface variations z_S of frequency of $1 \times 10^4\ rad\,s^{-1}$, an amplitude of $8 \times 10^{-10}\ m$ and in the presence of sensor noise n of $45\,mV\,Hz^{-0.5}$*

Figure 5.15 compares the results of the proposed H_∞ and classical PI control technique where surface variations (z_S) have an amplitude of 4×10^{-10} m in the presence of the same frequency and sensor noise n as in Figure 5.14. The result shows that, with PI control technique, the variations in distance d go outwith the acceptable bounds. This means that the desired positioning accuracy is not possible with the PI control technique when surface variations are fast. (e.g. with frequency $z_S = 1 \times 10^4\,\mathrm{rad\,s^{-1}}$). To observe the rapidity of these controllers, a step variation of sample surface (4×10^{-10} m) is simulated (Figure 5.16) where it can be seen that with the H_∞ control, the STM tip comes back to the desired position to keep the distance d constant much faster than for the classical PI control technique.

Finally, we have verified the RS and RP conditions as given in equations (5.32) and (5.33). Simulation results shows that the RS condition is satisfied (Figure 5.17), i.e. the closed-loop system remains stable for all perturbed plants around the nominal model up to the chosen worst-case model uncertainty. Figure 5.18 shows that RP is achieved according to the condition described in equation (5.33).

5.7. Conclusions

In this chapter, a mixed-sensitivity H_∞ control technique for the scanning tunneling microscope (STM) feedback loop is designed. Performance in terms of high positioning accuracy with high bandwidth and good robustness is analyzed. The results are compared with a commercially used classical PI control technique for STM.

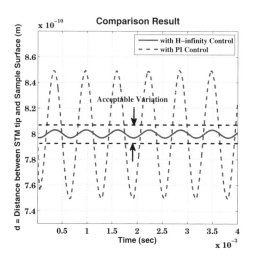

Figure 5.15. *Comparison between H_∞ and PI control having surface variations z_S of frequency of $1 \times 10^4\,rad\,s^{-1}$, an amplitude of $4 \times 10^{-10}\,m$ and in the presence of sensor noise n of $45\,mV\,Hz^{-0.5}$*

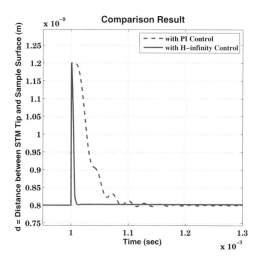

Figure 5.16. *Comparison between PI and H_∞ control having step surface variations z_S of $4 \times 10^{-10}\,m$ amplitude*

These results show how STM performance can indeed be significantly improved by appropriate control design, in terms of high positioning accuracy ($\pm 8 \times 10^{-12}$ m) with high bandwidth (the obtained closed-loop bandwidth is almost 15 times better than the bandwidth obtained with the PI control technique), which means that fast and

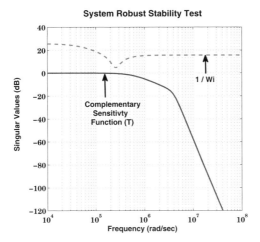

Figure 5.17. *System RS tested with the H_∞ control technique*

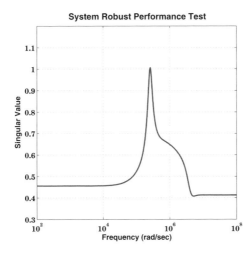

Figure 5.18. *System RP tested with the H_∞ control technique*

large sample surface variations z_s can be treated much better in that case. Real-time experimental validation of the H_∞ controller is currently in progress.

5.8. Bibliography

[ABR 07] ABRAMOVITCH D., ANDERSSON S., PAO L., SCHITTER G., "A tutorial on the mechanisms, dynamics, and control of Atomic Force Microscopes", *American Control Conference*, NY, USA, p. 3488–3502, 2007.

[AHM 08] AHMAD I., VODA A., BESANÇON G., "Controller design for a closed-loop scanning tunneling microscope", *4th IEEE Conference on Automation Science and Engineering*, Washington DC, USA, p. 971–976, August 2008.

[ANG 98] ANGUIANO E., OLIVA A., AGUILAR M., "Optimal conditions for imaging in scanning tunneling microscopy: Theory", *Rev. Sci. Instrum.*, vol. 69, num. 2, p. 3867–3874, 1998.

[BHI 07] BHIKKAJI B., RATNAM M., FLEMING A., MOHEIMANI S., "High-performance control of piezoelectric tube scanners", *IEEE Transactions on Control System Technology*, vol. 15, num. 5, p. 853–866, 2007.

[BIN 86] BINNING G., ROHRER H., "Scanning tunneling microscopy", *IBM J. Res. Develop.*, vol. 30, p. 355–369, 1986.

[BON 01] BONNAIL N., Analyse de données, modélisation et commande pour la microscopie en champ proche utilisant des actionneurs piézoélectriques, PhD thesis, Universite de la Mediterranee Aix-Marseille II, 2001.

[BON 04] BONNAIL N., TONNEAU D., JANDARD F., CAPOLINO G., DALLAPORTA H., "Variable structure control of a piezoelectric actuator for a scanning tunneling microscope", *IEEE Transactions on Industrial Electronics*, vol. 51, num. 2, p. 354–363, 2004.

[CHE 08] CHEN C., *Introduction to Scanning Tunneling Microscopy*, Oxford Science Publications, 2nd edition, 2008.

[KAT 03] KATZIR S., *The Discovery of the Piezoelectric Effect*, Springer Berlin, Heidelberg, 2003.

[LAN 77] LANDAU L., LIFSHITZ E., *Quantom Mechanics*, Pergamon Press, Oxford, 1977.

[LAN 98] LANDAU I., KARIMI A., "Robust digital control using pole placement with sensitivity function shaping method", *Int. J. Robust Nonlinear Control*, vol. 8, p. 191–210, 1998.

[LAN 06] LANDAU I., ZITO G., *Digital Control System: Design, Identification and Implementation*, Springer, 2006.

[MAT 05] MATHIES G., Analysis of STM Feedback System, Master of Science Thesis, Leiden University, 2005.

[OHA 95] OHARA T., YOUCEF-TOUMI K., "Dynamics and control of piezo tube actuators for subnanometer precision applications", *American Control Conference*, p. 3808–3812, 1995.

[OLI 95] OLIVA A., ANGUIANO E., DENISENKO N., AGUILAR M., PENA J., "Analysis of scanning tunneling microscopy feedback system", *Rev. Sci. Instrum.*, vol. 66, num. 5, p. 3196–3203, 1995.

[PRO 03] PROCHAZKA H., LANDAU I., "Pole placement with sensitivity function shaping using 2nd order digital notch filters", *Automatica*, vol. 39, p. 1103–1107, 2003.

[SAL 02] SALAPAKA S., SEBASTIAN A., CLEVELAND J., SALAPAKA M., "High bandwidth nano-positioner: A robust control approach", *Rev. Sci. Instrum.*, vol. 73, num. 9, p. 3232–3241, 2002.

[SCH 04] SCHITTER G., STEMMER A., "Identification and open-loop tracking control of a piezoelectric tube scanner for high-speed scanning probe microscopy", *IEEE Transactions on Control System Technology*, vol. 12, num. 3, p. 449–454, 2004.

[SCH 07] SCHITTER G., ASTROM K., DEMARTINI B., THURNER P., TURNER K., HANSMA P., "Design and modeling of a high-speed AFM-scanner", *IEEE Transactions on Control Systems Technology*, vol. 15, num. 5, p. 906–915, 2007.

[SKO 96] SKOGESTAD S., POSTLETHWAITE I., *Multivariable Feedback Control: Analysis and Design*, John Wiley & Sons, 1996.

[TAY 93] TAYLO M., "Dynamics of piezoelectric tube scanners for scanning probe microscopy", *Rev. Sci. Instrum.*, vol. 64, num. 1, p. 154–158, 1993.

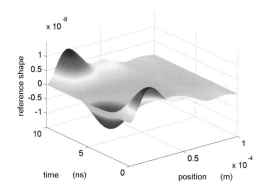

Figure 2.10

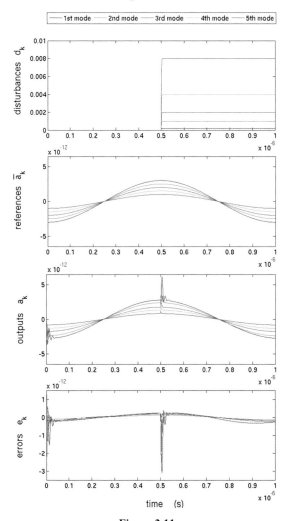

Figure 2.11

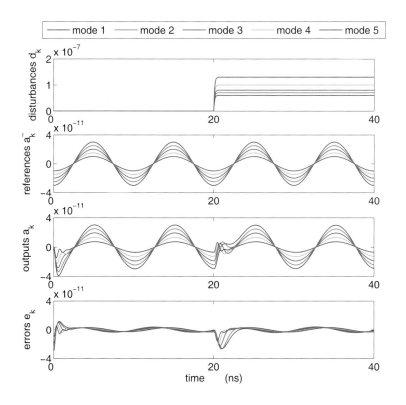

Figure 2.12

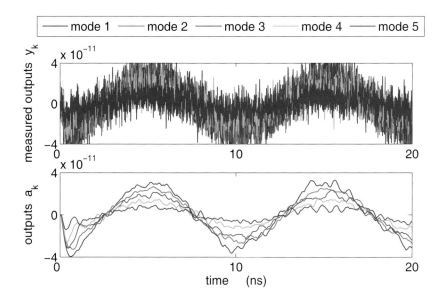

Figure 2.14

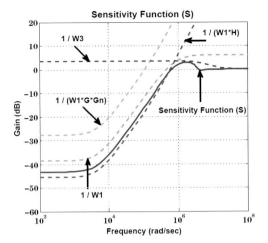

Figure 5.8

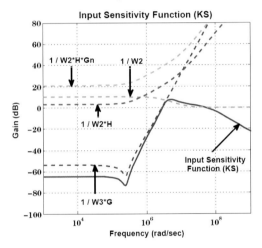

Figure 5.9

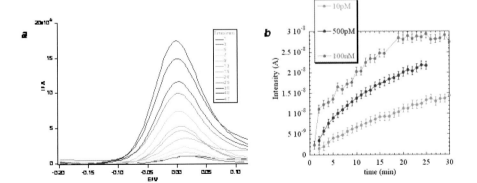

Figure 7.6

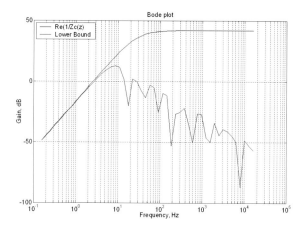

Figure 8.14b

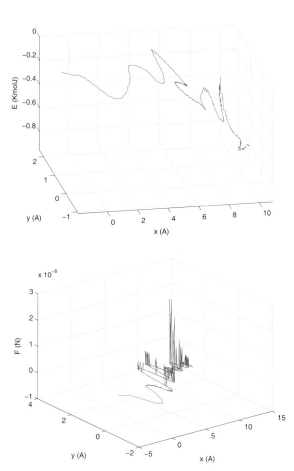

Figure 9.7a and b

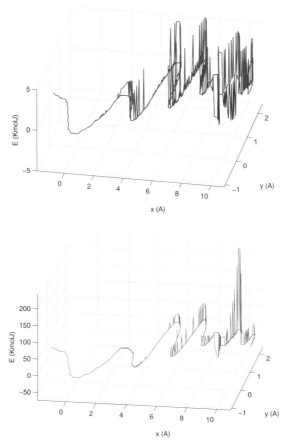

Figure 9.8a and b

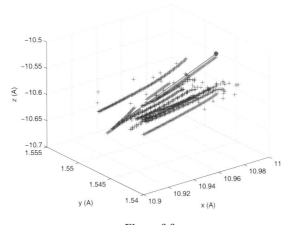

Figure 9.9a

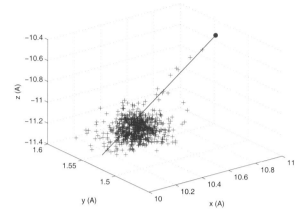

Figure 9.10a

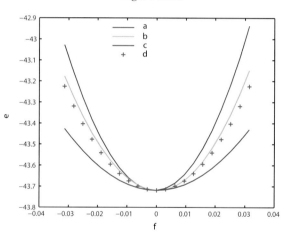

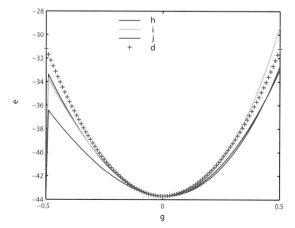

Figure 9.19a and b

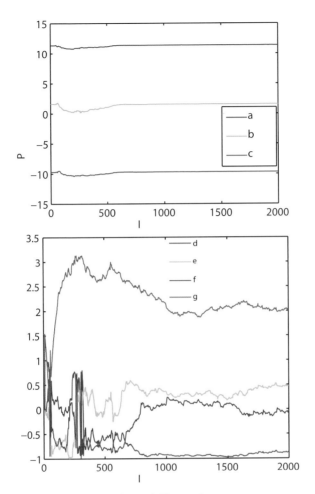

Figure 9.20 a and c

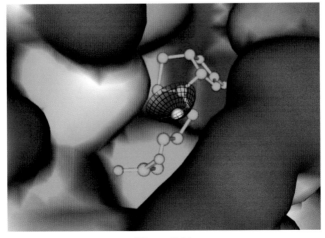

Figure 9.21

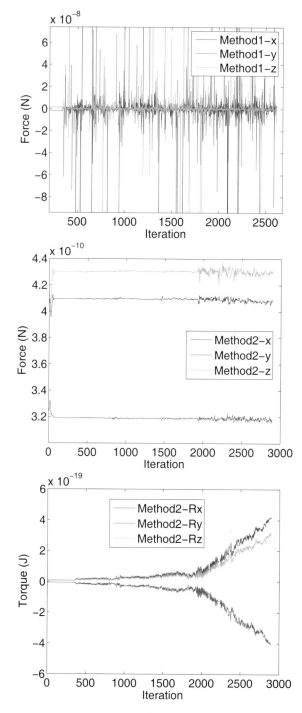

Figure 9.22 a, b and c

Chapter 6

Modeling, Identification and Control of a Micro-cantilever Array

We present a simplified model of mechanical behavior of large cantilever arrays with discoupled rows in the dynamic operating regime. Since the supporting bases are assumed to be elastic, cross-talk effect between cantilevers is taken into account. The mathematical derivation combines a thin plate asymptotic theory and the two-scale approximation theory, devoted to strongly heterogenous periodic systems. The model is not standard, so we present some of its features. We explain the method used for discretization and report results of its numerical validation with full 3D Finite Element simulations. In a second part, we apply a recently developed general theory of optimal control. The general theory applies to the field of finite length distributed systems where actuators and sensors are regularly spaced. It yields approximations implementable on semi-decentralized architectures. The practical implementation in a real-time device remains a critical point. One of the envisioned techniques is based on distributed analog electronic circuits. In a third part, we anticipate such implementation and show how they can be modeled through the two-scale approximation theory (at least in the linear static case). The simplified resulting model is found to be a system of a few partial differential equations. Its properties are inherited from the periodic cell composition and from electric conditions imposed at the boundaries. Its numerical solution, a vector of a few mean voltages, is weakly dependent on the array size. We present the model implementation.

Chapter written by Scott Cogan, Hui Hui, Michel Lenczner, Emmanuel Pillet, Nicolas Rattier and Youssef Yakoubi.

6.1. Introduction

Since its invention by Binnig [BIN 86], the atomic force microscope (AFM) has opened up new possibilities for a number of operations at the nanoscale, having an impact across various sciences and technologies. Today, the most popular application of AFM is in the materials sciences, biology and fundamental physics; see the reviews of Giessibl [GIE 03], Drakova [DRA 01] and Garcia and Perez [GAR 02], among others.

The AFM is also used for the manipulation of an object or materials at the nanoscale, for example the parallel Lithography of Quantum Devices [BUL 06, KAK 04], investigations into mechanical interactions at the molecular level in biology [CAR 00, RIE 02, ZLA 00], manipulation of nano-objects [DEC 03, SIT 04] and data storage e.g. [DES 00, HSI 05, KIM 03, LUT 99, YAN 06, YU 03]. A number of research laboratories are now developing large AFM arrays which can achieve the same kind of task in parallel. The most advanced system is the Millipede from IBM [DES 00] for data storage. A number of new architectures are emerging, however; see [BUL 04, DES 00, GRE 00, HSI 05, KAK 04, KIM 03, LUT 99, YAN 04, YAN 06, YU 03].

We are currently developing tools for the modeling, identification and control of microcantilever arrays such as those encountered in AFM arrays. In this chapter we report results in this area. The thread of our approach is to provide light computational methods for complex systems. This concerns modeling as well as control. Our mechanical structure model is based on a specific multiscale technique.

For control, we start with a general theory of optimal control applied to our simple cantilever array model and provide an approximation of the control law which may be implemented on a semi-decentralized computing architecture. In particular, it could be implemented in the form of a periodically distributed analog electronic circuit. Even although this implementation is incomplete, we present in advance a general model of such periodically distributed electronic circuits. It will be applied to fast simulations of electronic circuits realizing our control approximation.

The general model has been derived with a modified form of the multiscale technique used for mechanical structures. In the near future, we intend to couple both multiscale models to run light simulations for matrices of electromechanical systems. We also develop a variety of useful identification tools associated with our light models, allowing global sensitivity analysis (GSA), deterministic updating and inverse identification by Monte Carlo simulation. We take advantage of the simplicity of our AFM model to perform very quick GSA and Monte Carlo simulations, methods which are generally time consuming.

6.2. Modeling and identification of a cantilever array

We present a simplified model of mechanical behavior of large cantilever arrays with discoupled rows in the dynamic operating regime. Since the supporting bases are assumed to be elastic, cross-talk effect between cantilevers is taken into account. The mathematical derivation combines a thin plate asymptotic theory and the two-scale approximation theory, devoted to strongly heterogenous periodic systems. The model is not standard, so we present some of its features. We explain how each eigenmode is decomposed into the products of a base mode with a cantilever mode. We explain the method used for its discretization, and report results of its numerical validation with full 3D Finite Element simulations.

We perform GSA on the proposed model. Before any parametric identification, GSA is a necessary step to discard model parameters which are not influential. The results of a deterministic and stochastic identification are finally presented. The first is the updating of a dynamic model based on eigenelement sensitivities. The second is based on Bayesian inference.

6.2.1. *Geometry of the problem*

We consider a 2D array of cantilevers. It comprises rectangle parallelepiped bases crossing the array in which rectangle parallelepiped cantilever are clamped. Bases are assumed to be connected in the x_1 direction only, so that the system behaves as a set of discoupled rows. Each row is clamped at its ends. Concerning the other ends, we report two cases: one for free cantilevers and one for cantilevers equipped with a rigid tip (as in AFMs).

The whole array is a periodic repetition of the same cell in the directions x_1 and x_2 (see Figure 6.1a). We assume that the number of columns and rows of the array are sufficiently large, namely larger than or equal to 10. We then introduce the small parameter ε^* which equals the inverse of the number of cantilevers in a row $1/N$. We highlight the fact that the technique presented in the rest of the chapter can be extended to other geometries of cantilever arrays and even to other classes of microsystem arrays.

6.2.2. *Two-scale approximation*

Each point of the 3D space with coordinates $x = (x_1, x_2, x_3)$ is decomposed as $x = x^c + \epsilon y$, where x^c represents the coordinates of the center of the cell to which x belongs:

$$\epsilon = \begin{pmatrix} \varepsilon^* & 0 & 0 \\ 0 & \varepsilon^* & 0 \\ 0 & 0 & 1 \end{pmatrix}$$

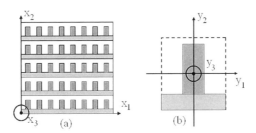

Figure 6.1. *(a) Finite Element Model (FEM) and two-scale model eigenvalues and (b) absolute errors*

and $y = \epsilon^{-1}(x - x^c)$ is the dilated relative position of x with respect to x^c. Points with coordinates y vary in the so-called *reference cell*; see the 2D view in Figure 6.1b obtained through a translation and the (x_1, x_2)-dilatation ϵ^{-1} of any current cell in the array.

We consider the distributed field $u(x)$ of elastic deflections in the array and we introduce its *two-scale transform*:

$$\widehat{u}^\varepsilon(\widetilde{x}, y) = u(x^c + \epsilon y)$$

for any $x = x^c + \epsilon y$ and $\widetilde{x} = (x_1, x_2)$. By construction the two-scale transform is constant, with respect to its first variable $\widetilde{x}$, over each cell. Since it depends on the ratio ε^* it may be approximated by the asymptotic field denoted u^0, obtained for a large number of cells (in both x_1 and x_2-directions) or, equivalently, when ε^* (mathematically) approaches 0:

$$\widehat{u}^\varepsilon = u^0 + O(\varepsilon^*).$$

The approximation u^0 is called the *two-scale approximation* of u. We mention that, as a consequence of the asymptotic process, the partial function $\widetilde{x} \mapsto u^0(\widetilde{x}, .)$ is continuous instead of being piecewise constant.

We now consider that the field of elastic deflections u is a solution of the Love-Kirchhoff thin elastic plate equation in the whole mechanical structure, including bases and cantilevers. Furthermore, we assume that the ratio of cantilever thickness h_C to base thickness h_B is very small, namely

$$\frac{h_C}{h_B} \approx \varepsilon^{*4/3}. \tag{6.1}$$

This assumption is formulated so that the ratio of cantilever stiffness to base stiffness is very small, namely of the order of ε^{*4}. The asymptotic analysis when

ε^* vanishes shows that u^0 does not depend on the cell variable y in bases and so only depends on the spatial variable $\widetilde{x}$.

We next remark that $u^0(\widetilde{x}, y)$ is a two-scale field, and therefore cannot be directly used as an approximation of the field $u(x)$ in the actual array of cantilevers. An inverse two-scale transform is therefore applied to u^0. However, we note that $\widetilde{x} \mapsto u^0(\widetilde{x}, y)$ is continuous, and so u^0 does not belong to the range of the two-scale transform operators and it has no preimage. Hence we introduce an approximated inverse of the two-scale transform $v(\widetilde{x}, y) \mapsto \overline{v}(x)$ in the sense that, for any sufficiently regular one-scale function $u(x)$ and two-scale function $v(\widetilde{x}, y)$, we have

$$\overline{\widehat{u}} = u + O(\varepsilon^*) \text{ and } \widehat{\overline{v}} = v + O(\varepsilon^*).$$

It emerges that $\overline{v}(x)$ is a mean over the cell including x with respect to $\widetilde{x} = (x_1, x_2)$ when x belongs to a cantilever:

$$\overline{v}(x) = \left\langle v(., \epsilon^{-1}(x - x^c)) \right\rangle_{\widetilde{x}}$$

and, with respect to x_2 when x belongs to a base,

$$\overline{v}(x) = \left\langle v(., \epsilon^{-1}(x - x^c)) \right\rangle_{x_2}.$$

We retain $\overline{u}^0$ as an approximation of u in the actual physical system. Note that for the model in dynamics, the deflection $u(t, x)$ is a time-space function. In our analysis we do not introduce a two-scale transformation in time, so the time variable t acts as a simple parameter.

6.2.3. *Model description*

We now describe the model satisfied by the two-scale approximation $u^0(t, \widetilde{x}, y)$ of $u(t, x)$. Note that as the deflection in the Kirchhoff–Love model u is independent of x_3, u^0 is independent of y_3. To increase simplicity, we neglect the effect of torsion i.e. the variations of $y_1 \mapsto u^0(t, \widetilde{x}, y)$ in cantilevers. Cantilever motion is governed by a classical Euler–Bernoulli beam equation in the microscopic variable y_2:

$$m^C \partial_{tt} u^0 + r^C \partial^4_{y_2 \ldots y_2} u^0 = f^C$$

where $r^C = \varepsilon^{*4} E^C I^C$, m^C is a linear mass, E^C is the cantilever elastic modulus, I^C is the second moment of cantilever section and f^C is a load per unit length in the cantilever. This model represents motion of an infinite number of cantilevers parameterized by all $\widetilde{x} = (x_1, x_2)$.

Bases are also governed by an Euler–Bernoulli equation in the macroscopic variable x_1 where part of the load comes from continuous distributions of cantilever shear forces:

$$m^B \partial_{tt} u^0 + r^B \partial_{x_1 \ldots x_1}^4 u^0 = -d^B \partial_{y_2 \ldots y_2}^3 u^0 + f^B$$

where $r^B = E^B I^B$, m^B, E^B, I^B, d^B and f^B are a linear mass, the base elastic modulus, the second moment of section of the base, a cantilever-base coupling coefficient and the load per unit length in the base, respectively.

In the model, cantilevers appear as clamped-in bases. At base-cantilever junctions,

$$u_{\text{cantilever}}^0 = u_{\text{base}}^0 \quad \text{and} \quad (\partial_{y_2} u^0)_{\text{cantilever}} = 0 \tag{6.2}$$

because $\partial_{y_2} u^0 = 0$ in bases. Other cantilever ends may be free and defined:

$$\partial_{y_2 y_2}^2 u^0 = \partial_{y_2 y_2 y_2}^3 u^0 = 0 \tag{6.3}$$

or may be equipped with a rigid part (usually a tip in AFMs) and defined:

$$J^R \partial_{tt} \begin{pmatrix} u^0 \\ \partial_{y_2} u^0 \end{pmatrix} + \varepsilon r^C \begin{pmatrix} -\partial_{y_2 y_2 y_2}^3 u^0 \\ \partial_{y_2 y_2}^2 u^0 \end{pmatrix} = \begin{pmatrix} f_3^R \\ F_3^R + F_2^R \end{pmatrix}$$

at junctions between elastic and rigid parts. Here, J^R is a matrix of moments of the rigid part about the junction plane, f_3^R is a load in the y_3 direction, F_3^R is a first moment of loads about the junction plane and F_2^R is the first moment of loads in the y_2 direction about the beam neutral plane. Finally, base ends are assumed to be clamped in a fixed support, i.e.

$$u^0 = \partial_{x_1} u^0 = 0. \tag{6.4}$$

The loads f^C, f^B and f^R in the model are asymptotic loads which are generally not defined from the physical problem. In practical computations, they are replaced by the two-scale transforms $\widehat{f}^C, \widehat{f}^B$ and $\widehat{f}^R$. For completeness, we mention that rows of cantilevers are discoupled; this is why x_2 only plays the role of a parameter.

6.2.4. Structure of eigenmodes

An infinite number of eigenvalues λ^A and eigenvectors $\varphi^A(x_1, y_2)$ are associated with the model. For convenience, we parameterize them with two independent indices i and j, both varying in the infinite countable set $\mathbb{N}$.

The first index i refers to the infinite set of eigenvalues λ_i^B and eigenvectors $\varphi_i^B(x_1)$ of the Euler–Bernoulli beam equation associated with a base. The eigenvalues

$(\lambda_i^B)_{i\in\mathbb{N}}$ constitute a sequence of positive numbers increasing towards infinity. At each such eigenvalue, an eigenvalue problem is associated with cantilevers. It also has a countable infinity of solutions denoted by λ_{ij}^C and $\varphi_{ij}^C(y_2)$.

Since the index i of λ_i^B is fixed, the sequence $(\lambda_{ij}^C)_{j\in\mathbb{N}}$ is a positive sequence increasing towards infinity. On the other side, for fixed j and large λ_i^B i.e. large i, the sequence $(\lambda_{ij}^C, \varphi_{ij}^C)_{i\in\mathbb{N}}$ converges to an eigenelement of the clamped-free cantilever model. The eigenvalues λ_{ij}^A of the model are proportional to λ_{ij}^C. Finally, each eigenvector $\varphi_{ij}^A(x_1, y_2)$ is the product of a mode in a base by a mode in a cantilever $\varphi_i^B(x_1)\varphi_{ij}^C(y_2)$.

6.2.5. *Model validation*

We report observations made of eigenmode computations. We consider a 1D silicon array of N cantilevers ($N = 10, 15$ or 20), with base dimensions $500 \times 16.7 \times 10\,\mu m^3$ and cantilever dimensions $41.7 \times 12.5 \times 1.25\,\mu m^3$. See Figure 6.2 for the two possible geometries (with or without tips).

Figure 6.2. *Cantilever array (a) with tips and (b) without tips*

We have carried out our numerical study on both cases, but we limit the following comparisons to cantilevers without tips because configuration including tips yields comparable results.

We restrict our attention to a finite number n^B of eigenvalues λ_i^B in the base. Computing the eigenvalues λ^A, we observe that they are grouped in bunches of size n^B accumulated around clamped-free cantilever eigenvalues. A number of eigenvalues are isolated far from the bunches. It is remarkable that the eigenelements in the same bunch share the same cantilever mode shape (close to a clamped-free cantilever mode) even if they correspond to different indices j. This is why these modes are referred to as 'cantilever modes'.

Isolated eigenelements also share a common cantilever shape, which initially looks like a clamped-free cantilever mode shape except that the clamped side is shifted far from zero. The induced global mode φ^A is then dominated by base deformations and will therefore be called 'base modes'. Densities of the square root of eigenvalues are reported in the second, fourth and sixth graphs (from top down) of Figure 6.3 for $n_B = 10, 15$ and 20, respectively. These figures show three bunches with size n_B and isolated modes that remain unchanged.

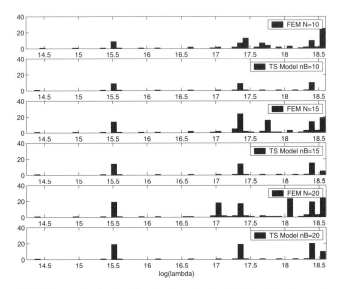

Figure 6.3. *Eigenmode density distributions for the FEM and the two-scale model*

We discuss the comparison with the modal structure of the 3D linear elasticity system for the cantilever array discretized by a standard finite element procedure. The eigenvalues of the 3D elasticity equations also constitute an increasing positive sequence that accumulate at infinity. The density distribution of the two-scale model exhibits a number of concentration points and also some isolated values. Here bunch sizes equal the number N of cantilevers. The first, third and fifth graphs of Figure 6.3 represent eigenmode distributions for $N = 10, 15$ and 20. Extrapolating this observation shows that, when the number of cantilevers increases to infinity, bunch size increases proportionally.

Since the two-scale model is an approximation in the sense of an infinitely large number of cantilevers, the two-scale model spectrum exhibits mode concentration with an infinite number of elements. This observation provides guidelines for operating mode selection in the two-scale model. In order to determine an approximation of the spectrum for an N-cantilevers array, we suggest operating a truncation in the mode list in order to retain a simple infinity of eigenvalues $(\lambda_{ij}^A)_{i=1,...,N \text{ and } j \in \mathbb{N}}$. We highlight the fact that N eigenvalue bunches generally do not correspond to a single column of the truncated matrix λ^A_{ij}. This comes from the base mode distribution in this list.

When considered in increasing order, base modes are located in consecutive lines of the matrix λ^A but not necessarily in the same column. We note that a number of eigenvalues in the FEM spectrum do not have a counterpart in the two-scale model spectrum. The missing elements correspond to physical effects not taken into account in the Euler–Bernoulli models for bases and cantilevers.

The next step in the discussion is to compare the eigenmodes, especially those belonging to bunches of eigenvalues. To compare an eigenvector from the two-scale model with an eigenvector of the elasticity system, we use the Modal Assurance Criterion (MAC) [ALL 03] which is equal to 1 when the shapes are identical and to 0 when they are orthogonal (Figure 6.4).

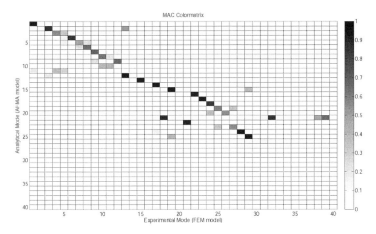

Figure 6.4. *MAC matrix between two-scale model modes and FEM modes*

We compare some eigenmodes which have a MAC value close to 1 in Figure 6.5.

This test has been applied to transverse displacement only and a further selection has been developed in order to eliminate modes corresponding to physical effects not modeled by the Euler–Bernoulli models. Following this procedure, mode pairing is successfully achieved.

Paired eigenvalues are represented in Figure 6.6a; the corresponding relative errors are plotted on Figure 6.6b. Note that errors are far from being uniform among eigenvalues. In fact, the main error source is the poor precision of the Euler–Bernoulli

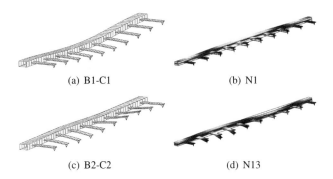

(a) B1-C1

(b) N1

(c) B2-C2

(d) N13

Figure 6.5. *Eigenmode shapes of analytical mode and FEM mode*

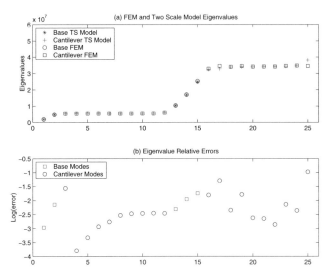

Figure 6.6. *(a) Superimposed eigenmode distributions of the simple two-scale model with the full 3D FEM and (b) errors in logarithmic scale*

model for representing base deformations in a few particular cases. Indeed, careful observation of finite element modes shows that base torsion is predominant for some modes. This is especially true for the first mode of the first cantilever mode bunch.

6.2.6. *Model identification*

6.2.6.1. *Global sensitivity analysis (GSA)*

The objective of GSA is to study the effect of the parameter variability on the model responses. While the classical local sensitivity analysis studies the effect of small perturbations around nominal parameter values, the GSA studies the effect of variations over all parameter space.

We denote the vector of parameters which describes the model as $m = [m_1\, m_2, \ldots, m_{n_p}]^T \in \mathfrak{M}$. $d = \{d_1, d_2, \ldots, d_{n_d}\} \in \mathfrak{D}$ describes the observable data. The exact relation between m and d is $d = g(m)$. In this model, the parameters are Young's modulus, the Poisson ratio, volume mass and the thickness, length and width of the base, cantilever and tip. All the parameters are used in GSA. The list of eigenmodes is $(\varphi_{ij}^A)_{i=1,\ldots,10}$ and $_{j=1,2}$. The indices i and j represent base modes and cantilever modes, respectively (Figure 6.7).

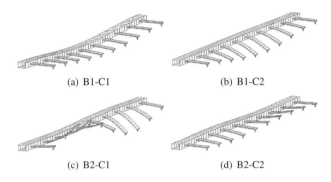

(a) B1-C1   (b) B1-C2

(c) B2-C1   (d) B2-C2

Figure 6.7. *Eigenmodes of model (B: base mode; C: cantilever mode)*

Qualitative and quantitative GSA methods can be found in the literature [SAL 00]. To analyze the AFMA model, we applied qualitative methods using the correlation coefficients of singular value decomposition (SVD). Each parameter varies according to a *uniform* probability law 0.8–1.2 times the nominal value, independently of the others. Five hundred samples are calculated for the first ten modes of base and two modes of cantilever. The correlation coefficients matrix is depicted in Figure 6.8a, where the horizontal base is the input parameters and the vertical base is the output eigenvalues. Figures 6.8b and c represent the SVD matrix and the singular values, respectively. Each column of the SVD matrix represents a singular vector.

From Figure 6.8a, we can see a strong correlation between the parameters hB and Lbeam and the model responses. For the SVD analysis, the number of influential

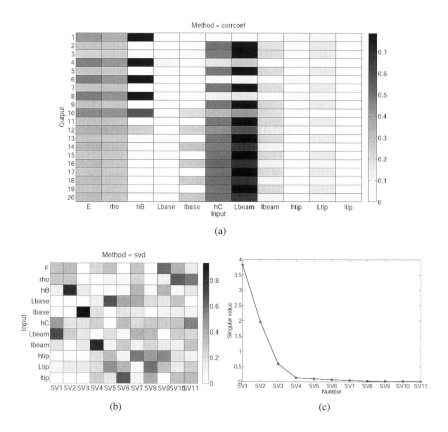

Figure 6.8. *(a) Correlation coefficients matrix, (b) SVD matrix and (c) singular values*

parameters is indicated by the singular values. Figure 6.8c depicts two significant singular values with respect to the others, which means that only two parameters are influential. The important parameters are then determined using the maximum absolute values of the singular vectors associated with the two maximal singular values. From Figure 6.8b, we deduce that hB and Lbeam are the most influential parameters. The analysis carried out by correlation matrix and SVD therefore agree. As hB and Lbeam appear to be the most important parameters, we only consider these two parameters in the following.

6.2.6.2. *Updating by sensitivity*

Parameter updating through sensitivity is an iterative procedure based on eigensolution sensitivities with respect to the model parameters. The convergence algorithm is governed by the evolution of a cost function which returns the computation of the minimum of the difference between experimental and calculated data. This algorithm was implemented in the AFM toolbox to perform deterministic identification.

According to previous analysis, we note that parameters hB and Lbeam are perturbed. We set hB to 1.3 and Lbeam to 0.8. After nine iterations, the convergence is reached and the exact value of the reference parameters (all equal to 1) is returned (Figure 6.9).

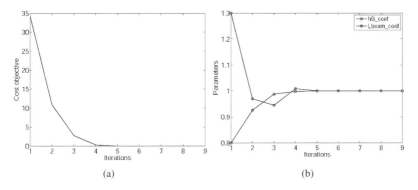

Figure 6.9. *Evolution of (a) cost objective function and (b) perturbed parameters*

6.2.6.3. *Inverse identification*

The aim of any inverse problem is to obtain model parameter values from observed data. Here, we use a probabilistic formulation of inverse problems developed by Tarantola [TAR 05]. This formulation is based on the notion of conjunction of states of information. *A priori* uncertainty information on the model parameters, represented by the probability density function (PDF) $\rho_M(m)$, experimental uncertainty information with the associated PDF $\rho_M(m)$ and theoretical uncertainty information $\Theta(d, m)$ are combined to produce *a posteriori* PDF $\sigma_M(m)$ on the set of model parameters. Since no analytic expression exists for these PDFs, a Markov Chain Monte Carlo (MCMC) algorithm is used to sample the *a posteriori* PDFs [MOS 02].

To put this approach into practice, we consider $m = \{m_1, m_2\} = \{hB, Lbeam\}$ as the set of model parameters. The set of observable data is $d^{\text{obs}} = \{d_1^{\text{obs}}, \ldots, d_{20}^{\text{obs}}\}$ where d_i^{obs} the eigenvalues are $(\lambda_{ij}^A)_{i=1,\ldots,10 \text{ and } j=1,2}$. In this application, no theoretical uncertainty is considered. This is the case of a classical Bayesian inference, where the marginal probability *a posteriori* of the model parameters $\sigma_M(m)$ represents the conditional probability of the observations d given any m. We assume that the experimental and model uncertainties are Gaussian. $\rho_M(m)$ and $\rho_D(d)$ are therefore Gaussian PDFs.

It is often difficult to calculate the *a posteriori* PDF $\sigma_M(m)$ and the associated marginals $\sigma_{m_k}(m_k)$ directly. We will estimate the densities by a Monte Carlo simulation. As proposed in [MOS 02], a MCMC algorithm of Metropolis–Hastings [MET 53] is utilized.

To check the convergence of the algorithm, we plot the convergence of average $\hat{\mu}_{n_s}^t$, $t = 1, \ldots, n_s$ where n_s is the number of samples. The convergence is reached after 124 iterations; see Figure 6.10. The densities are estimated with the last 500 samples and are plotted in Figure 6.11. The vertical line indicates the nominal value of the parameter from which the observations of d^{obs} have been simulated.

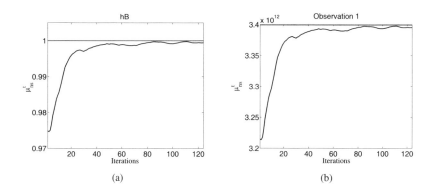

Figure 6.10. *Evolutions of $\hat{\mu}_{n_s}^t$ for (a) hB and (b) observation 1*

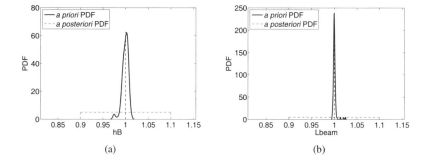

Figure 6.11. *Results of identification for the parameters (a) hB and (b) Lbeam*

The dispersion diagrams *a posteriori* between hB, Lbeam and observation 1 and between hB and Lbeam are also presented in Figure 6.12.

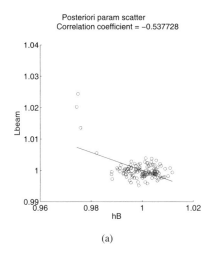

(a)

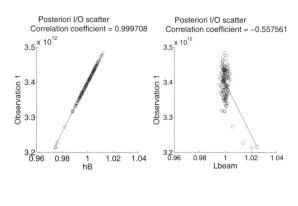

(b)

Figure 6.12. *Dispersion diagrams between (a) observation 1 and (b) parameters*

6.3. Semi-decentralized approximation of optimal control applied to a cantilever array

We apply a recently developed general theory of optimal control approximation to the cantilever array model. The theory applies to the field of finite length distributed systems where actuators and sensors are regularly spaced. It yields approximations implementable on semi-decentralized architectures. Our result is limited to the linear quadrature regulator (LQR), but its extension to other optimal control theories for linear distributed systems such as linear quadric Gaussian (LQG) or H_∞ controls is in progress.

We focus on illustrating the method rather than on providing a mathematically rigorous treatment. In the following, we begin with transforming the two-scale model of cantilever arrays into an appropriate form. All construction steps of the approximate LQR are fully presented. Finally, we report numerical simulation results.

6.3.1. *General notation*

The norm and the inner product of a Hilbert space E are denoted by $\|.\|_E$ and $(.,.)_E$. For a second Hilbert space F, $\mathcal{L}(E, F)$ denotes the space of continuous linear operators defined from E to F. In addition, $\mathcal{L}(E, E)$ is denoted by $\mathcal{L}(E)$. We say that $\Phi \in \mathcal{L}(E, F)$ is an isomorphism from E to F if Φ is a one-to-one continuous mapping with a continuous inverse.

6.3.2. *Reformulation of the two-scale model of cantilever arrays*

We reformulate the two-scale model presented in section 6.2 in a set of notation which is more usual in control theory of infinite dimensional systems.

We adopt the configuration of the cantilevers without tip; see Figure 6.13. The model expressed in the two-scale reference appears as in a rectangle $\Omega = (0, L_B) \times (0, L_C)$. The parameters L_B and L_C represent the base length in the macroscale direction x and the scaled cantilever length in the microscale variable y, respectively. The base is modeled by the line $\Gamma = \{(x, y) \mid x \in (0, L_B) \text{ and } y = 0\}$ and the rectangle Ω is filled by an infinite number of cantilevers.

We recall that the system motion is described by its bending displacement only. Since the base is governed by an Euler–Bernoulli beam equation, we consider two kinds of distributed forces: one exerted by the attached cantilevers and the other – denoted $u_B(t, x)$ – originating from an actuator distribution. The bending displacement, the mass per unit length, the bending coefficient and the width are denoted $w_B(t, x), \rho^B, R^B$ and ℓ_C, respectively. The base governing equation states

$$\rho^B \partial_{tt}^2 w_B + R^B \partial_{x \ldots x}^4 w_B = -\ell_\mathbf{C} R^C \partial_{yyy}^3 w_C - \partial_{xx}^2 u_B. \tag{6.5}$$

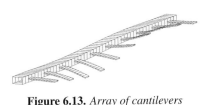

Figure 6.13. *Array of cantilevers*

The base is still assumed to be clamped, so the boundary conditions:

$$w_B = \partial_x w_B = 0 \tag{6.6}$$

are unchanged at both ends.

Cantilevers are oriented in the y-direction, and we recall that their motions are governed by an infinite number of Euler–Bernoulli equations distributed along the x-direction. Here, each cantilever is subjected to a control force $u_C(t, x)$ assumed, for simplicity, constant along cantilevers. This choice does not affect the method presented in the following, so it can be replaced by any other realistic force distribution. Denoting cantilever bending displacements, mass per unit length and bending coefficient by $w_C(t, x, y), \rho^C$ and R^C, respectively, the governing equation in $(x, y) \in \Omega$ is

$$\rho^C \partial_{tt}^2 w_C + R^C \partial_{y...y}^4 w_C = u_C.$$

The boundary conditions

$$\begin{cases} w_C = w_B \text{ and } \partial_y w_C = 0 & \text{at } y = 0 \\ \partial_{yy}^2 w_C = \partial_{yyy}^3 w_C = 0 & \text{at } y = L_C \end{cases} \tag{6.7}$$

represent an end clamped in the base and a free end. Finally, both equations are supplemented with initial conditions on displacements and velocities:

$$\begin{aligned} w_B &= w_{B,0}, \ \partial_t w_B = w_{B,1}, \\ w_C &= w_{C,0}, \text{ and } \partial_t w_C = w_{C,1}. \end{aligned}$$

The LQR problem is set for control variables $(u_B, u_C) \in U = H^2 \cap H_0^1(\Gamma) \times L^2(\Gamma)$ and for the cost function:

$$\mathcal{J}\left(w_{B,0}, w_{B,1}, w_{C,0}, w_{C,1}; u_B, u_C\right) \tag{6.8}$$

$$= \int_0^\infty \|w_B\|_{H_0^2(\Gamma)}^2 + \|\partial_{yy}^2 w_C\|_{L^2(\Omega)}^2 + \|u_B\|_{H^2 \cap H_0^1(\Gamma)}^2 + \|u_C\|_{L^2(\Gamma)}^2 \, dt.$$

6.3.3. *Model reformulation*

The first step of method application consists of transforming the control problem into another problem with internal distributed control and observation. To do so, we make additional assumptions yielding model simplifications. We set $\bar{w}_C = w_C - w_B$, the solution of an Euler–Bernoulli equation in cantilevers with homogenous boundary conditions

$$
\begin{cases}
\rho^C \partial_{tt}^2 \bar{w}_C + R^C \partial_{y...y}^4 \bar{w}_C = u_C - \rho^C \partial_{tt}^2 w_B & \text{in } \Omega, \\
\bar{w}_C = \partial_y \bar{w}_C = 0 & \text{at } y = 0, \\
\partial_{yy}^2 \bar{w}_C = \partial_{yyy}^3 \bar{w}_C = 0 & \text{at } y = L_C.
\end{cases}
\tag{6.9}
$$

We introduce the basis of normalized eigenfunction $(\psi_k)_k$, the solution of the corresponding eigenvalue problem

$$
\begin{cases}
\partial_{y...y}^4 \psi = \lambda^C \psi \text{ in } (0, L_C), \\
\psi(0) = \partial_y \psi(0) = 0, \\
\partial_{yy}^2 \psi(L_C) = \partial_{yyy}^3 \psi(L_C) = 0, \\
\|\psi_k\|_{L^2(0,L_C)} = 1.
\end{cases}
\tag{6.10}
$$

It is well known that, in most practical applications, a very small number of cantilever modes is sufficient to properly describe the system. For the sake of simplicity, we only take into account the first mode, keeping in mind that the method can handle more than one mode. We therefore adopt the approximation

$$
\bar{w}_C(t, x, y) \simeq \bar{w}_C^1(t, x)\, \psi_1(y),
$$

where $\bar{w}_C^1$ is the coefficient of the first mode ψ_1 in the modal decomposition of $\bar{w}_C$. Introducing the mean $\bar{\psi}_1 = \int_0^{L_C} \psi_1 dy$ and $u_C^1 = \int_0^{L_C} u_C \psi_1 dy$, we find that $\bar{w}_C^1$ is the solution of

$$
\rho^C \partial_{tt}^2 \bar{w}_C^1 + R^C \lambda_1^C \bar{w}_C^1 = u_C^1 - \rho^C \bar{\psi}_1 \partial_{tt}^2 w_B.
$$

In order to avoid the term $\partial_{tt}^2 w_B$, we introduce $\widetilde{w}_C = \bar{w}_C^1 + \bar{\psi}_1 w_B$ in order to make $\widetilde{w}_C$ the solution of

$$
\rho^C \partial_{tt}^2 \widetilde{w}_C + R^C \lambda_1^C \widetilde{w}_C - R^C \lambda_1^C \bar{\psi}_1 w_B = u_C^1.
\tag{6.11}
$$

Since

$$
\partial_y^3 w_C = \partial_y^3 (\bar{w}_C + w_B) = \partial_y^3 [\bar{w}_C^1 \psi_1 + w_B \psi_1] = \partial_y^3 \psi_1 \widetilde{w}_C,
$$

we set $c_1 = \partial_y^3 \psi_1(0)$ and determine that the couple $(w_B, \widetilde{w}_C)$ is a solution of the system of equations on Γ, i.e.

$$\begin{cases} \rho^B \partial_{tt}^2 w_B + R^B \partial_{x...x}^4 w_B + \ell_C R^C c_1 \widetilde{w}_C = -\partial_{xx}^2 u_B & \text{in } \Gamma, \\ \rho^C \partial_{tt}^2 \widetilde{w}_C + R^C \lambda_1^C \widetilde{w}_C - R^C \lambda_1^C \bar{\psi}_1 w_B = u_C^1 & \text{in } \Gamma, \end{cases} \quad (6.12)$$

with the boundary conditions equation (6.6). The cost functional is simplified accordingly, i.e.

$$\begin{aligned} \mathcal{J} \simeq \int_0^\infty \left\| \partial_{xx}^2 w_B(t,x) \right\|_{L^2(\Gamma)}^2 + \left\| \lambda_1^C \widetilde{w}_C(t,x) \right\|_{L^2(\Gamma)}^2 \\ + \left\| \partial_{xx}^2 u_B \right\|_{L^2(\Gamma)}^2 + \left\| u_C^1 \right\|_{L^2(\Gamma)}^2 \, dt. \end{aligned} \quad (6.13)$$

6.3.4. Classical formulation of the LQR problem

We now write the above LQR problem in a classical abstract setting [CUR 95]. We set the state variable as

$$z^T = \begin{pmatrix} w_B & \widetilde{w}_C & \partial_t w_B & \partial_t \widetilde{w}_C \end{pmatrix},$$

the control variable as

$$u^T = \begin{pmatrix} u_B & u_C^1 \end{pmatrix},$$

the state operator as

$$A = \begin{pmatrix} 0 & 0 & I & 0 \\ 0 & 0 & 0 & I \\ -R^B \partial_{x...x}^4 / \rho^B & -\ell_C R^C c_1 / \rho^B & 0 & 0 \\ R^C \lambda_1^C \bar{\psi}_1 / \rho^C & -R^C \lambda_1^C / \rho^C & 0 & 0 \end{pmatrix},$$

the control operator as

$$B = \begin{pmatrix} 0 & 0 \\ 0 & 0 \\ -\frac{\partial_{xx}^2}{\rho^B} & 0 \\ 0 & \frac{I}{\rho^C} \end{pmatrix},$$

the observation operator as

$$C = \begin{pmatrix} I & 0 & 0 & 0 \\ 0 & \lambda_1^C I & 0 & 0 \\ 0 & 0 & 0 & 0 \\ 0 & 0 & 0 & 0 \end{pmatrix},$$

the weight operator as $S = I$ and the functional operator as $J(z_0, u) = \int_0^{+\infty} \|Cz\|_Y^2 + (Su, u)_U \, dt$.

The LQR problem, which consists of minimizing the function according to the constraint equation (6.12), may be written under its usual form as

$$\frac{dz}{dt}(t) = Az(t) + Bu(t) \text{ for } t > 0 \text{ and } z(0) = z_0,$$

$$\min_{u \in U} J(z_0, u). \tag{6.14}$$

Here, A is the infinitesimal generator of a continuous semigroup on the separable Hilbert space $Z = H_0^2(\Gamma) \times L^2(\Gamma)^3$ with dense domain $D(A) = H^4(\Gamma) \cap H_0^2(\Gamma) \times L^2(\Gamma) \times H_0^2(\Gamma) \times L^2(\Gamma)$. It is known that the control operator $B \in \mathcal{L}(U, Z)$, the observation operator $C \in \mathcal{L}(Z, Y)$ and $S \in \mathcal{L}(U, U)$, where $Y = Z$. We also know that (A, B) is stabilizable and that (A, C) is detectable, in the sense that there exist $G \in \mathcal{L}(Z, U)$ and $F \in \mathcal{L}(Y, Z)$ such that $A - BG$ and $A - FC$ are the infinitesimal generators of two uniformly exponentially stable continuous semigroups. It follows that for each $z_0 \in Z$, the LQR problem (6.14) admits a unique solution:

$$u^* = -Kz \tag{6.15}$$

where $K = S^{-1}B^*Pz$ and $P \in \mathcal{L}(Z)$ is the unique self-adjoint non-negative solution of the operational Riccati equation:

$$\left(A^*P + PA - PBS^{-1}B^*P + C^*C\right)z = 0, \tag{6.16}$$

for all $z \in D(A)$.

The adjoint A^* of the unbounded operator A is defined from $D(A^*) \subset Z$ to Z by the equality $(A^*z, z')_Z = (z, Az')_Z$ for all $z \in D(A^*)$ and $z' \in D(A)$. The adjoint $B^* \in \mathcal{L}(Z, U)$ of the bounded operator B is defined by $(B^*z, u)_U = (z, Bu)_Z$; the adjoint $C^* \in \mathcal{L}(Y, Z)$ is defined similarly.

6.3.5. *Semi-decentralized approximation*

This section provides a step-by-step formulation of the method of approximation.

6.3.5.1. *Matrices of functions of a self-adjoint operator*

Since the approximation method of P is based on the concept of matrices of functions of a self-adjoint operator, this section is devoted to their definition. We only discuss the simplest case of compact operators, avoiding spectral theory technicalities (see [DAU 90] for the general theory). From this point onwards, we denote the separable Hilbert space $L^2(\Gamma)$ by X and the self-adjoint operator $\left(\partial_{x\ldots x}^4\right)^{-1}$ by Λ with domain

$$D(\Lambda) = H^4(\Gamma) \cap H_0^2(\Gamma) \text{ in } X.$$

As Λ is self-adjoint and compact, its spectrum $\sigma(\Lambda)$ is discrete, bounded and comprises real eigenvalues λ_k. They are solutions of the eigenvalue problem $\Lambda\phi_k = \lambda_k\phi_k$ with $\|\phi_k\|_X = 1$. In the following, $I_\sigma = (\sigma_{\min}, \sigma_{\max})$ refers to an open interval that includes $\sigma(\Lambda)$.

For a given real-valued function f, continuous on I_σ, $f(\Lambda)$ is the linear self-adjoint operator on X defined by

$$f(\Lambda)z = \sum_{k=1}^{\infty} f(\lambda_k) z_k \phi_k$$

where $z_k = (z, \phi_k)_X$, with domain

$$D(f(\Lambda)) = \{z \in X \mid \sum_{k=1}^{\infty} |f(\lambda_k)z_k|^2 < \infty\}.$$

If f is a $n_1 \times n_2$ matrix of real-valued functions f_{ij}, continuous on I_σ, $f(\Lambda)$ is a matrix of linear operators $f_{ij}(\Lambda)$ with domain

$$D(f(\Lambda)) = \{z \in X^{n_2} \mid \sum_{k=1}^{\infty} \sum_{j=1}^{n_2} |f_{ij}(\lambda_k)(z_j)_k|^2 < \infty \;\forall i = 1, \ldots, n_1\}.$$

6.3.5.2. Factorization by a matrix of functions of Λ

The second step in the semi-decentralized control approximation method is the factorization of K under the form of a product of a function of Λ with operators admitting a natural semi-decentralized approximation. To do so, we introduce three isomorphisms $\Phi_Z \in \mathcal{L}(X^4, Z)$, $\Phi_U \in \mathcal{L}(X^2, U)$ and $\Phi_Y \in \mathcal{L}(X^4, Y)$, mapping a power of X into Z, U and Y, respectively, so that

$$a(\Lambda) = \Phi_Z^{-1} A \Phi_Z, \; b(\Lambda) = \Phi_Z^{-1} B \Phi_U,$$
$$c(\Lambda) = \Phi_Y^{-1} C \Phi_Z, \text{ and } s(\Lambda) = \Phi_U^{-1} S \Phi_U$$

are matrices of functions of Λ. In the current example, we propose

$$\Phi_Z = \begin{pmatrix} \Lambda^{\frac{1}{2}} & 0 & 0 & 0 \\ 0 & I & 0 & 0 \\ 0 & 0 & I & 0 \\ 0 & 0 & 0 & I \end{pmatrix}, \; \Phi_U = \begin{pmatrix} (-\partial_{xx}^2)^{-1} & 0 \\ 0 & I \end{pmatrix} \text{ and } \Phi_Y = \Phi_Z.$$

This choice yields

$$
a\left(\lambda\right) = \begin{pmatrix} 0 & 0 & \lambda^{-1/2} & 0 \\ 0 & 0 & 0 & 1 \\ -\frac{R^B}{\rho^B}\lambda^{-1/2} & -\frac{\ell_C R^C c_1}{\rho^B} & 0 & 0 \\ \frac{R^C \lambda_1^C \bar{\psi}_1}{\rho^C}\lambda^{1/2} & -\frac{R^C \lambda_1^C}{\rho^C} & 0 & 0 \end{pmatrix},
$$

$$
b\left(\lambda\right) = \begin{pmatrix} 0 & 0 \\ 0 & 0 \\ \frac{1}{\rho^B} & 0 \\ 0 & \frac{1}{\rho^C} \end{pmatrix}, \quad c\left(\lambda\right) = \begin{pmatrix} 1 & 0 & 0 & 0 \\ 0 & \lambda_1^C & 0 & 0 \\ 0 & 0 & 0 & 0 \\ 0 & 0 & 0 & 0 \end{pmatrix} \quad \text{and} \quad \left(\lambda\right) = 1.
$$

Endowing Z, U and Y with the inner products $(z, z')_Z = \left(\Phi_Z^{-1} z, \Phi_Z^{-1} z'\right)_{X^4}$, $(u, u')_U = \left(\Phi_U^{-1} u, \Phi_U^{-1} u'\right)_{X^2}$ and $(y, y')_Y = \left(\Phi_Y^{-1} y, \Phi_Y^{-1} y'\right)_{X^4}$, we find the subsequent factorization of the controller K in equation (6.15) which plays a central role in the approximation.

Proposition 6.1. *The controller K admits the factorization*

$$
K = \Phi_U q\left(\Lambda\right) \Phi_Z^{-1},
$$

where $q\left(\lambda\right) = s^{-1}\left(\lambda\right) b^T\left(\lambda\right) p\left(\lambda\right)$ *and where, for all* $\lambda \in \sigma$, $p(\lambda)$ *is the unique self-adjoint non-negative matrix solving the algebraic Riccati equation:*

$$
a^T\left(\lambda\right) p + pa\left(\lambda\right) - pb\left(\lambda\right) s^{-1}\left(\lambda\right) b^T\left(\lambda\right) p + c^T\left(\lambda\right) c\left(\lambda\right) = 0. \tag{6.17}
$$

Proof. The algebraic Riccati equation can be found after replacing A, B, C and S by their decomposition in the Riccatti equation (6.16). □

In the following, we require that the algebraic Riccati equation (6.17) admits a unique solution for all $\lambda \in I_\sigma$, checked numerically.

Remark 6.1. In this example, Φ_Z is a matrix of function of Λ, as is $\Phi_U^{-1} K$:

$$
k(\Lambda) = \Phi_U^{-1} K. \tag{6.18}
$$

The approximation is therefore developed directly on $k(\Lambda)$ but we emphasize that, in more generic situations, it is pursued on $q(\Lambda)$.

Remark 6.2. Introducing the isomorphisms Φ_Z, Φ_Y and Φ_U allows a broad class of problems to be considered where the operators A, B, C and S are not strictly functions of the same operator. In this particular application, the control operator B is composed by using the operator $-\partial_{xx}^2$. This is taken into account in Φ_U in a manner in which $\Phi_Z^{-1} B \Phi_U$ is a function of Λ only.

Remark 6.3. We indicate how the isomorphisms Φ_Z, Φ_Y and Φ_U have been chosen. The choice of Φ_Z and Φ_Y results directly from the expression of the inner product $(z, z')_Z = \left(\Phi_Z^{-1} z, \Phi_Z^{-1} z'\right)_{X^4}$ and from

$$(z_1, z_1')_{H_0^2(\Gamma)} = \left(\left(\Delta^2\right)^{\frac{1}{2}} z_1, \ \left(\Delta^2\right)^{\frac{1}{2}} z_1'\right)_{L^2(\Gamma)}.$$

For Φ_Y, we start from $B = \Phi_Z b(\Lambda) \Phi_U^{-1}$ and from the relation $(u, u')_Y = \left(\Phi_U^{-1} u, \Phi_U^{-1} u'\right)_{X^2}$ which implies that $-\partial_{xx}^2 / \rho^B = b_{3,1} (\Phi_U)_{1,1}$ and $I/\rho^C = b_{4,2}(\Lambda)(\Phi_U)_{2,2}$. The expression of Φ_U follows.

6.3.5.3. *Approximation of the functions of Λ*

The third step in the method consists of an approximation of a general function of Λ by a simpler function of Λ easily discretized and implemented in a semi-decentralized architecture. The strategy must be general and, at the same time, the approximation must be accurate. A simple choice would be to adopt a polynomial or a rational approximation, but their discretization yields very high errors due to the powers of Λ.

This can be avoided when using the Dunford–Schwartz formula [YOS 95] which represents a function of an operator. It involves only the operator $(\zeta I - \Lambda)^{-1}$ which may be simply and accurately approximated. However, this formula requires the function be holomorphic inside an open vicinity of σ. Since the function is generally not known, this set cannot be easily determined so we prefer to proceed in two separate steps. First, the function is approximated through a highly accurate rational approximation. The Dunford–Schwartz formula is then applied to the rational approximation, with a path tracing out an ellipse including I_σ but no poles.

Since the interval I_σ is bounded, each function $k_{ij}(\lambda)$ has a rational approximation over I_σ which can be expressed as the global formulation:

$$k_N(\lambda) = \frac{\sum_{m=0}^{N^N} d_m \lambda^m}{\sum_{m'=0}^{N^D} d'_{m'} \lambda^{m'}} \tag{6.19}$$

where $d_m, d'_{m'}$ are matrices of coefficients and $N = \left(N^N, N^D\right)$ is the couple comprising the matrix N^N of numerator polynomial degrees and the matrix N^D of denominator polynomial degrees. The path C in the Dunford–Schwartz formula

$$k_N(\Lambda) = \frac{1}{2i\pi} \int_C k_N(\zeta)(\zeta I - \Lambda)^{-1} \, d\zeta$$

is chosen to be an ellipse parameterized by

$$\zeta(\theta) = \zeta_1(\theta) + i\zeta_2(\theta), \text{ with } \theta \in [0, 2\pi].$$

The parameterization is used as a change of variable, so the integral is rewritten in the form $I(g) = \int_0^{2\pi} g(\theta)\, d\theta$ and may be approximated by a quadrature formula involving M nodes $(\theta_l)_{l=1,...,M} \in [0, 2\pi]$ and M weights $(w_l)_{l=1,...,M}$, i.e.

$$I_M(g) = \sum_{l=1}^{M} g(\theta_l)\, w_l.$$

For each $z \in X^4$ and $\zeta \in \mathcal{C}$, we introduce the 4D vector field:

$$v^\zeta = -i\zeta' k_N(\zeta)(\zeta I - \Lambda)^{-1} z.$$

Decomposing v^ζ into its real part v_1^ζ and its imaginary part v_2^ζ, the couple (v_1^ζ, v_2^ζ) is a solution of the system

$$\begin{cases} \zeta_1 v_1^\zeta - \zeta_2 v_2^\zeta - \Lambda v_1^\zeta = Re\left(-i\zeta' k_N(\zeta)\right) z, \\ \zeta_2 v_1^\zeta + \zeta_1 v_2^\zeta - \Lambda v_2^\zeta = Im\left(-i\zeta' k_N(\zeta)\right) z. \end{cases} \tag{6.20}$$

Combining the rational approximation k_N and the quadrature formula therefore yields an approximate realization $k_{N,M}(\Lambda)$ of $k(\Lambda)$:

$$k_{N,M}(\Lambda)\, z = \frac{1}{2\pi} \sum_{l=1}^{M} v_1^{\zeta(\theta_l)} w_l. \tag{6.21}$$

This formula is central to the method, so is therefore the focus of our attention in the simulations. Note that a real-time realization $k_{N,M}(\Lambda)\, z$ requires M systems such as equation (6.20) be solved corresponding to the M nodes $\zeta(\theta_l)$. The matrices $k_N(\zeta(\theta_l))$ could be computed 'off-line' once and for all and stored in memory, so their determination would not penalize a rapid real-time computation. To summarize, the ultimate parameter responsible for accuracy in a real-time computation (apart from spatial discretization discussed in the next section) is M, the number of quadrature points.

6.3.5.4. *Spatial discretization*

The final step consists of a spatial discretization of equation (6.20). It does not represent a specific novelty, so we do not discuss it through numerical simulations. For the sake of simplicity, the interval Γ is meshed with regularly spaced nodes separated by a distance h. We introduce Λ_h^{-1}, the finite difference discretization of Λ^{-1}:

$$\Lambda_h^{-1} = \frac{1}{h^4} \begin{pmatrix} h^4 & 0 & 0 & 0 & 0 & 0 & \cdots & 0 \\ -\frac{3}{2}h^3 & 2h^3 & -\frac{1}{2}h^3 & 0 & 0 & 0 & \cdots & 0 \\ 1 & -4 & 6 & -4 & 1 & 0 & \cdots & 0 \\ 0 & \ddots & \ddots & \ddots & \ddots & \ddots & & 0 \\ \vdots & & \ddots & \ddots & \ddots & \ddots & \ddots & \vdots \\ 0 & \cdots & 0 & 1 & -4 & 6 & -4 & 1 \\ 0 & \cdots & 0 & 0 & 0 & -\frac{1}{2}h^3 & 2h^3 & -\frac{3}{2}h^3 \\ 0 & \cdots & 0 & 0 & 0 & 0 & 0 & h^4 \end{pmatrix}.$$

In practice, the discretization length h is chosen to be small compared to the distance between cantilevers. z_h then denotes the vector of nodal values of z. For each ζ we introduce $(v_{1,h}^\zeta, v_{2,h}^\zeta)$, a discrete approximation of (v_1^ζ, v_2^ζ), a solution of the discrete set of equations:

$$\begin{cases} \zeta_1 v_{1,h}^\zeta - \zeta_2 v_{2,h}^\zeta - \Lambda_h v_{1,h}^\zeta = Re\left(-i\zeta' k_N(\zeta)\right) z_h, \\ \zeta_2 v_{1,h}^\zeta + \zeta_1 v_{2,h}^\zeta - \Lambda_h v_{2,h}^\zeta = Im\left(-i\zeta' k_N(\zeta)\right) z_h. \end{cases}$$

An approximate optimal control, intended to be implemented in a set of spatially distributed actuators, can finally be estimated from the nodal values:

$$\Phi_{U,h} k_{N,M,h} z_h = \Phi_{U,h} \frac{1}{2\pi} \sum_{l=1}^{M} v_{1,h}^{\zeta_l} w_l,$$

estimated at mesh nodes, where $\Phi_{U,h}$ is the discretization of Φ_U which requires the discretization of $-\partial_{xx}^2$. This can be carried out as for Λ by using a finite difference method.

6.3.6. Numerical validation

To build a rational interpolation k_N of the form equation (6.19) over I_σ, we mesh the interval with $L + 1$ distinct nodes $\lambda_0, \ldots, \lambda_L$.

All $p(\lambda_n)$ solutions of the algebraic Riccati equation are then accurately computed with a standard solver. To compute the rational approximation, we start by imposing $L + 1$ conditions

$$k_N(\lambda_n) = k(\lambda_n),$$

or, equivalently, that

$$\sum_{m=0}^{N^N} d_m \lambda_n^m - k(\lambda_m) \sum_{m'=0}^{N^D} d'_{m'} \lambda_n^{m'} = 0$$

for $n = 0, \ldots, L+1$. When L is large enough, the resulting system with $N^N + N^D + 2$ unknowns $[d, d'] = [d_0, \ldots, d_{N^N}, d'_0, \ldots, d'_{N^D}]$ is then overdetermined, so is solved in the mean square sense.

In a numerical experiment, we have set all coefficients $R^B, \rho^B, \ell_C, R^C, \rho^C$ and L_C to 1 and $L_B = 4.73$. All eigenvalues of Λ are therefore included in $(0, 1)$, the first cantilever eigenvalue is equal to $\lambda_1^C = 12.36$, $\bar{\psi}_1 = -0.78$ and $c_1 = 9.68$. Moreover, we have chosen $L = 100$ nodes logarithmically distributed along $I_\sigma = (10^{-2}, 1)$. Note that the shapes of all spectral functions k_{ij} involved in K, represented in Figure 6.14, exhibit a singular behavior at the origin. This demonstrates that this example is not trivial.

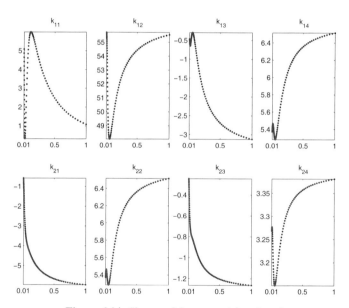

Figure 6.14. *Shapes of the spectral functions k*

In Table 6.1, we report polynomial degrees $N = (N^N, N^D)$ and relative errors

$$e_{ij} = \frac{\|k_{ij,N} - k_{ij}\|_{L^2(I_\sigma)}}{\|k_{ij}\|_{L^2(I_\sigma)}}$$

between the exact k and its rational approximation k_N. The degrees N^N and N^D can be chosen to be sufficiently large so that errors are sufficiently small, since this has no effect on on-line control computation time.

(i,j)	N_{ij}	$e_{ij} \times 10^{-7}$
$(1,1)$	$(7,19)$	4.78
$(1,2)$	$(7,20)$	0.69
$(1,3)$	$(13,8)$	3.83
$(1,4)$	$(7,19)$	1.19
$(2,1)$	$(8,20)$	1.81
$(2,2)$	$(7,19)$	1.19
$(2,3)$	$(20,10)$	0.89
$(2,4)$	$(19,7)$	0.53

Table 6.1. *Errors in rational approximations*

Numerical integrations were performed with a standard trapezoidal quadrature rule. Relative errors, between the exact functions and final approximations,

$$E_{ij} = \frac{\|k_{ij,N,M} - k_{ij}\|_{L^2(I_\sigma)}}{\|k_{ij}\|_{L^2(I_\sigma)}}$$

are reported in Figure 6.15 in logarithmic scale for M varying from 10 to 10^3. The results are satisfactory. Accuracy is proportional to the number of nodes. It may be easily tuned without changing spatial complexity governed by the operator Λ.

6.4. Simulation of large-scale periodic circuits by a homogenization method

This section focuses on the simulation of spatially periodic circuits e.g. which result from the realization of our control approximations. The periodic unit cell is limited to linear and static components but its number can be very large. Our theory allows us to simulate arrays of electronic circuits which are far removed from the possibility of regular circuit simulators such as Spice.

This is an adaptation of the two-scale approach used in section 6.2 and has been introduced in [LEN 06]. The resulting model consists of a partial differential equation (PDE), related to a macroscopic electric potential coupled with local circuit equations.

In the following, we present the general framework illustrated through a simple example. The PDE can be resolved with the usual computational tools. Solving this PDE and postprocessing its solution leads to an approximation of all voltages and currents. Theoretically, the larger the number of cells, the more accurate the model. The method is illustrated on a basic circuit to allow hand calculations, which are mostly matrix multiplications.

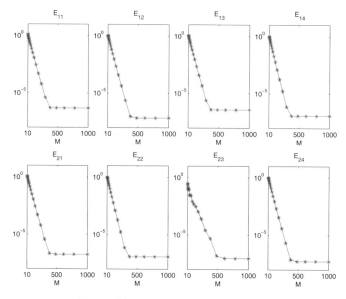

Figure 6.15. *Errors between k and $k_{N,M}$*

6.4.1. *Linear static periodic circuits*

We consider the class of periodic circuits in d space dimensions. An example of such a circuit in two-space dimensions is shown in Figure 6.16. The circuit cell is detailed in Figure 6.17. Some voltage or current sources, whose value may be zero, are incorporated as boundary conditions. We assume that the number of cells is large in all the d directions. Mathematically, it is easier to formalize the problem by considering that the whole circuit occupies a unit square $\Omega = (0,1)^d$ and that the period lengths, in all directions, are equal to an identical small parameter ε (see Figure 6.16).

We limit ourselves to the study of circuits whose cell is linear and static. The components of a cell are limited to the Spice elements R, V, I, E, F, G and H. All ports of any multiport component E, F, G and H must belong to the same cell. The expanded cell is arbitrarily defined in a unit cell $Y = (-1/2, +1/2)^d$ (see Figure 6.17). We map any discrete node n onto continuous coordinates $(y_1, \ldots, y_d)$. The vector $y(n) \in \mathbb{R}^d$ is the coordinate vector of a node n. For example, the coordinates of the nodes in Figure 6.17 are:

$$y(1,\ldots,6) = \begin{pmatrix} -1/2 & 0 & 1/2 & 0 & 0 & 1/4 \\ 0 & 0 & 0 & 1/2 & -1/2 & -1/4 \end{pmatrix}.$$

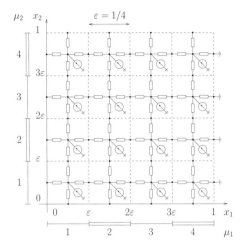

Figure 6.16. *Circuit example*

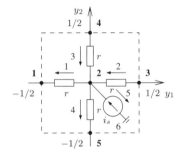

Figure 6.17. *Expanded cell of the circuit*

In particular, the coordinates of the node $n = 3$ are the vector $(1/2, 0)^T$.

The maps of voltages and currents from the whole circuit (global network) to the cell circuit (local network) are defined as follows:

 – $\mathcal{E}$ denotes the branch set of the whole circuit;

 – $\mathcal{N}$ denotes the node set of the whole circuit;

 – E denotes the branch set of the unit cell circuit; and

 – N denotes the node set of the unit cell circuit.

We define three indices:

– the global index $\mathcal{I}$ references all the branches of the entire circuit;

– the multi-integer $\mu = (\mu_1, \ldots, \mu_d) \in \{1, \ldots, m\}^d$ references all the cells Y_μ^ε in the circuit Ω; and

– the local index $j \in \{1, \ldots, |E|\}$ references all the branches of the unit cell Y.

Each branch voltage or current can then be referenced by the index $\mathcal{I}$ or by the couple (μ, j). This is a one-to-one correspondence denoted by $\mathcal{I} \sim (\mu, j)$. Using this correspondence, for each vector $\mathbf{u} \in \mathbb{R}^{|\mathcal{E}|}$, we may define a unique tensor $U_{\mu j}$ with $(\mu, j) \in \{1, \ldots, m\}^d \times \{1, \ldots, |E|\}$ by $U_{\mu j} = \mathbf{u}_{\mathcal{I}}$ for $(\mu, j) \sim \mathcal{I}$.

6.4.2. *Circuit equations*

The electrical state of a circuit can be charaterized [CHU 87] by the vectors $(\varphi, \mathbf{v}, \mathbf{i})$ where

$$\varphi \in \mathbb{R}^{|\mathcal{N}|} \quad = \quad \text{the nodal voltages (or electric potentials);}$$

$$\mathbf{v} \in \mathbb{R}^{|\mathcal{E}|} \quad = \quad \text{the branch voltages; and}$$

$$\mathbf{i} \in \mathbb{R}^{|\mathcal{E}|} \quad = \quad \text{the branch currents.}$$

We can formulate the circuit equations in the form

$$\mathbf{v} \quad = \quad \mathcal{A}^T \varphi, \tag{6.22}$$

$$\mathcal{R}\mathbf{i} + \mathcal{M}\mathbf{v} \quad = \quad \mathbf{u}_s, \tag{6.23}$$

$$\mathbf{i}^T \mathbf{w} \quad = \quad 0, \ \forall \mathbf{w} = \mathcal{A}^T \psi \text{ with } \psi \in \Psi \tag{6.24}$$

where $\mathbf{u}_s \in \mathbb{R}^{|\mathcal{E}|}$ represents voltage and current sources merged in a single vector completed with zeroes. Equation (6.22) is Kirchhoff's Voltage Law. Equation (6.23) represents the constitutive equations and equation (6.24) corresponds to the Tellegen theorem. Here Ψ is the set of admissible potentials for the circuit problem, that is

$$\Psi = \left\{ \psi \in \mathbb{R}^{|\mathcal{N}|} \text{ such that } \psi_{\mathcal{I}} = 0 \text{ for all ground nodes } n_{\mathcal{I}} \right\}.$$

As the matrices $\mathcal{M} \in \mathbb{R}^{|\mathcal{E}|} \times \mathbb{R}^{|\mathcal{E}|}$, $\mathcal{R} \in \mathbb{R}^{|\mathcal{E}|} \times \mathbb{R}^{|\mathcal{E}|}$ and the vector $\mathbf{u}_s \in \mathbb{R}^{|\mathcal{E}|}$ are deduced exclusively from the branch equations of the circuit, they can be expressed in terms of two reduced matrices $M \in \mathbb{R}^{|E|} \times \mathbb{R}^{|E|}$ and $R \in \mathbb{R}^{|E|} \times \mathbb{R}^{|E|}$ and a reduced vector $u_s \in \mathbb{R}^{|E|}$. The reduced matrices and vector are simply derived from the constitutive equations of the unit cell, which in the example are

$$
\begin{aligned}
-v_1 + ri_1 &= 0, \\
-v_2 + ri_2 &= 0, \\
-v_3 + ri_3 &= 0, \\
-v_4 + ri_4 &= 0, \\
i_5 &= i_s.
\end{aligned}
$$

The transpose $\mathcal{A}^T \in \mathbb{R}^{|\mathcal{E}|} \times \mathbb{R}^{|\mathcal{N}|}$ of the incidence matrix can also be expressed in terms of a reduced matrix denoted by A^T (with a little abuse of notation). Note that we cannot find a reduced matrix for the incidence matrix itself. We introduce the local (complete) incidence matrix $A \in \mathbb{R}^{|N|} \times \mathbb{R}^{|E|}$:

$$
A_{ij} = \left\{ \begin{array}{ll}
+1 & \text{if branch } j \text{ leaves node } i, \\
-1 & \text{if branch } j \text{ enters node } i, \\
0 & \text{if branch } j \text{ does not touch node } i.
\end{array} \right.
$$

The solution of the simplified model introduced in this section is an approximation of the solution of equations (6.22)–(6.24) for small values of ε ($\varepsilon \ll 1$). It is derived as a limit of the latter when the cell length ε diminishes towards zero.

6.4.3. *Direct two-scale transform T_E*

The general idea of the two-scale transform is based on gathering the voltages or currents, both denoted $\widehat{u}$, of a branch j of all cells. Indeed, the voltages or currents of all branches j are defined by a function $x \mapsto \widehat{u}_j(x)$, which depends on the parameter ε and whose limit when $\varepsilon \to 0$ will be calculated.

Let us first denote the characteristic function of the cell Y_μ^ε by $\chi_{Y_\mu^\varepsilon}(x)$, equal to 1 when $x \in Y_\mu^\varepsilon$ and 0 otherwise. As an example, the characteristic function $\chi_{Y_{32}^\varepsilon}$ of the cell $\mu = (3, 2)$ is depicted in Figure 6.18.

The two-scale transform $\widehat{u}$ of the branch vector $\mathbf{u} \in \mathbb{R}^{|\mathcal{E}|}$ is the vector of Y_μ^ε-piecewise constant functions $\widehat{\mathbf{u}} \in \mathbb{P}^0(\Omega)^{|E|}$:

$$
\widehat{\mathbf{u}}_j(x) \quad = \quad \sum_{\mu \in \{1,\dots,m\}^d} \chi_{Y_\mu^\varepsilon}(x) U_{\mu j} \tag{6.25}
$$

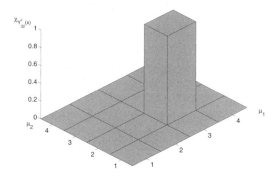

Figure 6.18. *Characteristic function* $\chi_{Y^\varepsilon_{32}}$

where $U_{\mu j} = \mathbf{u}_{\mathcal{I}}$ with $(\mu, j) \sim \mathcal{I}$.

For example, $\widehat{\mathbf{v}}_j(x)$ is the voltage $V_{\mu j}$ of the branch referred to by the local index j of the cell μ to which x belongs. By construction, the function $x \mapsto \widehat{\mathbf{v}}_j(x)$ is constant over all cells.

Figure 6.19 illustrates this concept by representing a component of an arbitrary vector $\widehat{\mathbf{v}}$. The figure indicates that the voltage $\widehat{\mathbf{v}}_2(x)$ related to the branch $j = 2$ (cf. Figure 6.17) of the cell $(\mu_1, \mu_2) = (1, 4)$ is equal to 2 V.

We denote the linear map $\mathbf{u} \mapsto \widehat{\mathbf{u}}$ from $\mathbb{R}^{|\mathcal{E}|}$ to $\mathbb{P}^0(\Omega)^{|E|} \subset L^2(\Omega)^{|E|}$ by T_E, where $\mathbb{P}^0(\Omega)$ is the set of piecewise constant functions over the cells. Our model is derived for the limit when $\varepsilon \to 0$ of all vectors involved in the circuit equations. The actual circuit voltages and currents are then computed by inverting the two-scale transform with the physical value of ε. The following section is devoted to the construction of T_E^{-1}.

6.4.4. *Inverse two-scale transform* T_E^{-1}

The calculation of the inverse two-scale transform T_E^{-1} is carried out by computing the adjoint T_E^* and then providing two identity properties between these transforms. The notation for inner products and norms in $\mathbb{R}^{|\mathcal{E}|}$ and $L^2(\Omega)^{|E|}$ is listed in Table 6.2,

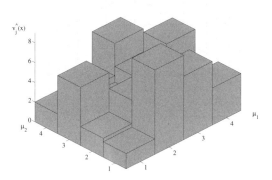

Figure 6.19. *One component $\widehat{\mathbf{v}}_2(x)$ of a two-scale transform*

where

$$[\mathbf{u}, \mathbf{v}] = \varepsilon^d \mathbf{u}^T.\mathbf{v},$$

$$(u, v) = \sum_{j=1}^{|E|} \int_\Omega u_j(x) v_j(x) dx.$$

	$\mathbf{u}, \mathbf{v} \in \mathbb{R}^{|\mathcal{E}|}$	$u, v \in L^2(\Omega)^{|E|}$
Inner product	$[\mathbf{u}, \mathbf{v}]$	(u, v)
Norm	$|\mathbf{v}| = [\mathbf{v}, \mathbf{v}]^{1/2}$	$||u|| = (u, u)^{1/2}$

Table 6.2. *Inner products and norms*

For all $u \in L^2(\Omega)^{|E|}$, the adjoint $T_E^* u$ is defined:

$$[T_E^* u, v] = (u, T_E v) \text{ for all } v \in \mathbb{R}^{|\mathcal{E}|}. \tag{6.26}$$

The calculation of T_E^* from equation (6.26) is given in appendices A1 and A2 (section 6.6) and leads to

$$(T_E^* u)_{\mathcal{I}} \;=\; \varepsilon^{-d} \int_{Y_\mu^\varepsilon} u_j(x) dx. \qquad (6.27)$$

Moreover, appendices A1, A3 and A4 (section 6.6) prove that $T_E^* T_E = I_{\mathcal{E}}$ on $\mathbb{R}^{|\mathcal{E}|}$ and $T_E T_E^* = I_E$ on $\mathbb{P}^0(\Omega)^{|E|}$. As T_E is one-to-one from $\mathbb{R}^{|\mathcal{E}|}$ to $\mathbb{P}^0(\Omega)^{|E|}$, these two identities show that

$$T_E^{-1} \;=\; T_E^*.$$

6.4.5. Two-scale transform T_N

The two-scale transform $\widehat{\varphi}$ of the nodal vector $\varphi \in \mathbb{R}^{|\mathcal{N}|}$ is the vector of Y_μ^ε-piecewise constant functions $\widehat{\varphi} \in \mathbb{P}^0(\Omega)^{|N|}$ defined by

$$\widehat{\varphi}_j(x) \;=\; \sum_{\mu \in \{1,\dots,m\}^d} \chi_{Y_\mu^\varepsilon}(x) \Phi_{\mu j}, \qquad (6.28)$$

where $\Phi_{\mu j} = \varphi_{\mathcal{I}}$ with $(\mu, j) \sim \mathcal{I}$. We denote the linear map $\varphi \mapsto \widehat{\varphi}$ from $\mathbb{R}^{|\mathcal{N}|}$ to $\mathbb{P}(\Omega)^{|N|} \subset L^2(\Omega)^{|N|}$ by T_N. As the nodes located on the cell boundary belong to two adjacent cells, T_N is not one-to-one.

6.4.6. Behavior of 'spread' analog circuits

We begin by illustrating the scaling of currents and voltages in a 1D circuit. A circuit spread over a large region may have some paths linking opposite sides. To derive a PDE for the electric potential, we assume that voltages are increments of the order ε along such paths. Flowing current results in numerous $(1/\varepsilon)$ additive sources, so it has a magnetude of 1 as long as the sources are of the order ε (Figure 6.20).

A branch which does not belongs to any crossing path is necessarily part of a path to the ground, so its voltage magnitude is 1. We set the order of the current magnitude to be ε as it may be a source for a crossing path (Figure 6.21).

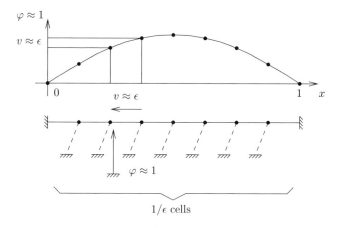

Figure 6.20. *Illustration of the magnitude orders of φ and v*

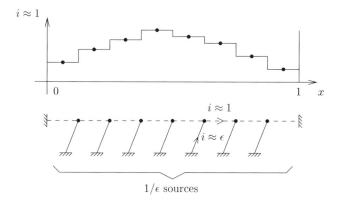

Figure 6.21. *Illustration of the magnitude order of i*

The periodicity of the circuit implies that each node n located on the boundary of the unit cell has its counterpart n' on the opposite side. We assume that each such couple is linked by at least a crossing path. We introduce the set $E_C \subset E$ comprised of all the branches of at least one path linking each couple (n, n'). Of course, a link between (n, n') which includes a ground node is not considered as a path. The complementary set $E - E_C$ is denoted by E_{NC} (non-crossing paths).

In the case where many crossing paths link n and n', the designer is free to decide which are included in E_C and which are not regarding the above discussion about current and voltage magnitudes. The subset E_C is partitioned into its n_c connected components $E_C = \cup_{p=1}^{n_c} E_{Cp}$. In the following, the main result on the circuit equations will be derived for the connected components of E_C and not for E_C itself.

The subsets N_C and N_{NC} of N are defined as the set of nodes involved in at least one of the branches of E_C and E_{NC}, respectively. Since the branches of E_C and E_{NC} have common nodes, these two subsets N_C and N_{NC} are not a partition of N, $N_C \cap N_{NC} \neq \varnothing$. N_{Cp} is the set of nodes involved in the branches of E_{Cp}. The subsets N_{Cp} constitute a partition of N_C, $N_C = \cup_{p=1}^{n_c} N_{Cp}$ and the subsets E_{Cp} constitute a partition of E_C; the two subsets are disconected. The definitions and some properties of these sets are depicted in Figure 6.22.

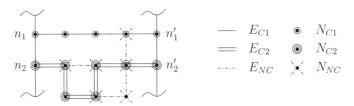

Figure 6.22. *Depiction of node and branch sets*

Finally, $N_{C\times1}$ is a set of n_c nodes comprising one arbitrary node of each connected component N_{Cp}. N_0 is the set containing only the cell ground node.

6.4.7. *Cell equations (micro problem)*

The model formulation is decomposed into four parts. We first formulate the linear relation between mean electric potentials φ_C^0 along crossing paths and the other fields as branch currents and voltages. This relation is strictly local in each cell. In the next section, the linear relation is simply rewritten introducing linear operators. They are then used for coefficients of the boundary value problem on φ_C^0. Finally, actual voltages and currents are computed from the inverse two-scale transform.

The previous assumptions about voltage and current magnitudes are formulated using the scaling matrices S_v, S_c and S_s applied to the two-scale transforms:

$$\widehat{\mathbf{i}}^\varepsilon = S_c \widehat{\mathbf{i}},$$
$$\widehat{\mathbf{v}}^\varepsilon = S_v \widehat{\mathbf{v}},$$
$$\widehat{\mathbf{u}}_s^\varepsilon = S_s \widehat{\mathbf{u}}_s,$$

with the $|E| \times |E|$ scaling matrices defined as

$$
\begin{aligned}
S_v &= \varepsilon^{-1} I_{E_C} + I_{E_{NC}}, & (6.29) \\
S_c &= I_{E_C} + \varepsilon^{-1} I_{E_{NC}}, & (6.30) \\
S_s &= \Pi_c S_c + \Pi_v S_v. & (6.31)
\end{aligned}
$$

Here the $|E| \times |E|$ matrices I_{E_C} and $I_{E_{NC}}$ are the projectors on the subspaces of $\mathbb{R}^{|E|}$ generated by vectors with non-vanishing values on E_C and E_{NC}:

$$
\begin{aligned}
(I_{E_C})_{jk} &= \begin{cases} \delta_{jk} & \text{if } e_j \in E_C, \\ 0 & \text{otherwise}, \end{cases} \\
(I_{E_{NC}})_{jk} &= \begin{cases} \delta_{jk} & \text{if } e_j \in E_{NC}, \\ 0 & \text{otherwise}. \end{cases}
\end{aligned}
$$

Moreover, each branch in equation (6.23) is homogenous to a current or to a voltage. This leads to a partition of E into two subsets. The $|E| \times |E|$ matrices Π_c and Π_v (for currents and voltages, respectively) are defined as the projectors of these two subsets.

The transform $\widehat{\varphi}$ is not scaled; it is rewriten as $\widehat{\varphi}^\varepsilon$ for consistency in notation, i.e.

$$
\widehat{\varphi}^\varepsilon = \widehat{\varphi}.
$$

The reduced matrices M and R of $\mathcal{M}$ and $\mathcal{R}$ are scaled in a consistent manner:

$$
\begin{aligned}
M^\varepsilon &= S_s M S_v^{-1}, \\
R^\varepsilon &= S_s R S_c^{-1}.
\end{aligned}
$$

The scaled reduced matrices M^ε and R^ε are assumed to converge towards some limit M^0 and R^0 when $\varepsilon \to 0$. If the norms $\|\widehat{\mathbf{i}}^\varepsilon\|, \|\widehat{\mathbf{v}}^\varepsilon\|, \|\widehat{\varphi}^\varepsilon\|$ and $\|\widehat{\mathbf{u}}_s^\varepsilon\|$ are bounded, then $(\widehat{\mathbf{i}}^\varepsilon, \widehat{\mathbf{v}}^\varepsilon, \widehat{\varphi}^\varepsilon$ and $\widehat{\mathbf{u}}_s^\varepsilon)$ are weakly converging when $\varepsilon \to 0$ towards a limit $(i^0, v^0, \varphi^0, u_s^0)$ in $L^2(\Omega)$ [YOS 95].

We prove that the vector of electric potential $\varphi^0(x)$ is a constant $\varphi^0_{Cp}(x)$ in each connected component of cell-crossing paths. We therefore split it according to $\varphi^0 = I^0\varphi^0_C + \varphi^0_{NC}$, I^0 being defined by equation (6.37), with $\varphi^0_C = (\varphi^0_{Cp})_{p=1,\ldots,n_c}$ and $\varphi^0_{NC}(x)$ being the electric potentials at nodes not at crossing paths. Electric potential variations within connected components of crossing paths are recovered using the corrector φ^1_C:

$$\varphi_C = \varphi^0 + \varepsilon\varphi^1_C.$$

We are now ready to state the cell equations. We begin by assuming that φ^0_C is known.

For a given $\varphi^0_C \in \Psi^H$, Ψ^H defined in equation (6.45) and $u^0_s \in L^2(\Omega)^{|E|}$, there exist $\varphi^1_C \in L^2(\Omega; \mathbb{R}^{|N|}_{per})$ such that $\varphi^0_{NC} \in L^2(\Omega; \mathbb{R}^{|N|})$, $i^0 \in L^2(\Omega)^{|E|}$ and $v \in L^2(\Omega)^{|E|}$ are solutions of the algebraic cell circuit equations at each location of Ω:

$$v = I_{E_C}A^T\varphi^1_C + I_{E_{NC}}A^T\varphi^0_{NC}, \tag{6.32}$$
$$R^0i^0 + M^0v = u^0_s - M^0(\tau\nabla\varphi^0_C + I_{E_{NC}}A^T I^0\varphi^0_C), \tag{6.33}$$
$$i^{0T}w = 0, \forall w = I_{E_C}A^T\psi^1_C + I_{E_{NC}}A^T\psi^0_{NC} \text{ with } (\psi^1_C, \psi^0_{NC}) \in \Psi^m. \tag{6.34}$$

Moreover, the vector $v^0 \in L^2(\Omega)^{|E|}$ is expressed by

$$v^0 = v + \tau\nabla\varphi^0_C + I_{E_{NC}}A^T I^0\varphi^0_C.$$

We assume that the solution is unique. This assumption is generally satisfied when the global circuit equations have a unique solution.

The admissible nodal voltage set is

$$\Psi^m = \{(\psi^1_C, \psi^0_{NC}) \in L^2(\Omega; \mathbb{R}^{|N|}_{per}) \times L^2(\Omega; \mathbb{R}^{|N|})$$
$$\text{such that } I_{(N-N_C)\cup N_{C\times 1}}\psi^1_C = 0 \text{ and } I_{N_C\cup N_0}\psi^0_{NC} = 0\}.$$

The set $\mathbb{R}^{|N|}_{per}$ is defined as

$$\mathbb{R}^{|N|}_{per} = \{\phi \in \mathbb{R}^{|N|} \text{ such that } \phi_j = \phi_{j'} \text{ for all couples } (n_j, n_{j'}) \text{ of opposite nodes}\}.$$

The $|E| \times d \times n_c$ tensor τ is defined by

$$\tau_{lkp} = \begin{cases} \sum_{j:n_j \in N_{Cp}} y_k(n_j) A_{jl} & \text{for } e_l \in E_{Cp}, \\ 0 & \text{otherwise.} \end{cases} \tag{6.35}$$

We recall that $y(n) \in \mathbb{R}^d$ is the coordinate vector of a node n and we use the tensor product notation:

$$(\tau\theta)_l = \sum_k \sum_p \tau_{lkp}\theta_{kp} \tag{6.36}$$

where the summation is over the two last indices of τ.

The $|N| \times n_c$ matrix I^0 is defined:

$$I_{jp}^0 = \begin{cases} 1 & \text{if } n_j \in N_{Cp}, \\ 0 & \text{otherwise,} \end{cases} \tag{6.37}$$

where N_{Cp} is the set of nodes involved in the branches of E_{Cp}.

6.4.8. Reformulation of the micro problem

In the following section, we state that φ_C^0 is the solution of a PDE. Once φ_C^0 is known, i^0 and v^0 can be computed. Since equations (6.32)–(6.34) are linear, there exist some matrices $\mathcal{L}_x, \mathcal{H}_x$ and a third-order tensor $\mathcal{P}_x$ such that i^0, φ_{NC}^0 and v can be expressed as function of φ_C^0, its gradient $\nabla\varphi_C^0$ and the vector source u_s^0, i.e.

$$i^0 = \mathcal{L}_i\varphi_C^0 + \mathcal{P}_i\nabla\varphi_C^0 + \mathcal{H}_i u_s^0, \tag{6.38}$$
$$\varphi_{NC}^0 = \mathcal{L}_\varphi\varphi_C^0 + \mathcal{P}_\varphi\nabla\varphi_C^0 + \mathcal{H}_\varphi u_s^0, \tag{6.39}$$
$$v = \mathcal{L}_v\varphi_C^0 + \mathcal{P}_v\nabla\varphi_C^0 + \mathcal{H}_v u_s^0. \tag{6.40}$$

The computation of the vector v^0 is then unchanged:

$$v^0 = v + \tau\nabla\varphi_C^0 + I_{E_{NC}}A^T I^0\varphi_C^0. \tag{6.41}$$

The terms $\mathcal{L}_\alpha, \mathcal{P}_\alpha$ and $\mathcal{H}_\alpha$ are of course independent of $\varphi_C^0, \nabla\varphi_C^0$ and u_s^0 and can therefore be used to express the coefficients in the equation of φ_C^0.

6.4.9. *Homogenized circuit equations (macro problem)*

In this section, we state the equation satisfied by φ_C^0.

The vector $\varphi_C^0 \in \Psi^H$ is a solution of the n_c partial differential equations (referred to as homogenized equations) with boundary conditions:

$$A^H(\mathcal{P}_i\nabla\varphi_C^0 + \mathcal{L}_i\varphi_C^0) \quad = \quad -A^H\mathcal{H}_i u_s^0, \tag{6.42}$$

$$\varphi_{Cp}^0 \quad = \quad 0 \text{ on } \Gamma_{0p}, \tag{6.43}$$

$$(\mathcal{P}_i\nabla\varphi_C^0 + \mathcal{L}_i\varphi_C^0)n_\tau \quad = \quad 0 \text{ on } \Gamma - \Gamma_{0p}. \tag{6.44}$$

Γ_{0p} is the part of the boundary Γ of Ω where the pth connected component is grounded. The operator A^H is defined:

$$A^H \quad = \quad -\partial_{\tau^*} + I^{0T}AI_{E_{NC}},$$

where $\partial_{\tau^*}i = \tau^*\nabla i$ with $\tau_{pkl}^* = \tau_{lkp}$ and the use of convention (6.36). The derivative $\partial_\tau\varphi_C^0$ and the normal n_τ are defined:

$$\partial_\tau\varphi_C^0 \quad = \quad \tau\nabla\varphi_C^0,$$

$$(n_\tau)_{lp} \quad = \quad \sum_{k=1}^{d}\tau_{lkp}n_k,$$

where ∇ is the gradient $(\partial_{x_k})_{k=1,...,d}$ and $n = (n_k)_{k=1,...,d}$ is the outward unit normal vector to the boundary Γ of Ω. Note that the coefficients A^H and the derivatives ∇_τ depend on node coordinates inherited from equation (6.35) of τ.

Finally, the admissible set of macroscopic potential is

$$\Psi^H \quad = \quad \{\psi \in L^2(\Omega)^{n_c} \text{ such that } \partial_\tau\psi \in L^2(\Omega)^{|E|} \text{ and } \psi_k(x) = 0 \text{ on } \Gamma_{0k}\}. \tag{6.45}$$

Let us turn to the example depicted in Figure 6.16. φ_C^0 has only one component φ_{C1}^0 ($n_c = 1$) and we assume that $r = \varepsilon r^0$ and $i_s = \varepsilon i_s^0$. φ_C^0 is then a solution of the PDE:

$$\frac{\partial^2 \varphi_{C1}^0}{\partial x_1^2} + \frac{\partial^2 \varphi_{C1}^0}{\partial x_2^2} = -2r^0 i_s^0 \text{ in } \Omega,$$

$$\varphi_{C1}^0 = 0 \text{ on } \Gamma_{0,1},$$

$$\nabla \varphi_{C1}^0 . n_\tau = 0 \text{ on } \Gamma - \Gamma_{0,1}.$$

Once the solution φ_{C1}^0 is computed, the two-scale limits (v^0, i^0) are expressed by equations (6.38)–(6.41). For the example, the two-scale current and voltage are given by

$$v^0 = -\frac{1}{2} \left(\frac{\partial \varphi_{C1}^0}{\partial x_1}, \frac{\partial \varphi_{C1}^0}{\partial x_1}, \frac{\partial \varphi_{C1}^0}{\partial x_2}, \frac{\partial \varphi_{C1}^0}{\partial x_2}, 2\varphi_{C1}^0 \right)^T,$$

$$i^0 = -\frac{1}{2} \left(\frac{1}{r^0} \frac{\partial \varphi_{C1}^0}{\partial x_1}, \frac{1}{r^0} \frac{\partial \varphi_{C1}^0}{\partial x_1}, \frac{1}{r^0} \frac{\partial \varphi_{C1}^0}{\partial x_2}, \frac{1}{r^0} \frac{\partial \varphi_{C1}^0}{\partial x_2}, -2i_s^0 \right)^T.$$

6.4.10. Computation of actual voltages and currents

Actual voltages and currents may then be recovered through the inverse two-scale transform equation (6.27) and inverse scalings equations (6.29)–(6.31):

$$\mathbf{v} \approx T_E^{-1} S_v^{-1} v^0,$$

$$\mathbf{i} \approx T_E^{-1} S_i^{-1} i^0.$$

The approximation of the node voltages φ is achieved in a different manner. From the solution φ_C^0 of equations (6.42)–(6.44), the approximation of the node voltages is built as follows (neglecting the first-order correction):

$$\varphi_\mathcal{I} \approx \varphi_C^0(x_\mu^\varepsilon + \varepsilon y(n_j)) \text{ for } \mathcal{I} \sim (\mu, j) \text{ and } n_j \in N_C,$$

where $x_\mu^\varepsilon \in [0, 1]^d$ is the coordinate vector of the center of the cell μ (Figure 6.16). We recall that $y(n_j) \in [-1/2, 1/2]^d$ is the coordinate vector of the node n_j (Figure 6.17).

For the voltage at the nodes which belong to a non-crossing path, the approximation is simpler because it does not need to refer to the spatial location in the cell:

$$\varphi_{\mathcal{I}} \approx \varphi_C^0(x_\mu^\varepsilon) \text{ for } \mathcal{I} \sim (\mu, j) \text{ and } n_j \in N - N_C - N_0.$$

A comparison of the solutions computed by the two-scale model with those obtained from a direct circuit simulation has been done for the example circuit with 10×10 cells. In the following simulation results, all the circuit boundaries are connected to ground and the component values are $r^0 = 10 \, \mathrm{k\Omega}$ and $i_s^0 = 1 \, \mathrm{mA}$. The comparison focuses only on node voltages magnitude; their location on the domain is depicted in Figure 6.23.

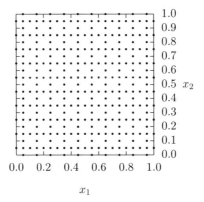

Figure 6.23. *Location of node voltages*

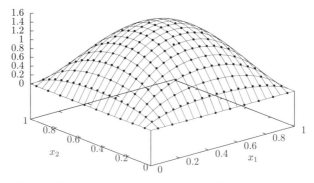

Figure 6.24. *Two-scale model compared to Spice computation*

The computation of φ_C^0 has been carried out using a FEM on a regular mesh of 40×40 squares (see Figure 6.24). We must emphasize that the mesh size is chosen to obtain an accurate numerical solution of the PDE and is not at all related to the number of the cells of the circuit. The maximum amplitude is $1.4742\,\text{V}$. A direct simulation of the periodic circuit has been made with Spice. The maximum amplitude is $1.4723\,\text{V}$. In Figure 6.24, the continuous FEM solution $\varphi_{\mathcal{I}} = \varphi_C^0(x_\mu^\varepsilon + \varepsilon y(n_j))$ is represented by the mesh while all voltage nodes computed by Spice are depicted by bullets. These results show a good qualitative agreement between the two methods, even if the number of cells is not large (10 in one direction, which corresponds to $\varepsilon = 0.1$).

6.5. Bibliography

[ALL 03] ALLEMANG R. J., "The modal assurance criterion: Twenty years of use and abuse", *S V Sound and Vibration*, vol. 37, num. 8, p. 14–23, 2003.

[BIN 86] BINNIG G., QUATE C., GERBER C., "Atomic force microscope", *Physical Review Letters*, vol. 56, num. 9, p. 930–933, 1986.

[BUL 04] BULLEN D., CHUNG S.-W., WANG X., ZOU J., MIRKIN C. A., LIU C., "Parallel dip-pen nanolithography with arrays of individually addressable cantilevers", *Applied Physics Letters*, vol. 84, num. 5, p. 789–791, 2004.

[BUL 06] BULLEN D., LIU C., "Electrostatically actuated dip pen nanolithography probe arrays", *Sensors and Actuators, A: Physical*, vol. 125, num. 2, p. 504–511, 2006.

[CAR 00] CARRION-VAZQUEZ M., OBERHAUSER A., FISHER T., MARSZALEK P., LI H., FERNANDEZ J., "Mechanical design of proteins studied by single-molecule force spectroscopy and protein engineering", *Progress in Biophysics; Molecular Biology*, vol. 74, num. 1–2, p. 63–91, 2000.

[CHU 87] CHUA L., DESOER A., KUH S., *Linear and Nonlinear Circuits*, Series in Electrical Engineering, McGraw–Hill, 1987.

[CUR 95] CURTAIN R. F., ZWART H., *An Introduction to Infinite-Dimensional Linear Systems Theory*, vol. 21 of *Texts in Applied Mathematics*, Springer-Verlag, New York, 1995.

[DAU 90] DAUTRAY R., LIONS J.-L., *Mathematical Analysis and Numerical Methods for Science and Technology*, Springer-Verlag, Berlin, 1990.

[DEC 03] DECOSSAS S., PATRONE L., BONNOT A., COMIN F., DERIVAZ M., BARSKI A., CHEVRIER J., "Nanomanipulation by atomic force microscopy of carbon nanotubes on a nanostructured surface", *Surface Science*, vol. 543, num. 1–3, p. 57–62, 2003.

[DES 00] DESPONT M., BRUGGER J., DRECHSLER U., DURIG U., HABERLE W., LUTWYCHE M., ROTHUIZEN H., STUTZ R., WIDMER R., BINNIG G., ROHRER H., VETTIGER P., "VLSI-NEMS chip for parallel AFM data storage", *Sensors and Actuators, A: Physical*, vol. 80, num. 2, p. 100–107, 2000.

[DRA 01] DRAKOVA D., "Theoretical modelling of scanning tunnelling microscopy, scanning tunnelling spectroscopy and atomic force microscopy", *Reports on Progress in Physics*, vol. 64, num. 2, p. 205–290, 2001.

[GAR 02] GARCIA R., PEREZ R., "Dynamic atomic force microscopy methods", *Surface Science Reports*, vol. 47, num. 6–8, p. 197–301, 2002.

[GIE 03] GIESSIBL F., "Advances in atomic force microscopy", *Reviews of Modern Physics*, vol. 75, num. 3, p. 949–983, 2003.

[GRE 00] GREEN J.-B. D., LEE G. U., "Atomic force microscopy with patterned cantilevers and tip arrays: Force measurements with chemical arrays", *Langmuir*, vol. 16, num. 8, p. 4009–4015, 2000.

[HSI 05] HSIEH G.-W., TSAI C.-H., LIN W.-C., LIANG C.-C., LEE Y.-W., "Bond-and-transfer scanning probe array for high-density data storage", *IEEE Transactions on Magnetics*, vol. 41, num. 2, p. 989–991, 2005.

[KAK 04] KAKUSHIMA K., WATANABE T., SHIMAMOTO K., GOUDA T., ATAKA M., MIMURA H., ISONO Y., HASHIGUCHI G., MIHARA Y., FUJITA H., "Atomic force microscope cantilever array for parallel lithography of quantum devices", *Japanese Journal of Applied Physics, Part 1: Regular Papers and Short Notes and Review Papers*, vol. 43, num. 6 B, p. 4041–4044, 2004.

[KIM 03] KIM Y.-S., NAM H.-J., CHO S.-M., HONG J.-W., KIM D.-C., BU J. U., "PZT cantilever array integrated with piezoresistor sensor for high speed parallel operation of AFM", *Sensors and Actuators, A: Physical*, vol. 103, num. 1–2, p. 122–129, 2003.

[LEN 06] LENCZNER M., "Homogenization of linear spatially periodic electronic circuits", *Netw. Heterog. Media*, vol. 1, num. 3, p. 467–494 (electronic), 2006.

[LUT 99] LUTWYCHE M., ANDREOLI C., BINNIG G., BRUGGER J., DRECHSLER U., HABERLE W., ROHRER H., ROTHUIZEN H., VETTIGER P., YARALIOGLU G., QUATE C., "5x5 2D AFM cantilever arrays a first step towards a Terabit storage device", *Sensors and Actuators, A: Physical*, vol. 73, num. 1–2, p. 89–94, 1999.

[MET 53] METROPOLIS N., ROSENBLUTH A. W., ROSENBLUTH M. N., TELLER A. H., TELLER E., "Equation of state calculations by fast computing machines", *JCP J. Chem. Phys.*, vol. 1, num. 6, p. 1087–1092, 1953.

[MOS 02] MOSEGAARD K., TARANTOLA A., *International Handbook of Earthquake and Engineering Seismology*, Academic Press, 2002.

[RIE 02] RIEF M., GRUBMÜLLER H., "Single molecule force spectroscopy in biology using the atomic force microscope", *European Journal of Chemical Physics and Physical Chemistry*, vol. 3, num. 3, p. 255–261, 2002.

[SAL 00] SALTELLI A., CHAN K., SCOTT M., *Sensitivity Analysis*, Probability and Statistics Series, John Wiley & Sons, 2000.

[SIT 04] SITTI M., "Atomic force microscope probe based controlled pushing for nanotribological characterization", *IEEE/ASME Transactions on Mechatronics*, vol. 9, num. 2, p. 343–348, 2004.

[TAR 05] TARANTOLA A., *Inverse Problem Theory and Methods for Model Parameter Estimation*, SIAM, 2005.

[YAN 04] YANG Z., LI X., WANG Y., BAO H., LIU M., "Micro cantilever probe array integrated with piezoresistive sensor", *Microelectronics Journal*, vol. 35, num. 5, p. 479–483, 2004.

[YAN 06] YANG Z., YU Y., LI X., BAO H., "Nano-mechanical electro-thermal probe array used for high-density storage based on NEMS technology", *Microelectronics Reliability*, vol. 46, num. 5–6, p. 805–810, 2006.

[YOS 95] YOSIDA K., *Functional Analysis*, Classics in Mathematics, McGraw–Hill, Berlin, 1995.

[YU 03] YU X., ZHANG D., LI T., WANG X., RUAN Y., DU X., "Fabrication and analysis of micromachined cantilever array", *Pan Tao Ti Hsueh Pao/Chinese Journal of Semiconductors*, vol. 24, num. 8, p. 861–865, 2003.

[ZLA 00] ZLATANOVA J., LINDSAY S., LEUBA S., "Single molecule force spectroscopy in biology using the atomic force microscope", *Progress in Biophysics; Molecular Biology*, vol. 74, num. 1–2, p. 37–61, 2000.

6.6. Appendix

A1: Basic properties of some integrals on cells

$$\int_{Y_\mu^\varepsilon} dx' \;=\; \varepsilon^d$$

$$\int_{Y_\mu^\varepsilon} \chi_{Y_\lambda^\varepsilon}(x')dx' \;=\; \varepsilon^d \delta_{\mu\lambda}$$

A2: Derivation of the expression for T_E^*

$$(T_E\mathbf{v}, u) = \int_\Omega (T_E\mathbf{v}).u(x)dx$$

$$= \sum_{j=1}^{|E|} \int_{Y_\mu^\varepsilon} (T_E\mathbf{v})_j(x).u_j(x)dx$$

$$= \sum_{\mu\in\{1,\ldots,m\}^d} \sum_{j=1}^{|E|} \varepsilon^{-d}\int_{Y_\mu^\varepsilon} \chi_{Y_\mu^\varepsilon}(x)u_j(x)dxV_{\mu j}$$

$$= \varepsilon^d \sum_{\mu\in\{1,\ldots,m\}^d} \sum_{j=1}^{|E|} \varepsilon^{-d}\int_{Y_\mu^\varepsilon} u_j(x)dxV_{\mu j}$$

$$[T_E^*u, v] = \varepsilon^d (T_E^*u)^T.\mathbf{v}$$

$$= \varepsilon^d \sum_{\mu\in\{1,\ldots,m\}^d} \sum_{j=1}^{|E|} (T_E^*u)_{\mu j}V_{\mu j}$$

$$\Rightarrow (T_E^*u)_{\mu j} = \varepsilon^{-d}\int_{Y_\mu^\varepsilon} u_j(x)dx$$

A3: Proof that $T_E^*T_E = I_{\mathcal{E}}$ on $\mathbb{R}^{|\mathcal{E}|}$

Let $\mathbf{u} \in \mathbb{R}^{|\mathcal{E}|}$ and $\mathcal{I} \sim (\mu, j)$,

$$(T_E^*T_E\mathbf{u})_{\mathcal{I}} = T_E^*\left(\sum_{\lambda\in\{1,\ldots,m\}^d} U_{\lambda j}\chi_{Y_\lambda^\varepsilon}(x)\right)$$

$$= \varepsilon^{-d}\int_{Y_\mu^\varepsilon} \sum_{\lambda\in\{1,\ldots,m\}^d} \chi_{Y_\lambda^\varepsilon}(x)dxU_{\lambda j}$$

$$= \varepsilon^{-d}\varepsilon^d U_{\mu j}$$

$$= \mathbf{u}_{\mathcal{I}}$$

A4: Proof that $T_E T_E^* = I_E$ on $\mathbb{P}^0(\Omega)^{|E|}$

Let $u \in \mathbb{P}^0(\Omega; \mathbb{R}^{|E|})$,

$$
\begin{aligned}
(T_E T_E^* u)_j(x) &= (T_E(\varepsilon^{-d} \int_{Y_\mu^\varepsilon} u_j(x')dx'))_j(x) \\[2mm]
&= \sum_{\mu \in \{1,\ldots,m\}^d} \varepsilon^{-d} \int_{Y_\mu^\varepsilon} u_j(x')dx' \chi_{Y_\mu^\varepsilon}(x) \\[2mm]
&= \sum_{\mu \in \{1,\ldots,m\}^d} \sum_{\lambda \in \{1,\ldots,m\}^d} \varepsilon^{-d} \int_{Y_\mu^\varepsilon} \chi_{Y_\lambda^\varepsilon}(x')dx' U_{\lambda j} \chi_{Y_\mu^\varepsilon}(x) \\[2mm]
&= \sum_{\mu \in \{1,\ldots,m\}^d} \sum_{\lambda \in \{1,\ldots,m\}^d} \delta_{\mu\lambda} U_{\lambda j} \chi_{Y_\mu^\varepsilon}(x) \\[2mm]
&= \sum_{\mu \in \{1,\ldots,m\}^d} U_{\mu j} \chi_{Y_\mu^\varepsilon}(x) \\[2mm]
&= u_j(x)
\end{aligned}
$$

Chapter 7

Fractional Order Modeling and Identification for Electrochemical Nano-biochip

This chapter deals with fractional order modeling and identification of the electrochemical processes of a biochip. A generalized gray-box fractional order model is proposed to better describe the dynamic behavior of this type of process. Assuming *a priori* fixed (possibly estimated) values of the fractional order derivatives and using a discrete-time approximation of the fractional order model, a recursive instrumental variable algorithm was applied to estimate its parameters. The feasibility of the proposed approach is illustrated through the identification of a real electrochemical biochip.

7.1. Introduction

Electrochemical processes have the presence of phenomena in common, such as anomalous relaxation and diffusion, which can be seen as incorporating memory into the systems. In a formal way, memory can be incorporated into the constitutive equations through a causal convolution. It has been experimentally observed and analytically found that both the time domain and frequency domain behaviors of this type of processes do not fit the standard laws, i.e. exponential evolution in time domain or integer order slopes in their frequency responses [TOV 84, VAN 88]. Non-integer order slopes are therefore more suitable to describe in the frequency domain as such phenomena are present in electrochemical processes.

Chapter written by Abdelbaki Djouambi, Alina Voda, Pierre Grangeat and Pascal Mailley.

Moreover, non-integer order slopes in the frequency responses can be better fitted by transfer functions constructed as products of zeroes and poles of fractional power, or ratios of polynomials in s^α, α real, in agreement with the expressions of the Laplace transforms of the mentioned functions.

All these observations lead us to consider fractional calculus as an appropriate tool to phenomenologically describe the richness of dynamic features exhibited by electrochemical systems (such as the biochip considered in this chapter). The resulting models exhibit possible unknown (or time-varying) coefficients, which call for appropriate identification methods to be applied.

Identification of diffusion interfaces is a fundamental problem which has already received much attention. Because of the nature of available data – frequency or temporal – two experimental and very different situations are encountered. Collecting frequency data requires adequate experiments; it is mainly used in electrochemistry where special devices are employed to measure impedances at different frequencies [FEL 97]. On the other hand, time data are more easy to collect by conventional data acquisition systems.

Fitting a model (with integer or non-integer derivatives) to frequency data is a relatively simple problem. Two classes of techniques can be used. The simplest is Levy's approach [LEV 59]: the derivative orders have to be postulated, then the parameters are estimated by classical least-squares method and appropriate software. The main drawback of this technique is that parameter estimates are biased because of equation error [LJU 87]. On the other hand, output-error approach based on non-linear optimization is more complex to implement but is able to give unbiased estimates, either for parameters or derivative orders [KHA 01].

Fitting a fractional model to time data is a more general and much more complex problem. It has already received some solutions based on off-line fractional system identification adapted to particular classes of models [BAT 01, MAL 06, OUS 05]. The diffusion interface is modeled using derivators of order equal to 0.5 and of its successive multiples up to an order N. The value of N is empirically selected in order to obtain the best approximation. With this method, it is possible to approach the input-output behavior of the diffusion interface with excellent accuracy. Nevertheless, the resulting model does not give information about the value of the non-integer orders of the real system. This is because the approach applies a basic order equal to 0.5, but gives no information on the value of the fractional order that would be better adapted to the problem.

Because of the long memory behavior of fractional systems, off-line identification algorithms (which use the whole patch of the acquired data) can also have serious computational problems. To solve this problem, on-line identification methods are performed with a gradual update of the parameter estimates. The main advantage of these methods over off-line methods is that they can be tuned to track changes of model parameter values over time.

In this chapter, a generalized gray-box fractional order model is proposed to better physically describe the underlying electrochemical process of a biochip. Assuming *a priori* fixed (possibly estimated) values of the fractional order derivatives and using a discrete-time approximation of the fractional order model, it is possible to estimate its parameters using a recursive instrumental variable algorithm. Repeating this operation with different values of the fractional orders, their optimal values corresponding to the minimal value of the quadratic criterion can be selected.

The chapter is organized as follows: in section 7.2 we briefly introduce fractional differentiation and fractional order system representation in the form of transfer functions. Section 7.3 presents the recursive identification method of fractional order models with some of its possible extensions. In section 7.4, we propose a gray-box fractional order structure to model an electrochemical process based on a Randle's generalized circuit. Section 7.5 is devoted to the illustration of the method on a real electrochemical biochip. We end the chapter with some concluding remarks.

7.2. Mathematical background

7.2.1. *Brief review of fractional differentiation*

The concept of differentiation to an arbitrary order $\alpha \in R_+^*$ was defined in the 19th century by Riemann and Liouville as [MIL 93, OLD 74]:

$$D^\alpha = \left(\frac{d}{dt}\right)^\alpha. \tag{7.1}$$

The α fractional derivative of $x(t)$ is defined as being an integer derivative of order $m = [\alpha] + 1$ ([.] represents the floor operator) of a non-integer integral of $1 - (m - \alpha)$:

$$D^\alpha x(t) = D^m(I^{m-\alpha})x(t) = \frac{1}{\Gamma(m-\alpha)}\left(\frac{d}{dt}\right)^m \int_0^t \frac{x(\tau)d\tau}{(t-\tau)^{1-(m-\alpha)}} \tag{7.2}$$

where $t > 0, \alpha \in R_+^*$ and Euler's function Γ is defined as:

$$\Gamma(x) = \int_0^\infty e^{-t}t^{x-t}dt. \tag{7.3}$$

A discrete-time definition of fractional derivative was proposed by Grünwald (1867) as:

$$D^\alpha x(t) = \lim_{h \to 0} \frac{1}{h^\alpha} \sum_{k=0}^{[t/h]} (-1)^k \binom{\alpha}{k} x(t - kh) \tag{7.4}$$

where h is the sampling time. Newton's binomial $\binom{\alpha}{k}$ is generalized to non-integer orders by use of Euler's function as:

$$\binom{\alpha}{k} = \frac{\Gamma(\alpha+1)}{\Gamma(k+1)\Gamma(\alpha-k+1)}. \tag{7.5}$$

Equation (7.4) is generally used in time-domain simulations of fractional differentiation. As Newton's binomial $\binom{\alpha}{k}$ does not converge rapidly to zero with k when α is a non-integer, the computation of $D^\alpha x(t)$ depends on all values of $x(t)$ between 0 and t (assuming that $x(t) = 0$ for $t \le 0$). Since fractional derivatives of a function depend on its whole past, fractional operators are known to have long-memory behavior.

For a real implementation of equation (7.4), only the recent past behavior of $x(t)$ is taken into account as described by the so-called short-memory principle [POD 99] recalled here.

Theorem 7.1. *Short-memory principle: if function x is bounded in $[0, t]$, i.e. if a value X exists verifying:*

$$|x(\xi)| < X, \forall \xi \in [0, t], \tag{7.6}$$

then the approximation over the memory length T

$$D^\alpha x(t) \approx_{t-T} D_t^\alpha x(t) \tag{7.7}$$

results in an error ϵ bounded by

$$|\epsilon| \le \frac{XT^{-\alpha}}{|\Gamma(1-\alpha)|}. \tag{7.8}$$

Remark 7.1. From equation (7.8) it results that, for the error to be smaller than a certain desired value $|\epsilon|$, we must have:

$$T \ge \sqrt[\alpha]{\frac{X}{|\epsilon\Gamma(1-\alpha)|}} \tag{7.9}$$

where $t - T$ is a moving lower limit and T is the *memory length*.

According to the theorem given above, equation (7.4) can be approximated by:

$$D^\alpha x(t) = \frac{1}{h^\alpha} \sum_{k=0}^{N} (-1)^k \binom{\alpha}{k} x(t-kh) \tag{7.10}$$

where $N = [T/h]$ is the number of addends in the approximation.

7.2.2. *Fractional order systems*

Fractional order systems are generally represented by the generalized fractional differential equation:

$$y(t) + \sum_{i=1}^{n_a} a_i D^{\alpha_i} y(t) = \sum_{j=0}^{n_b} b_j D^{\beta_j} u(t) \tag{7.11}$$

where differentiation orders $\alpha_1 < \alpha_2 < \ldots < \alpha_{n_a}$, $\beta_0 < \beta_1 < \ldots < \beta_{n_b}$, are allowed to be non-integer positive numbers and $(a_i, b_j) \in R^2$, $i = 1, 2, \ldots, n_a$, $j = 0, 1, \ldots, n_b$.

A more concise algebraic tool can be used to represent fractional systems: the Laplace transform [OLD 74]. If $x(t) = 0 \ \forall t \leq 0$, the Laplace transform of the α fractional order derivative of $x(t)$ can be given as:

$$\mathcal{L}[D^\alpha x(t)] = s^\alpha X(s). \tag{7.12}$$

This property allows equation (7.11) to be true, provided $u(t)$ and $y(t)$ are relaxed at $t = 0$, in a transfer function form:

$$G(s) = \frac{\sum_{j=0}^{n_b} b_j s^{\beta_j}}{1 + \sum_{i=1}^{n_a} a_i s^{\alpha_i}}. \tag{7.13}$$

Definition 7.1. A transfer function $G(s)$ is commensurate of order α if it can be written as $G(s) = F(s^\alpha)$, where $F = T/R$ is a rational function and T and R are two co-prime polynomials. Moreover, the commensurate order α is the biggest number satisfying the previously mentioned condition.

In other words, the commensurate order α is defined as the biggest real number such that all differentiation orders are integer multiples of α.

A modal form transfer function can then be obtained, providing equation (7.13) is strictly proper:

$$G(s) = \sum_{k=1}^{K} \sum_{q=1}^{\nu_k} \frac{A_{k,q}}{(s^\alpha - s_k)^q} \tag{7.14}$$

where $s_k, k = 1, \ldots, K$ are known as the s^α-poles of integer multiplicity q.

The following results are given without proof.

Theorem 7.2. *Stability theorem [MAT 96]: a commensurate (of order α) transfer function $G(s)$ is BIBO (bounded-input, bounded-output) stable if and only if (iff)*

$$0 < \alpha < 2 \tag{7.15}$$

and for every s^α-pole, $s_k \in C$ of $G(s)$:

$$|arg(s_k)| > \alpha \frac{\pi}{2}. \tag{7.16}$$

7.3. Prediction error algorithm for fractional order system identification

Consider the class of stable SISO (single-input, single-output) continuous-time systems modeled by equation (7.13) and characterized by the coefficient vector:

$$\theta_c = (a_1, \ldots a_{n_a}, b_0, \ldots, b_{n_b})^T. \tag{7.17}$$

A priori knowledge is generally used to fix the differentiation orders $\alpha_1, \ldots, \alpha_{n_a}$, $\beta_0, \ldots, \beta_{n_b}$. The fractional differential equation related to equation (7.13) can be given by equation (7.11):

$$y(t) + \sum_{i=1}^{n_a} a_i D^{\alpha_i} y(t) = \sum_{j=0}^{n_b} b_j D^{\beta_j} u(t). \tag{7.18}$$

In order to formulate a recursive prediction algorithm, equation (7.18) should be first approximated by a difference equation in discrete time. By applying the Grünwald–Letnikov approximation given by equation (7.10), the output can be written in a linear prediction form as [OUS 05]:

$$y(k+1) = -\sum_{i=1}^{n_a} a'_i Y_i(k) + \sum_{j=0}^{n_b} b'_j U_j(k) \tag{7.19}$$

where

$$a'_i = \frac{\frac{a_i}{h^{\alpha_i}}}{1 + \sum_{k=1}^{n_a} \frac{a_k}{h^{\alpha_k}}}, \quad b'_j = \frac{\frac{b_j}{h^{\beta_j}}}{1 + \sum_{k=1}^{n_a} \frac{a_k}{h^{\alpha_k}}}, \quad 1 \le i \le n_a, \ 0 \le j \le n_b \tag{7.20}$$

and

$$Y_i(k) = \sum_{j=1}^{N} (-1)^j \binom{\alpha_i}{j} y(k+1-j), \quad U_j(k) = \sum_{i=0}^{N} (-1)^i \binom{\beta_j}{i} u(k+1-i). \tag{7.21}$$

Consider observed data $u(t)$ and $y^*(t) = y(t) + p(t)$, where $p(t)$ is a perturbation signal. The prediction equation (7.19) can be rewritten in a disturbed form as:

$$y^*(k+1) = -\sum_{i=1}^{n_a} a'_i Y_i^*(k) + \sum_{j=0}^{n_b} b'_j U_j(k) + e(k+1) \tag{7.22}$$

where

$$Y_i^*(k) = \sum_{j=1}^{N} (-1)^j \binom{\alpha_i}{j} y^*(k+1-j) \tag{7.23}$$

and

$$e(k+1) = p(k+1) + \sum_{i=1}^{n_a} a'_i \sum_{j=1}^{N} (-1)^j \binom{\alpha_i}{j} p(k+1-j). \tag{7.24}$$

As model (7.22) is linear versus coefficients a'_i and b'_j ($i = 1, \ldots, n_a$, $j = 0, \ldots, n_b$), it can be given in a linear regression form as:

$$y^*(k+1) = \theta^T \phi(k) + e(k+1) \tag{7.25}$$

where

$$\theta = (a'_1, \ldots, a'_{n_a}, b'_0, \ldots, b'_{n_b})^T \tag{7.26}$$

and

$$\phi(k) = [-Y_1^*(k), \ldots, -Y_{n_a}^*(k), U_0(k), \ldots, U_{n_b}(k)]^T. \tag{7.27}$$

Regression equation (7.25) represents an accurate discrete-time representation of the considered system. However, in this expression the parameter vector θ is assumed to be unknown. The fractional orders α_i and β_j ($i = 1, \ldots, n_a$, $j = 0, \ldots, n_b$) are assumed known (fixed) by the user (as is the case for many diffusion systems [BAT 01]). If the disturbance term $e(k)$ is a white noise, we can consider the *a posteriori* prediction output $\hat{y}(k+1)$ computed on the basis of the new estimated parameter vector $\hat{\theta}(k+1)$ and the former input/output measurements inside $\phi(k)$ as:

$$\hat{y}(k+1) = \hat{\theta}(k+1)^T \phi(k) \tag{7.28}$$

where $\phi(k)$ is given by equation (7.27) and

$$\hat{\theta}(k+1) = (\hat{a}'_1(k+1), \ldots, \hat{a}'_{n_a}(k+1), \hat{b}'_0(k+1), \ldots, \hat{b}'_{n_b}(k+1))^T. \tag{7.29}$$

The estimated parameters vector $\hat{\theta}$ is obtained by minimizing the quadratic least-squares criterion:

$$\min_{\hat{\theta}(k)} J_k(\hat{\theta}) = \min_{\hat{\theta}(k)} \frac{1}{k} \sum_{i=1}^{k} [y^*(i) - \hat{y}(i, \hat{\theta}(k))]^2. \tag{7.30}$$

Provided the inverse $[\sum_{i=1}^{k} \phi(i-1)\phi^T(i-1)]^{-1}$ exists, the solution of this problem can be given by the least-squares estimate (as in the classical integer-order models [SOD 89]):

$$\hat{\theta}(k) = \left[\sum_{i=1}^{k} \phi(i-1)\phi^T(i-1) \right]^{-1} \sum_{i=1}^{k} \phi(i-1)y(i). \tag{7.31}$$

A recursive version of equation (7.31) can be given as [LAN 98]:

$$\begin{cases} \hat{\theta}(k+1) = \hat{\theta}(k) + F(k)\phi(k)\varepsilon(k+1) \\[2mm] F(k+1) = F(k) - \dfrac{F(k)\phi(k)\phi^T(k)F(k)}{1 + \phi^T(k)F(k)\phi(k)} \\[2mm] \varepsilon(k+1) = \dfrac{y^*(k+1) - \hat{\theta}^T(k)\phi(k)}{1 + \phi^T(k)F(k)\phi(k)} \end{cases} \tag{7.32}$$

where the adaptation gain matrix $F(k)$ is generally started with:

$$F(0) = \frac{1}{\delta}I; \quad 0 < \delta \ll 1. \tag{7.33}$$

In the case of systems with slowly varying parameters, a 'forgetting' factor λ ($0 < \lambda < 1$) is introduced to give more weight to recently observed data compared to older data. The recursive least-squares algorithm is then given as [LAN 98]:

$$\begin{cases} \hat{\theta}(k+1) = \hat{\theta}(k) + F(k)\phi(k)\varepsilon(k+1) \\[2mm] F(k+1) = \dfrac{1}{\lambda}\left[F(k) - \dfrac{F(k)\phi(k)\phi^T(k)F(k)}{\lambda + \phi^T(k)F(k)\phi(k)} \right] \\[2mm] \varepsilon(k+1) = \dfrac{y^*(k+1) - \hat{\theta}^T(k)\phi(k)}{1 + \phi^T(k)F(k)\phi(k)}. \end{cases} \tag{7.34}$$

As in the classical case for integer-order models, Cois *et al.* [COI 01] showed that the least-squares estimator equation (7.31) of non-integer models is biased in the presence of noisy output. To eliminate the bias, we proposed a recursive instrumental variable method [DJO 07]:

$$
\begin{cases}
\hat{\theta}(k+1) = \hat{\theta}(k) + F(k)\psi(k)\varepsilon(k+1) \\[2mm]
F(k+1) = F(k) - \dfrac{F(k)\psi(k)\phi^T(k)F(k)}{1 + \phi^T(k)F(k)\psi(k)} \\[3mm]
\varepsilon(k+1) = \dfrac{y^*(k+1) - \hat{\theta}^T(k)\phi(k)}{1 + \phi^T(k)F(k)\psi(k)}
\end{cases}
\tag{7.35}
$$

where ψ is the *instrumental variable regression vector* obtained by simulation of an *auxiliary fractional model* which has similar dynamics to those of the identified system (as for an integer-order model, such as in [SOD 89]). A selected model in this context can be given by the discrete-time regression:

$$
y^{IV}(k+1) = -\sum_{i=1}^{n_a} \hat{a}'_i(k)Y_i^{IV}(k) + \sum_{j=0}^{n_b} \hat{b}'_j(k)U_j(k)
\tag{7.36}
$$

where $\hat{a}'_i(k)$ and $\hat{b}'_j(k)$ $(i = 1, \ldots, n_a;\ j = 0, \ldots, n_b)$ are the estimated parameters at time k and

$$
Y_i^{IV}(k) = \sum_{j=1}^{N} (-1)^j \binom{\alpha_i}{j} y^{IV}(k+1-j).
\tag{7.37}
$$

The instrumental variable regression vector ψ is then given by:

$$
\psi(k) = [-Y_1^{IV}(k), \ldots, -Y_{n_a}^{IV}(k), U_0(k), \ldots, U_{n_b}(k)]^T.
\tag{7.38}
$$

Stability and convergence properties of the parameter adaptation algorithm given above have already been investigated for linear predictors arising from integer order ARX (autoregressive with exogenous inputs) model structures [LAN 98]. For a fractional order model, it has been shown that the sampled model can be represented in a linear regression form such as equation (7.28). The proposed prediction error algorithm is therefore asymptotically stable (i.e. global asymptotic convergence to zero of the *a posteriori* predictor) for any finite value of the adaptation gain $F > 0$.

The convergence towards zero of the prediction error does not imply in every case that the estimated parameters will converge towards the true parameters. The following result is quoted without proof.

Theorem 7.3. *[DJO 08] Given a sampled model of the form equation (7.25) obtained by discretization of the continuous-time model equation (7.18) with N addends, and using the adjustable predictor given by equation (7.28), the parametric convergence, i.e.*

$$\lim_{k \to \infty} \hat{a}'_i(k) = a'_i, \quad i = 1, \dots, n_a$$

$$\lim_{k \to \infty} \hat{b}'_j(k) = b'_j, \quad j = 0, \dots, n_b$$

is ensured if:

1) we use a stable PAA $(F > 0)$;

2) the number of parameters $n_a + n_b$ and the number of addends of the discrete approximation N are known such that $n_a + n_b + 1 \leq 2N$;

3) the sampled model to be identified is characterized by an irreducible transfer operator in q^{-1}; and

4) the input $u(k)$ is a persistently exciting signal of order $2N$.

From equation (7.20), the original parameters a_i $(i = 1, \dots, n)$ of the continuous-time fractional order model can be obtained from the equation:

$$\begin{pmatrix} \frac{a'_1 - 1}{h^{\alpha_1}} & \frac{a'_1}{h^{\alpha_2}} & \cdots & \frac{a'_1}{h^{\alpha_{n_a}}} \\ \frac{a'_2}{h^{\alpha_1}} & \frac{a'_2 - 1}{h^{\alpha_2}} & \cdots & \frac{a'_2}{h^{\alpha_{n_a}}} \\ \cdot & \cdot & \cdots & \cdot \\ \frac{a'_{n_a}}{h^{\alpha_1}} & \frac{a'_{n_a}}{h^{\alpha_2}} & \cdots & \frac{a'_{n_a} - 1}{h^{\alpha_{n_a}}} \end{pmatrix} \begin{pmatrix} a_1 \\ a_2 \\ \cdot \\ a_{n_a} \end{pmatrix} = \begin{pmatrix} -a'_1 \\ -a'_2 \\ \cdot \\ -a'_{n_a} \end{pmatrix}.$$

The coefficients b_j, $j = 0, 1, \dots, n_b$ can therefore be obtained using the expression:

$$b_j = b'_j + b'_j \sum_{i=1}^{n} a_i h^{\beta_j - \alpha_i}. \tag{7.39}$$

7.4. Fractional order modeling of electrochemical processes

One of the most useful methods to experimentally study electrochemical processes is the impedance measurement method [BRE 83]. This method consists of applying small sinusoidal input signals (current or potential) to excite the system (electrochemical cell). With this small input signals method, it is possible to use linearized equations to model the physical system.

Measuring the impedance or the admittance (magnitude and phase) allows the electrode process to be analyzed in relation to the contribution from diffusion, kinetics, double layer, etc. For comparison with the electrochemical cell, equivalent electrical circuits are usually employed. The elements of these circuits represent the relevant phenomena in the process [HUA 03, MAG 06, SVE 00]. Among these equivalent circuits, the most used is the so-called Randle's equivalent circuit presented in Figure 7.1, where C_d is a pure capacitor representing the double layer, R_Ω is an uncompensated resistance which is (usually) the solution resistance between working and reference electrodes and Z_f is an impedance of Faradic process.

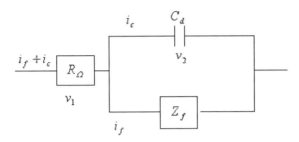

Figure 7.1. *Randle's equivalent circuit*

The faradic impedance Z_f can be subdivided into a pure resistive element representing the resistance to charge transfer and an element representing the difficulty of mass transport of the electroactive species, called the Warburg impedance. We can extend the validity of the Randle's circuit if we take into account the influence in the double layer of the electrodes rugosity and porosity, representing it by the so-called constant phase element Z_{CPE} [AGA 92]. We therefore obtain the extended *Randle's equivalent circuit* given in Figure 7.2, where $Z_w = a/(jw)^{1/2}$ is the Warburg impedance and $Z_{CPE} = b/(jw)^\alpha$, with $\alpha = 0.5$ for porous electrodes and $\alpha = 1$ for smooth electrodes.

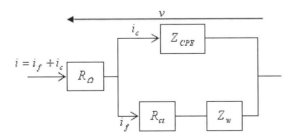

Figure 7.2. *Extended Randle's equivalent circuit*

Using the same notation as in [SCH 95] for viscoelastic models, we propose the generalized Randle's equivalent circuit shown in Figure 7.3 where Y_i ($i = 1, 2, \ldots, 4$) denotes a fractional order admittance defined by:

$$Y_i(jw) = c_i(jw\tau_i)^{\alpha_i}, \qquad 0 \le \alpha_i \le 1 \tag{7.40}$$

from which all the elements of the traditional and the extended Randle's circuits can be obtained as particular cases.

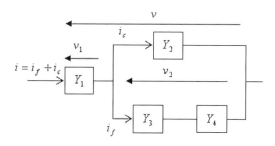

Figure 7.3. *Generalized Randle's equivalent circuit (in admittance form)*

The total admittance of the generalized Randle's circuit of Figure 7.3 is:

$$Y_{\text{tot}}(jw) = \frac{Y_1 Y_2 Y_3 + Y_1 Y_2 Y_4 + Y_1 Y_3 Y_4}{Y_1 Y_3 + Y_1 Y_4 + Y_2 Y_3 + Y_2 Y_4 + Y_3 Y_4} \tag{7.41}$$

where every element $Y_i, i = 1, 2, \ldots, 4$ is of course a function of (jw).

From equation (7.41), using the given notation for fractional operators and the law of exponents for the fractional differential operators, we obtain the equation that describes the general relation between applied potential $v(t)$ and current $i(t)$:

$$
\begin{aligned}
i(t) + k_1 D^{\alpha_4 - \alpha_3} i(t) \quad &+ \quad k_2 D^{\alpha_2 - \alpha_1} i(t) + k_3 D^{\alpha_4 - \alpha_1} i(t) + k_4 D^{\alpha_4 + \alpha_2 - \alpha_3 - \alpha_1} i(t) \\
&= \quad k_5 D^{\alpha_2} v(t) + k_6 D^{\alpha_4} v(t) + k_7 D^{\alpha_4 + \alpha_2 - \alpha_3} v(t)
\end{aligned}
$$

where

$$k_1 = \frac{c_4 \tau_4^{\alpha_4}}{c_3 \tau_3^{\alpha_3}}, \quad k_2 = \frac{c_2 \tau_2^{\alpha_2}}{c_1 \tau_1^{\alpha_1}}, \quad k_3 = \frac{c_4 \tau_4^{\alpha_4}}{c_1 \tau_1^{\alpha_1}}, \quad k_4 = \frac{c_2 \tau_2^{\alpha_2} c_4 \tau_4^{\alpha_4}}{c_1 \tau_1^{\alpha_1} c_3 \tau_3^{\alpha_3}},$$

$$k_5 = c_2 \tau_2^{\alpha_2}, \quad k_6 = c_4 \tau_4^{\alpha_4}, \quad k_7 = \frac{c_2 \tau_2^{\alpha_2} c_4 \tau_4^{\alpha_4}}{c_3 \tau_3^{\alpha_3}}. \tag{7.42}$$

Model (7.42) can be simplified given some suitable approximations of fractional derivative orders α_i i.e.:

– generalized Warburg impedance: $\alpha_4 = \alpha, 0 \leq \alpha \leq 0.5$;
– generalized constant phase element: $\alpha_2 = \beta, 0.5 \leq \beta \leq 1$; and
– dominant resistor behavior: $\alpha_1 = \alpha_3 \approx 0$.

This yields

$$i(t) + a_1 D^\alpha i(t) + a_2 D^\beta i(t) + a_3 D^{\alpha+\beta} i(t) = b_1 D^\alpha v(t) + b_2 D^\beta v(t) + b_3 D^{\alpha+\beta} v(t)$$

(7.43)

where $a_1 = k_1 + k_3, a_2 = k_2, a_3 = k_4, b_1 = k_6, b_2 = k_5, b_3 = k_7$.

Assuming that the process is relaxed at $t = 0$, the corresponding transfer function model can be given as a particular case of equation (7.13) by:

$$Y(s) = \frac{I(s)}{V(s)} = \frac{b_1 s^\alpha + b_2 s^\beta + b_3 s^{\alpha+\beta}}{1 + a_1 s^\alpha + a_2 s^\beta + a_3 s^{\alpha+\beta}}.$$

(7.44)

7.5. Identification of a real electrochemical biochip

Many studies have been carried out on the impedance analysis of electrochemical biochip cells [AGA 92, BRE 83]. In most of these, the impedance measurement has been carried out using a transfer function analyzer. It is well known that the phenomena behind the dynamic behavior of these processes are very complex and difficult to explain. In some of these projects, the fractional order character of the process dynamic behavior was pointed out and explained through the fractal geometry of the relation which controls the mass transport of the electroactive species.

To illustrate the utility of the proposed fractional model structure and the efficiency of the proposed identification method in electrochemical process modeling and identification, a real electrochemical biochip cell was considered in this section. For a fuller description of this system, see [CHI 05, CHI 06].

7.5.1. Experimental set-up

Among the different methodologies dedicated to DNA hybridization transduction, electrochemistry has received much attention due to its intrinsic capabilities including ease of integration or sensitivity. Indeed, electrochemical transduction/detection relies on the immobilization at the individualized electrode surface of oligonucleotide sequences (ODN) that specifically recognize their complementary strand to form, through the well-known hybridization process, the associated double strand. However, such recognition processes do not involve any metabolism (e.g. there is no change in the chemical nature of species surrounding the sensing surface). Different strategies have therefore been developed to electrochemically translate this biological response into interpretable electrical signals either directly [COS 08, KAR 07] or indirectly. The latter strategy indeed allows signal amplification using DNA hybridization multiple labeling including metal particles [ROC 06, WIL 07], intercalators [MAR 07, WAN 04] or redox labels [FLE 07].

Of these methodologies, enzyme labeling has received much attention since this strategy is analogous to classically encountered immunoassays based on the detection of enzymatically generated product, DNA hybridization being amplified due to the enzyme turnover. In such a context, horseradish peroxidase or glucose oxidase were classically involved in hybridization electrochemical detection [DJE 07, ION 06, KAV 06]. More recently, alkaline phosphatase (AlP) was implemented in DNA hybridization detection due to its large turnover [ELS 06] that enables large amplification of the hybridization event.

We used the previously mentioned enzyme as a label here. Indeed, AlP is involved in the dephosphatation mechanism of phosphated substrates. In such a context, Figure 7.4 shows the detection principle of AlP-based DNA hybridization assay.

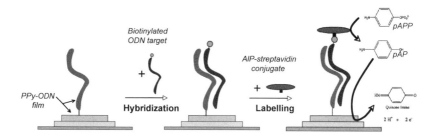

Figure 7.4. *Schematic of hybridization electrochemical reading protocol using AlP as a label*

Oligonucleotide probes were electrochemically immobilized at the transducing surface (included within an array of eight detection microelectrodes coupled to one working electrode and one reference electrode; Figure 7.5) using previously described polypyrrole (electro) chemistry and electrospotting [MAI 05]. Following hybridization with the specific complementary biotynilated target, hybridization was labeled with AlP due to avidin-biotin recognition process, using commercially available AlP-avidin conjugate. Finally, hybridization detection was effected by adding the phosphated substrate of AlP, p-aminophenyl phosphate (pAPP). The latter was metabolized by AlP to generate the redox active molecule p-aminophenol (pAP), electrochemically detected by square wave voltammetry at the underlying electrode surface for a potential of nearly 0 V versus Ag/AgCl.

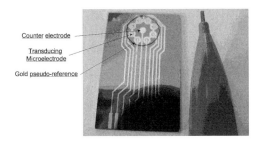

Figure 7.5. *Picture of the API-T8^{TM} electrochemical chip used for DNA hybridization assay. The chip, which was designed by Apibio company Biomerieux group [GAR 07], consists of an array of eight working gold-disc microelectrodes (150 μm diameter) circularly repartitioned around one gold-disc counter electrode (1 mm diameter) and surrounded by a gold multiring pseudoreference electrode*

In biosensing applications, the biological event is generally detected through the utilization of low-frequency electrochemical signals (e.g. cyclic voltammetry or amperometry) as well as combinations of these signals with pulsed modulation (e.g. square wave voltammetry (SWV) and differential pulse voltametry (DPV)). Indeed, these latter methodologies were generally used as physical filters to extract undesirable background components such as interface capacitance (high frequency) or background fluctuations (low frequencies), thus allowing better definition of the specific signal and so decreasing the detection.

In this chapter, the SWV technique has been used as a reference method to delimit the analytical contour of DNA hybridization detection before investigation with random-pulsed excitation coupled to fractional derivative analysis. The protocol of DNA detection and revelation utilized here is a multistep process that involves complex physico-chemical behavior linked to the association of electrochemical detection, enzyme kinetic, diffusion process and time dependence due to detected-species depletion.

The latter aspect has a crucial impact since this assay was designed to work in extremely low reactive volumes (according to the target utilization of the biochip format in medical analysis laboratories). A complete set of relevant parameters was therefore assayed to obtain the best analytical conditions: DNA probe spot-density; hybridization time and temperature; AlP concentration utilized for the revelation; solution, temperature and time required for AlP coupling to the hybridized spots; and concentration of pAPP and incubation temperature used for the AlP-based revelation. Table 7.1 summarizes these different parameters, fully analyzed elsewhere [DUB 09].

Detection step	Analytical parameter	Value
Hybridization	Temperature	37°C
	Sample volume	100 μL
	pH	7.4
	Hybridization time	30 min
AlP coupling	Temperature	20°C
	Sample volume	100 μL
	AlP concentration	50 ng mL^{-1}
	Coupling time	15 min
Biochip reading	Temperature	21°C
	Volume of analysis	400 μL
	pH	8.6
	pAPP concentration	4 mM

Table 7.1. *Analytical parameters fixed for the hybridization, coupling and reading process*

Since this assay works in a drop of solution that excludes any convection behavior and makes diffusion the unique mass transfer phenomena, reading time following pAPP injection has a great impact on the sensor response. This is because pAPP depletion near the electrode surface could be reached and since the product of AlP metabolism, pAP, may accumulate at the surface. In such a context, Figure 7.6a displays a set of SWV signals recorded over incubation time. Figure 7.6b depicts the time evolution of the SWV current peak recorded along the revelation process.

Indeed, such a response is generated from a complex mechanism involving a series of equilibria that makes analytical modeling of the response rather difficult. Nevertheless, whatever the DNA target concentration in solution, a similar time evolution of the SWV amplitude as presented in Figure 7.6a was recorded.

Such an evolution cannot be fitted using the classically used Randle's model due to the complexity of the reading process. However, as complex as this reading process appears, it exhibits good repeatability. It also exhibits a similar time evolution for the different assayed concentrations of ODN target (Figure 7.6b) with a direct dependency of the signal amplitude and kinetic evolution on DNA target concentration and therefore on formed duplex quantities at the electrode surface. This latter behavior allows DNA detection using impedance methods enabling the different electroenzymatic contributions (diffusion, enzyme kinetic, double layer capacitance and electrochemical rate) to be calibrated and therefore the more relevant analytical signal associated with DNA hybridization to be exploited.

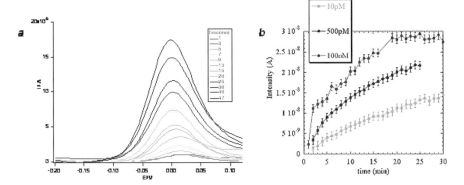

Figure 7.6. *(a) SWV evolution with incubation time recorded for a PPy-ODN film electropolymerized from a 1/80000 ratio solution of pyrrole Zip9 and pyrrole Zip 9comp (ODN target concentration was 100 nM) and (b) SWV peak current evolution with time for three different DNA target concentrations (100 nM: green line; 500 pM: blue line; and 10 pM: orange line) (see color section)*

However, due to pAp accumulation with time and therefore the relatively rapid evolution of the signal with time, such impedance-based analysis has to be prompt to avoid any instability of the acquired data. Random pulse excitation was therefore used (instead of classical impedance spectroscopy) after 15 minutes of incubation of the overall assembly in pAPP solution. The random pulsation was computed to scan the overall frequency range associated with the reading process. The pulsating signal was centered at the half-wave potential of pAP which corresponds to the peak potential of SWV signal and, more particularly, to the equivalent concentrations of the oxidized and reduced forms of pAP at the electrode (in the case of reversible electrochemical behavior). The pulse amplitude was therefore fixed to ± 30 mV around the previously mentioned working potential (see Figure 7.7).

7.5.2. *Fractional order model identification of the considered biochip*

The model considered here represents the total admittance Y_{tot} of the electrode mixture. The mixture was subjected to an excitation potential input of amplitude 30 mV in a sequence of pulses with variable duration. The current through the circuit is measured with a sample time $h = 25\,\mu$s to build a data file of 800 pairs.

The 800 (input-output) dataset (depicted in Figure 7.7) was divided into two equal-sized sequences. The first part was used for parameter estimation and the second part was used for model validation.

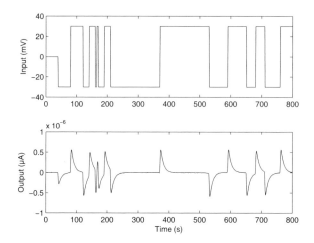

Figure 7.7. *Input-output experimentally measured data*

By considering the process as a gray-box, the objective is to show how to drive a generalized transfer function model of the form equation (7.44) which captures its dynamic behavior. Using the described recursive instrumental variable identification algorithm, we simulate the experimental data for different values of fractional orders α and β such that: $0 < \alpha < 0.5$ and $0.5 < \beta < 1$. (The particular case $\alpha = 0.5$ and $\beta = 0.75$ corresponds to the extended Randle's equivalent circuit model depicted in Figure 7.2).

The optimal coefficients will be obtained with the optimal orders α_{op} and β_{op}, minimizing the criterion:

$$(\alpha_{op}, \beta_{op}) = \arg \min_{\alpha,\beta}\{\min_{\hat{\theta}}[J(\hat{\theta}, \alpha, \beta)]\} \tag{7.45}$$

where J is the least-squares criterion and $\hat{\theta} = (\hat{a}_1, \hat{a}_2, \hat{a}_3, \hat{b}_1, \hat{b}_2, \hat{b}_3)$.

Estimation results are given by Tables 7.2 and 7.3. In order to evaluate its validity, we test the model with measured data differently from those which allowed the model identification (second part). The comparison is given in Figures 7.8 and 7.9.

From the previous simulations, we observe a good agreement between the real system behavior and the identified models which capture the dynamic behavior of the considered process. However, we can clearly seen that the generalized model gives the best results. In addition, it has the advantage of modeling the double-layer effect of the electrode rugosity and porosity β separately from the mass transport α effect.

	a_1	a_2	a_3	b_1	b_2	b_3
RIV estimate	-0.0195	0.0017	4.5411 $\times 10^{-17}$	2.9468 $\times 10^{-12}$	1.1437 $\times 10^{-11}$	-4.1617 $\times 10^{-14}$

Table 7.2. *Estimated parameters of the extended Randle's equivalent circuit model ($\alpha = 0.5, \beta = 0.75$) using the RIV method*

	α_{op}	β_{op}	a_1	a_2	a_3	b_1	b_2	b_3
RIV estimate	0.30	0.60	-0.09195	0.0049	3.1360 $\times 10^{-16}$	-2.3779 $\times 10^{-10}$	7.3824 $\times 10^{-11}$	-2.4615 $\times 10^{-12}$

Table 7.3. *Estimated parameters of the generalized Randle's equivalent circuit model using the RIV method*

Figure 7.10 compares the Bode plots of the identified generalized model and the real process (data). From this figure we can observe that the admittance Bode plot (the proposed model) agrees with some physical study and interpretation on electrochemical processes [BRE 83].

7.6. Conclusion

In this chapter, a fractional order model to represent the dynamic behavior of electrochemical processes using generalized Randle's equivalent circuit has been proposed. Such a model is very helpful for electrical engineers, since it allows them to

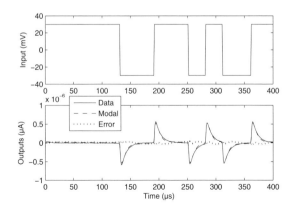

Figure 7.8. *Validation results of the extended Randle's equivalent circuit model*

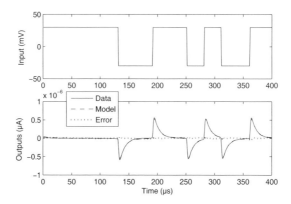

Figure 7.9. *Validation results of the generalized Randle's equivalent circuit model*

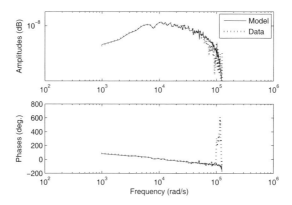

Figure 7.10. *Model and real-system Bode plots*

think in terms of electrical elements instead of electrochemical phenomena. A time-domain identification algorithm for parameter estimation of the proposed model was also presented.

The proposed methodology has also been illustrated on data from a real electrochemical biochip used for DNA hybridization assay, designed by Apibio company Biomerieux Group. The obtained results validate the modeling and identification strategy and also demonstrate its applicability for such complex processes.

7.7. Bibliography

[AGA 92] AGARWAL P., ORAZEM M., "Measurement models for electrochemical impedance spectroscopy", *J. Electrochem.*, vol. 139, num. 7, p. 1917–1927, 1992.

[BAT 01] BATTAGLIA J., COIS O., PUIGSEGUR L., OUSTALOUP A., "Solving an inverse heat conduction problem using a noninteger identified model", *Int. J. Heat Mass Transfer*, vol. 44, num. 14, p. 2671–2680, 2001.

[BRE 83] BRETT M., OLIVEIRA A., *Electrochemistry: Principles, Methods and Applications*, Oxford University Press, 1983.

[CHI 05] CHIBANE A., GRANGEAT P., DESBAT L., VODA A., "Application de modèles à dérivée non entière à la détection électrochimique sur biopuce", *GRETSI, 20ème colloque sur le Traitement du signal et des images*, Louvain la Neuve, Belgium, September 2005.

[CHI 06] CHIBANE A., DUBUISSON E., GRANGEAT P., MAILLEY P., "Détection électrochimique d'ADN sur biopuce: du marquage redox de l'hybridation à la modélisation du signal ampérométrique", *19ième entretiens du Centre Jacques Cartier Rhône-Alpes, Nanobiotechnologies pour l'analyse et la conversion d'énergie*, Grenoble, France, November 2006.

[COI 01] COIS O., LEVRON F., OUSTALOUP A., "Complex-fractional systems: modal decomposition and stability condition", *In Proc. ECC'2001 European Control Conference*, Porto, Portugal, 2001.

[COS 08] COSNIER S., MAILLEY P., "Recent advances in DNA sensors", *Analyst*, vol. 133, p. 984–991, 2008.

[DJE 07] DJELLOULI N., ROCHELET-DEQUAIRE M., LIMOGES B., DRUET M., BROSSIER P., "Evaluation of the analytical performances of avidin-modified carbon sensors based on a mediated horseradish peroxidase enzyme label and their application to the amperometric detection of nucleic acids", *Biosensors and Bioelectronics*, vol. 22, p. 2906–2913, 2007.

[DJO 07] DJOUAMBI A., VODA A., CHAREF A., "Fractional system identification using recursive algorithms approach", *European Control Conference ECC'07*, Kos, Greece, p. 1436–1441, 2007.

[DJO 08] DJOUAMBI A., VODA A., CHAREF A., Recursive identification of a class of fractional order models, Technical Report num. 03–2009, University of Oum El Bouaghi, Algeria, 2008.

[DUB 09] DUBUISSON E., CHIBANE A., GRANGEAT P., MAILLEY P., "Electrochemical DNA-hybridization detection via enzymatic amplification at microelectrode array modified with polypyrrole-oligonucleotide films", *Sensor Letters*, 2009, in press.

[ELS 06] ELSHOLZ B., WORL R., BLOHM L., ALBERS J., FEUCHT H., GRUNWALD T., JURGEN B., SCHWEDER T., HINTSCHE R., "Automated detection and quantitation of bacterial RNA by using electrical microarrays", *Analytical Chemistry*, vol. 78, p. 4794–4802, 2006.

[FEL 97] FELIU V., FELIU S., "A method of obtaining the time domain response of an equivalent circuit model", *Journal of Electroanalytical Chemistry*, vol. 435, p. 1–10, 1997.

[FLE 07] FLECHSIG G., RESKE T., "Electrochemical detection of DNA hybridization by means of osmium tetroxide complexes and protective oligonucleotides", *Analytical Chemistry*, vol. 79, p. 2125–2130, 2007.

[GAR 07] GARNIER F., BOUABDALLAOUI B., P.SRIVASTAVA, MANDRAND B., CHAIX C., "Conjugated polymer-based DNA chip with real time access and femtomol detection threshold", *Sensors and Actuators*, vol. 12, p. 313–320, 2007.

[HUA 03] HUANG X., GREVE D., NGUYEN D., DOMACH M. M., "Impedance based biosensor array for monitoring mammalian cell behavior", *Proceedings of IEEE*, p. 304–309, Oct 2003.

[ION 06] IONESCU R., HERMANN S., COSNIER S., MARKS R., "A polypyrrole cDNA electrode for the amperometric detection of the West Nile Virus", *Electrochem. Commun.*, vol. 8, p. 1741–1748, 2006.

[KAR 07] KARA P., CAVDAR S., MERIC B., ERENSOY S., OZSOZ M., "Electrochemical probe DNA design in PCR amplicon sequence for the optimum detection of microbiological diseases", *Bioelectrochemistry*, vol. 71, p. 204–210, 2007.

[KAV 06] KAVANAGH P., LEECH D., "Redox polymer and probe DNA tethered to gold electrodes for enzyme-amplified amperometric detection of DNA hybridization", *Analytical Chemistry*, vol. 78, p. 2710–2716, 2006.

[KHA 01] KHAORAPAPONG T., Modélisation d'ordre non entier des effets de fréquence dans les barres rotoriques d'une machine asynchrone, PhD Thesis, INP Toulouse, France, 2001.

[LAN 98] LANDAU I., LOZANO R., M'SAAD M., *Adaptive Control*, Springer, London, 1998.

[LEV 59] LEVY E., "Complex curve fitting", *IRE Transactions on Automatic Control*, vol. 4, p. 37–43, 1959.

[LJU 87] LJUNG L., *System Identification: Theory for the User*, Prentice Hall, Englewood Cliffs, New Jersey, 1987.

[MAG 06] MAGIN R., OVADIA M., "Modeling the cardiac tissue electrode interface using fractional calculus", *Proceedings of the 2nd IFAC Workshop on Fractional Differentiation and its Applications*, Porto, Portugal, 2006.

[MAI 05] MAILLEY P., LIVACHE T., ROGET A., "Conducting polymers for DNA sensors and DNA chips; from fabrication to molecular detection", PALECEK E., SCHELLER F., WANG J., Eds., *Electrochemistry of Nucleic Acids and Proteins. Towards Electrochemical Sensors for Genomics and Proteomics*, p. 297–344, Elsevier Publishing, 2005.

[MAL 06] MALTI R., AOUN M., SABATIER J., OUSTALOUP A., "Tutorial on system identification using fractional differentiation models", *Proceedings of the 2nd IFAC Workshop on Fractional Differentiation and its Applications*, Porto, Portugal, 2006.

[MAR 07] MARTI A., PUCKETT C., DYER J., STEVENS N., JOCKUSCH S., JU J., BARTON J., TURRO N., "Inorganic-organic hybrid luminescent binary probe for DNA detection based on spin-forbidden resonance energy transfer", *Journal of American Chemical Society*, vol. 129, p. 8680–8681, 2007.

[MAT 96] MATIGNON D., "Stability results for fractional differential equations with applications to control processing", *Proceedings of IEEE-SMC CESA'96*, Lille, France, p. 963–968, 1996.

[MIL 93] MILLER K., ROSS B., *An Introduction to Fractional Calculus and Fractional Diffrential Equations*, John Wiley & Sons, New York, 1993.

[OLD 74] OLDHAM K., SPANIER J., *The Fractional Calculus*, Academic Press, New York and London, 1974.

[OUS 05] OUSTALOUP A., *Représentation et Identification par Modèle Non Entier*, Hermés-Lavoisier, Paris, 2005.

[POD 99] PODLUBNY I., *Fractional Differential Equations*, Academic Press, San Diego, 1999.

[ROC 06] ROCHELET-DEQUAIRE M., LIMOGES B., BROSSIER P., "Subfemtomolar electrochemical detection of target DNA by catalytic enlargement of the hybridized gold nanoparticle labels", *Analyst*, vol. 131, p. 923–929, 2006.

[SCH 95] SCHIESSEL H., METZLER R., BLUMEN A., NONNENMACHER T., "Generalized viscoelastic models: their fractional equations with solutions", *Journal of Physics A: Mathematical and Theoretical*, vol. 28, p. 6567–6584, 1995.

[SOD 89] SODERSTROM T., STOICA P., *System Identification*, Prentice Hall International, UK, 1989.

[SVE 00] SVERRE G., MARTINSEN O. G., *Bioimpedance and Bioelectricity Basics*, Academic Press, New York/London, 2000.

[TOV 84] TOVIK P., "On the appearance of the fractional derivative in the behavior of real materials", *Transaction of the ASME*, vol. 51, p. 294–298, 1984.

[VAN 88] VAN DER ZIEL A., "Unified presentation of 1/f noise in electronic devices: fundamental 1/f noise sources", *Proceedings of IEEE*, p. 233–258, 1988.

[WAN 04] WANG B., BOUFFIER L., DEMEUNYNCK M., MAILLEY P., ROGET A., LIVACHE T., DUMY P., "New acridone derivatives for the electrochemical DNA-hybridization labelling", *Bioelectrochemistry*, vol. 63, p. 233–237, 2004.

[WIL 07] WILLNER I., WILLNER B., KATZ E., "Biomolecule-nanoparticle hybrid systems for bioelectronic applications", *Bioelectrochemistry*, vol. 70, p. 2–11, 2007.

PART III

From Nanoworld to Macro and Human Interfaces

Chapter 8

Human-in-the-loop Telemicromanipulation System Assisted by Multisensory Feedback

This chapter describes a multimodal interface for the teleoperation of a micro-manipulation system. AFM-based manipulation at the microscale has been investigated for several years. However, the scale of the environments and the complexity of the involved forces make the direct manipulation by the human operator complex, imprecise and very constraining for a long period. In the context of carrying out a pushing task using a micro-object, we propose a framework for intuitive and efficient manipulation. The proposed approach is based on a virtualized intermediate representation of the micro-environment. The 3D reconstruction is based on a robust and real-time tracking technique with subpixel accuracy. On the basis of the proposed 3D model, multimodal force feedback rendering assisted by virtual fixtures is proposed. We initially propose a full 3D immersive visual representation of the micro-environment to the operator, enhanced through haptic feedback. We complete the intermediate representation with a 3D audio feedback using auditive icons to represent microworld physical events (friction, contact, etc.) and physical auralization. Different levels of multisensory feedback have been evaluated. By combining visual, haptic and auditory feedback, we demonstrate experimentally that micromanipulation can be improved in different ways: task completion time, maximum force applied to the manipulated parts and number of collisions with the environment.

Chapter written by Mehdi AMMI and Antoine FERREIRA.

8.1. Introduction

In microscale manipulation, current microtelerobotic tasks require that the human performs high-precision, repeatable and safe operations in confined environments. Some examples can typically be found in microelectromechanical (MEMS) assembly systems [SIT 00] or in the injection of substances (DNA, RNA) in biological cells [KUN 06]. Currently, such tasks are performed under an optical microscope where forces are imperceptible and depth measurement limited. Tremor, fatigue and stress are magnified which affects the accuracy and efficiency of the micromanipulation tasks. The use of force feedback telemicromanipulation systems allows micro-objects to be manipulated by transferring both human motion and manipulation skills to the micromanipulator. However, the lack of dexterity during manipulation and the noisy visual information provided to the operator strongly limits their performances [FAH 02, FOK 05, SIT 00].

Virtual Reality interfaces have recently been investigated for efficient telemicro-manipulation systems. However, it was rapidly found that modeling the nanoscale world was unsuccessful due to strong uncertainties, noisy visual sensing information or unpredictable dynamic effects (adhesion, friction and van der Waals forces) [FER 04, KAW 01, OHB 00].

Automating the process of moving a large number of microcomponents in real-time is necessary to make such microrobotic tasks possible. By following the generated motion paths, the tip can either follow the topography of the surface or move across the surface by avoiding collisions with bumps. Automatic strategies with vision-based controlled pushing techniques have been tested successfully for simple tasks [LYN 07]. For complex 3D planning tasks, the authors in [MAK 01] developed specific heuristic algorithms. Different solutions have been proposed. Despite the large effort that has been expended on this problem, efficient fully automatic solutions at microscale work for very limited situations.

Several human-machine interfaces (HMI) designed to assist AFM-based nano-manipulation systems have been developed in order to improve the reliability of manipulations tasks. Augmented Reality systems for AFM-based micromanipulation have considerably enhanced the efficiency interaction of the operator [LI 04, LI 05, VOG 06].

The ultimate goal of augmented reality is to blend parts seamlessly together so that the user is made to believe that the whole micro/nano-environment is real [AMM 04]. It assumes a state of 'full immersion' of the operator senses (vision, force, haptic and auditory) for assisting as well as guiding the human operator from monitoring level (passive) up to human reaction level (active) in planning micromanipulation tasks. Bringing multimedia techniques into virtual reality enables us to go beyond pure graphics in emulating reality. With the inclusion of visual, haptic and auditory interfaces such as head-mounted displays (HMD), data gloves and force-reflecting haptics, operators can visualize, manipulate and interact with micro/nano objects in the virtual world more naturally.

The use of multimodal feedback has been motivated by human physiological studies that indicate that complementary feedback channels can be used to help the operator complete the task [EME 99, MAR 05, TOK 96]. In this study, an immersive telemanipulation system based on virtualized reality is developed for real-time micromanipulation. We examine the role of multimodal feedback to the operator during the micromanipulation phase by addressing the roles of visual, force, auditory and tactile feedback in a virtualized environment. We integrated vision-based virtual fixtures in order to overcome human limitations by providing guidance and assistance tools to robot-assisted micromanipulation tasks.

As proposed in [BET 04], virtual fixtures have been designed to have different levels of motion guidance ranging from complete free guidance (hard fixture), limited guidance (soft fixture) and no guidance. We demonstrated that most of the micromanipulation tasks required a mixture of these three types of fixtures. These results are in accordance with those reported by the authors in [AMM 07].

The chapter is summarized as follows. In section 8.2, we describe a multi-modal human-machine interface based on virtualized reality techniques for real-time telemicromanipulation with vision, force and sound feedback. The high-speed image processing techniques allowing the real-time reconstruction of augmented virtuality environment are presented in section 8.3. Finally, section 8.4 presents haptic-based path guiding strategies based on potential fields for human-centered telemicromanipulation.

8.2. Haptic-based multimodal telemicromanipulation system

8.2.1. *Global approach*

An immersive HMI system allowing interaction with a complex microscale environment is depicted in Figure 8.1 for AFM-based micromanipulation strategy. It is basically composed of virtual reality input/output devices (force feedback, 3D visual feedback, audio feedback), a virtualized reality interface and a piezoresistive AFM-based micromanipulator. We used a piezoresistive AFM cantilever (AFM-tip) in the experiments, with its tip used as an end-effector and force sensor.

The goal of the developed HMI [VOG 06] is the improvement of the communication between the operator and the micro-environment through adequate interaction and optimal exploitation of human perception (haptic, visual and audio channel). Moreover, the multimodal HMI proposes various assistance tools well adapted to the

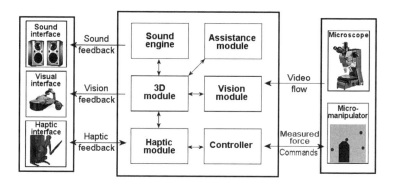

Figure 8.1. *Multimodal human-machine interface concept*

operational context of micromanipulation tasks through virtual fixtures mechanisms. These assistance metaphors are based on different active and passive guidance strategies.

The proposed interface is based on the concept of virtualization of the micro-environment. The generation of the virtual scene is based on three information sources: (i) real images provided by the optical microscopes; (ii) the piezoresistive force sensor integrated in the AFM-tip; and (iii) the position sensors of the micro/nano-manipulators.

Applying sensing fusion techniques, a faithful synthetic representation of the remote microworld is generated. In this way, the operator has several methods of navigation and interaction in order to explore and understand intuitively the microrobotic task. In addition, as the operator does not act directly on the real microscene but only on its virtual equivalent, the developed HMI ensures a safe and efficient decoupling interface between the teleoperator site (active part) and the micro-environment (passive part). In this way the adequate gesture (filtering, optimization, etc.) of the operator is then retransmitted in real-time to the AFM-based micromanipulator, according to the user skills.

8.2.2. *Telemicromanipulation platform and manipulation protocol*

The telemicromanipulation platform comprises three main parts (Figure 8.1). On the right, we have the micro-environment with an optical microscope to observe the environment and a micromanipulator to interact with the micro-objects. On the left, the operator is connected to the platform through several sensori-motor interfaces (HMD,

3D tracker, haptic interfaces, etc.). The proposed HMI is the junction between these two environments.

The software architecture of the HMI comprises six modules. The first of these is the vision module. The first function of this component is to extract information from the visual sensor (optical microscope). The second mission of this module is to calibrate the optical microscope to ensure a good registration between the virtual and real scene. The controller module is in charge of the bilateral controller that couples the haptic interface and the piezoresistive AFM-based micromanipulator. The 3D module exploits the information provided by the vision module to generate the 3D real-time scene. This module also integrates the navigation strategies and the visual metaphors.

The haptic modules manage two types of information. The first is provided by the force sensor mounted on the AFM-tip through the bilateral coupling. The second type of information displayed by the haptic module concerns the active virtual fixtures generated by the assistance module (potential field, optimal path, etc.).

In this study, the considered task concerns the manipulation of polystyrene microspheres through a pushing strategy (Figure 8.2). The goal of this manipulation is to change the microspheres from an initial configuration to a final one by considering several criteria (execution time, path optimization, operator comfort, etc.). In addition to microspheres, the scene comprises dust particles to simulate obstacles. The operator must avoid these elements during the manipulation.

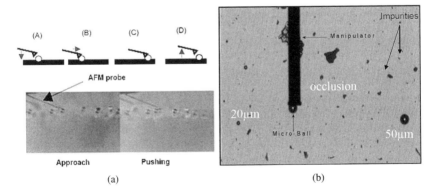

Figure 8.2. *Micromanipulation of microscaled objects using pushing strategy with AFM probe: (a) side view and (b) frontal view of the micromanipulation workspace*

The manipulation is carried out with a hybrid micromanipulator composed of three linear translation stages (x, y, z). It is driven by DC motors for the large displacement, combined with a 3 degree-of-freedom (dof) ultra-high-resolution piezomanipulator

(x, y, z) for fine positioning. The end-effector consists of a piezoresistive AFM cantilever integrating a full-bridge strain gauge sensor. The observation of the microscene is supported by a Mitutoyo FS70Z optical microscope equipped with high aperture objectives. Furthermore, the micromanipulation platform is equipped with a TIMM-150 optical microscope for lateral observation. The second microscope also allows the calibration of the vertical displacement of the micromanipulator.

The micromanipulator is controlled by an haptic interface (PHANToM Desktop). The haptic feedback interface displays two types of information. The first is based on the real scene and corresponds to the contact force measured by the force microsensor. This feedback is based on a bilateral coupling between the micromanipulator and the haptic arm. The second type of displayed information is based on the generation of virtual fixtures to assist the operator during real-time micromanipulation. These virtual information (virtual fixtures, metaphors, etc.) are based on several algorithms, i.e. SDK for collision detection, ordinary differential equation (ODE) for some dynamic effect, A* optimization algorithm and Voronoï graph for path planning. The 3D visual feedback is supported by the OpenInventor library.

For psychophysical studies, we consider three level of visual immersion: (i) not immersive with a simple computer screen (20 inches); (ii) semi-immersive with a large screen (100 inches); and (iii) a total immersive visual feedback with a head-mounted display (V6 from Virtual Research Systems). The 6-dof (3 translations and 3 rotations) head-tracking system is supported by a flock-of-birds magnetic position sensor. The audio feedback is based entirely on the virtual scene. It displays auditive icons corresponding to physical events (contact, friction, etc.), and auralization of manipulated data (distance, exerted force, etc.).

8.3. 3D visual perception using virtual reality

8.3.1. *Limitations of microscopy visual perception*

The operational efficiency of the human operator in the achievement of everyday tasks is essentially based on the flexibility and the performance of perception. For humans, the perception of the environment is dominated by the visual modality. This sense can quickly extract important information such as geometric features, spatial location or object identity. With teleoperation systems, the visual perception of the operator is greatly reduced since the observation is made using a 2D screen, which inhibits the stereoscopic perception and navigation mechanisms. With optical-based telemicromanipulation systems, other constraints restrict even more perception. Since the numerical aperture of the objectives are much lower than the macro-objectives, the depth-of-field is very low (0.9 μm with a magnification of ×50).

Real-time microcamera systems which can achieve 3D micromodeling and the 'all-in-focus' texture of objects simultaneously, with 'depth-from-focus' (defocus) criteria, are currently being developed. Real-time microcamera systems which can achieve 3D visualization with the defocus criteria have been considered in [ARA 00, LIE 02]. However, previous reports do not consider matching the virtual reality space and the real space while taking into account the variation of the environment in real-time, the tracking of micro-objects with different dimensions and visual sensing uncertainties.

We propose a 3D reconstruction environment for real-time observation, based on image processing and immersive multimodal techniques. In this section, the different steps of image processing techniques are proposed for 3D reconstruction: (i) localization of micro-objects and impurities, (ii) fine localization with subpixel accuracy, (iii) classification and labeling, and (iv) 3D reconstruction.

8.3.2. Coarse localization of microspheres

In order to be able to locate partially occluded microspheres, we used the pattern matching method. As this method is time consuming, we used the properties of specular reflection of light on the microspheres to decrease the processing time. Specular points are visualized on the center of each microsphere (Figure 8.3a) due to the alignment of the light source with the field view of the microscope. In order to isolate and amplify this frequency, three consecutive low pass–high pass filtering operations are applied to the original image (Figure 8.3c). Finally, a Laplacian operator with 8-connections is used to extract the specular points from the rest of the scene (Figure 8.3d). Since the scene is composed mainly of spheres with different diameters, a classification according to their radius is necessary. The radius (expressed in pixels) corresponds to the distance between the local maximum and the edge of the microspheres on the pattern. However, this tracking technique is not robust because of changes in lighting.

8.3.3. Fine localization using image correlation techniques

Taking into account the possibility of occlusion by the micromanipulator, we choose an image correlation technique for precise and robust localization (at pixel level). We consider a reference template of image data $M(u, v)$ and a test image $I(x, y)$. Correlation is carried out by comparing the template image to all parts of the test image of the same size. The site of the correlation peak is selected as the position of the target. In order to make the correlation insensitive to global luminosity variation, we use the Normalized Correlation Coefficient (NCC):

$$NCC = \frac{\sum_{i=1}^{m} \sum_{j=1}^{n} I_1(i,j) \times I_2(i,j)}{\sqrt{\sum_{i=1}^{m} \sum_{j=1}^{n} (I_1(i,j))^2 \times \sum_{i=1}^{m} \sum_{j=1}^{n} (I_2(i,j))^2}}. \qquad (8.1)$$

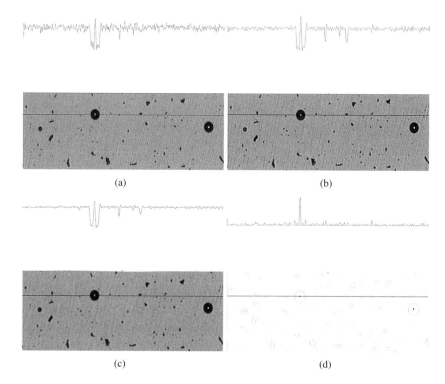

Figure 8.3. *Image processing steps for localization of targets (560×420 pixels): (a) original image; (b) high-pass filter; (c) high-pass + low-pass filter and (d) Laplacian operator*

To reduce the processing time, we tried to reduce the number of correlation tests by only considering a small area (99 pixels) around the local maximum detected during the previous image processing steps (see Figure 8.4a).

8.3.4. *Subpixel localization*

Using a correlation approach to locate a target instance only returns an integral location; the values of x and y are always an integer value. Assuming that the correlation surface is relatively smooth, it is possible to interpolate between sample values to estimate a subpixel localization for target. We propose a method using paraboloid surface for the interpolation (Figure 8.4b). Once the integral location is found, the eight neighbors on the correlation surface are also computed in order to fit $z(x, y)$ to a function of the form:

$$z = a\,x^2 + b\,y^2 + c\,x\,y + d\,x + e\,y + f. \tag{8.2}$$

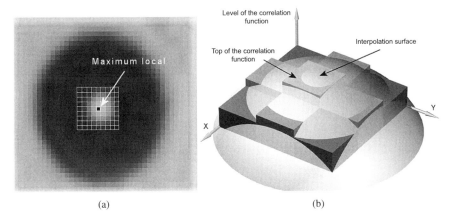

Figure 8.4. *(a) Space of calculation for correlation data and (b) paraboloid surface for interpolation*

The solution for the coefficient of the paraboloid can be found by solving the system equation

$$A\,x = b \tag{8.3}$$

where

$$A = \begin{bmatrix} x_0^2 & y_0^2 & x_0 y_0 & x_0 & y_0 & 1 \\ x_1^2 & y_1^2 & x_1 y_1 & x_1 & y_1 & 1 \\ . & . & . & . & . & . \\ . & . & . & . & . & . \\ x_8^2 & y_8^2 & x_8 y_8 & x_8 & y_8 & 1 \end{bmatrix},$$

$$b = \begin{bmatrix} z_0 \\ z_1 \\ . \\ . \\ z_8 \end{bmatrix} \quad \text{and} \quad x^T = \begin{bmatrix} a \\ b \\ c \\ d \\ e \\ f \end{bmatrix}.$$

Because A is a rectangular matrix and cannot be inverted to solve for x, a least-squares regression such as

$$x = (A^T\,A)^{-1}\,A^T\,b \tag{8.4}$$

must be used.

Once the coefficients of the surface are known, the maximum of the paraboloid can be found by taking the gradient of equation (8.2) with respect to x and y:

$$\frac{\delta z}{\delta x} = 2ax + cy + d = 0$$

$$\frac{\delta z}{\delta y} = 2by + cx + e = 0. \tag{8.5}$$

The positional coordinates (x, y) of the curve maximum are given by:

$$x = \frac{2db - ce}{c^2 - 4ab}$$

$$y = \frac{2ae - dc}{c^2 - 4ab}. \tag{8.6}$$

Note that this is a closed-form solution for the maximum. No iterative steps are involved, so the execution time is therefore deterministic. The application of the algorithm can be summarized in the following list of steps:

1) Determine the best integer pixel match between the reference template and the feature of interest.

2) Find the normalized correlation at the peak and eight surroundings points $(z_0, \ldots, z_8)$ using equation (8.2).

3) Set up the matrices for the system as shown in equation (8.3) using the correlation data points and their associated (x, y) positions.

4) Solve the coefficients of the paraboloid $a, b, \ldots, f$ using the numerical method of equation (8.4).

5) Use equation (8.6) to calculate the position of the surface maximum.

6) Add this subpixel value to the integer pixel location found in step (1) to precisely locate the specular reflection center of the microspheres.

A mean accuracy of at least 1/10 of a pixel (with a pixel size of 1.6 μm) is required for microworld recognition. Practical trials have shown that an accuracy of better than 1/16 of a pixel is possible.

8.3.5. *Localization of dust and impurities*

Impurities and dust particles located in the environment could be potential obstacles during pushing-based micromanipulation. We must therefore determine the exact location and dimensions of potential obstacles. The content of the image scene is composed of three types of objects: substrate, microspheres and dust particles. From the initial knowledge of positions, dimensions and shape of microspheres, it is possible to eliminate them from the scene. By applying a binary threshold, we only measure dust particles. In order to optimize the 3D visualization of the scene, virtual encapsulators (wireframe boxes) are created to encapsulate all detected dust particles, represented by black boxes in Figure 8.5.

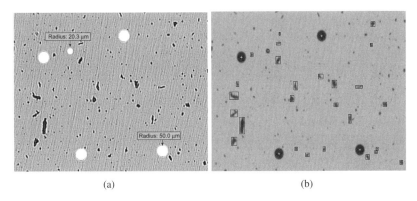

(a)   (b)

Figure 8.5. *Detection and localization of impurities in the micro-environment: (a) erasing microspheres and (b) representation of particle boundaries through virtual encapsulators*

Computation times for each image processing step are listed in Table 8.1.

Image processing operation	T1 (ms)	T2 (ms)
Calculation of local maxima	35.98	39.00
Classification	1.04	1.50
Correlation	23.11	23.37
Subpixel localization	0.54	0.61
Impurities localization	10.14	13.45
Tracking	0.76	1.10
Cycle time	71.57	79.03

Table 8.1. *Computation times*

8.3.6. Calibration of the microscope

The workspace of the AFM-based manipulator defined by the x, y, z micro-positioning stage needs to be calibrated to the image space acquired by the camera. Indeed, inherent rotations or non-linearities between the camera and the positioning stage axes should be taken into account, otherwise accurate motion of the AFM end-effector with respect to vision is not possible. For the calibrating micromanipulation system, we developed a virtual calibration pattern [BET 04] constructed using the micromanipulator with a subpixel localization in the image space.

8.3.7. 3D reconstruction of the microworld

The aim of the microscope calibration is to allow faithful registration of a 3D real-time reconstruction of an AFM-based micromanipulation. The reconstruction is mainly carried with the images returned from the frontal microscope; the lateral microscope is only used to extract lateral information (Figure 8.6), such as contact detection between the AFM-based micromanipulator and the microsphere or the micromanipulator z-axis calibration. All these data are then merged to obtain a virtual scene.

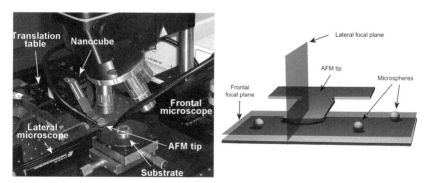

Figure 8.6. (a) Micromanipulation setup and (b) representation of the frontal and lateral focused planes

The required coordinates system transformation between the two microscopes and the virtual scene is defined. As explained above, the small depth-of-field of the microscope implies that the focal plane must be located on the observed object. In the case of the frontal microscope, the focal plane is positioned on the median plane of the manipulated microspheres. However, for the lateral microscope, the focal plane must be on the manipulated microspheres. Once the microscope is calibrated, the lateral microscope is bound with the manipulator. The handled microspheres are therefore always focused on the image plane and the necessary information can be easily extracted.

The homogenous transformation between the coordinates system of the microscopes and the virtual scene is depicted in Figure 8.7. The frames R_{o1} and R_{o2} are the initial objective coordinate systems of the frontal and lateral microscopes, respectively.

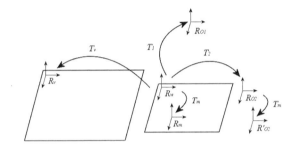

Figure 8.7. *Coordinate system transformation*

R'_{o2} is the coordinate system of the lateral microscope when the manipulator moves, R_w is the global coordinate system in the real microworld, R_v is the coordinate system of the virtual scene and R_m is the coordinate system of the manipulator. The transformations between these coordinate systems are as follows:

– T_1 and T_2 are the transformations between R_w and R_{o1} and between R_w and R_{o2}, respectively. These transformations are returned from calibration and comprise a translation and rotation.

– T_m is the transformation between the frames R_w and R_m. This transformation represents the coordinates of the end-effector of the micromanipulator in R_w during the manipulation. This is the same transformation as that between R_{o2} and R'_{o2} (the lateral microscope is linked with the manipulator via a second manipulator fixed under this microscope).

– T_v is the transformation between R_w and R_v. This transformation is composed of a rotation, a translation and a scaling. During the manipulation, the total transformations ($\mathbf{T}_{tot1}$ and $\mathbf{T}_{tot2}$) between the two microscopes and the virtual scene can therefore be expressed as:

$$\mathbf{T}_{tot1} = \mathbf{T}_v \mathbf{T}_1^{-1}$$
$$\mathbf{T}_{tot2} = \mathbf{T}_v \mathbf{T}_2^{-1} \mathbf{T}_m^{-1}. \tag{8.7}$$

An immersive user interface requires the real-time interaction with the microworld. From the previous acquisition, calibration and processing steps of 2D images, a 3D virtual scene is reconstructed exactly as for a real environment (Figure 8.8). When the spheres are moved to or removed from different locations, a regular update is performed at the image processing frequency. In order to reduce the computational time, we consider that the different impurities are static in the environment. This greatly simplifies and optimizes the 3D representation of the working space.

We choose to represent dust by encapsulated boxes. Experimental results show that faithful representation requires a large amount of computation time. Since we do not know the height of elementary dust, we assigned arbitrary heights. The 3D graphic rendering is based on OPEN-INVENTOR C++ graphic library on Win32 platform. This library provides powerful functions for graphical immersion and software architecture (stereo viewing, hierarchical representation, shadow, multithreading and 3D texture). Once the microworld is reconstructed, we can obtain perspective views of the virtual scene from any viewpoint. Here we used a Pentium IV-2.66 GHz CPU with 512 Mo DDRAM on a Windows 2000 platform.

On the basis of this 3D intermediate representation, we integrate several depth-perception cues (texture, shadow, etc.) to improve the depth perception of the operator. Moreover, the operator is immersed at several levels (full-immersion, semi-immersion, etc.) to give the impression of being physically present in the micro-environment [SEK 05]. The visual immersion allows the operator of the task environment to be brought closer; see Figure 8.8.

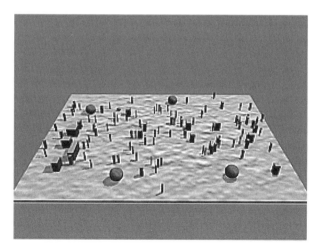

Figure 8.8. *Three-dimensional virtualized scene reconstructed in real time after the calibration step*

Furthermore, we propose several navigation techniques to facilitate the exploration of the micro-environment (gaze direction, scene in hand, camera in hand, etc.) [BOW 09]. These navigation metaphors are adapted to the several operational contexts of the intervention (scene exploration, object manipulation, etc.) [AUG 94]. Finally, the 3D scene also includes several passive assistance metaphors to help the operator during the manipulation (application of transparency to some objects, effect distance electrostatic field, etc.).

8.4. Haptic rendering for intuitive and efficient interaction with the micro-environment

If the visual mode allows the interpretation of an important part of implicated physical phenomena in teleoperation tasks, and thus plays an important role in the control of operator action, the haptic modality equally has an important function. In addition to the other senses, haptic perception through the epistemic and ergotic functions is essential to understand the micro-environment during the exploratory phase and for the regulation of gesture during the micromanipulation.

On the basis of the sensorial modes (kinesthesic, tactile) and haptic modalities (ergotic, epistemic), we classify metaphors into two types:

– Physical-scene-based metaphor: based on the exploitation of a piezoresistive force sensor fixed on the cantilever. This feedback allows the operator, through kinestesic and ergotic functions, to carry out the micromanipulation tasks with a high level of dexterity.

– Virtual-scene-based metaphor: based on the virtual scene. Its objective is to complete the real information provided by the force microsensor by adding synthetic feedback in order to compensate the sensing limitations. Moreover, the virtual feedback can be a support for several virtual fixtures to assist the operator during the micromanipulation tasks.

In the next sections, we develop several proposed haptic rendering feedbacks.

8.4.1. *Haptic-based bilateral teleoperation control*

The proposed micromanipulator structure depicted in Figure 8.9 is composed of three linear translation stages (x, y, z) driven by DC motors for coarse motion (range 25 mm and accuracy 100 nm) combined with a 3-dof ultra-high-resolution piezomanipulator (x, y, z) for fine positioning (range 100 μm and accuracy 1 nm). This hybrid micropositioning system combines the advantages of ultra-low inertia, high speed and the long travel range. The end-effector is constituted by a piezoresistive AFM cantilever integrating a full-bridge strain gauge sensor.

Figure 8.9. *Left: configuration of a 6-dof hybrid micromanipulator (magnetic and piezoelectric actuators) and right: AFM cantilever with piezoresistive force sensor*

To enhance the feeling of immersion, the operator can use a haptic interface (Sensable PHANToM Desktop) with 6-dof positional input and 3-dof force output for force-feedback interaction. Here, the operator is assumed to move smoothly and slowly for undesired instabilities. The operator controls the cantilever contact (x, y, z) position while feeling the normal contact force between the AFM tip and the object. A kinesthetic force feedback (KFF) bilateral controller allows the operator to feel the microforces sensed by the AMF cantilever (see Figure 8.10).

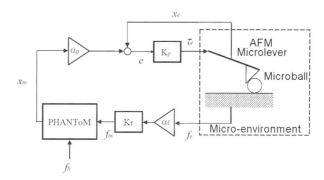

Figure 8.10. *Bilateral controller for kinesthetic force feedback*

The 'ideal' controller response is given as:

$$x_e \rightarrow \alpha_p x_m$$
$$f_m \rightarrow \alpha_f f_e$$

where $\alpha_p > 0$ and $\alpha_f > 0$ are the position and force scaling factors, respectively. The bilateral controller is chosen such that:

$$
\begin{aligned}
f_m &= \alpha_f\, K_f\, f_e \\
\tau_e &= K_p\,(\,\alpha_p\, x_m\, -\, x_e)
\end{aligned}
$$

where K_p and K_f are the position and the force compensation gains, respectively.

8.4.2. *Active operator guidance using potential fields*

During telemicromanipulation tasks, the operator can potentially collide with dust and/or sphere particles which are present in the working space. Adhesive forces such as van der Waals, electrostatic and surface tension have been studied in the area of materials science and physics [ISR 92]. The interaction between an AFM cantilever tip and a micro-object involves a variety of forces such as electrostatic and atomic forces for the non-contact regime and indentation and adhesion and capillary forces for the contact regime.

We propose a motion guidance strategy for microrobotic manipulation tasks to combine vision-based global and repulsive potential fields for path planning. Sensing data is acquired by the virtualized reality-based interface for observing the position and orientation of pushed objects and to haptically guide the AFM-based micromanipulator. To deal with the problem of real-time collision-free path planning, virtual repulsive forces are generated around obstacles from discrete potential fields.

The objective of this type of assistance is to achieve guided motion paths for the AFM tip without touching the obstacles (see Figure 8.11). The potential fields are virtual constraints that are implemented in the master's haptic control interface (PHAMToM stylus). For example, a virtually generated workpath generates virtual resistance to human operators; such resistance ensures the operator functions smoothly in maintaining an optimal and safe path. Potential fields are used because they are a straightforward method of dealing with difficult micro-environments without a complex set of path-planning rules.

8.4.2.1. *Virtual potential fields for global motion*

In our approach the robot is modeled as a particle acting under the combined influence of two major potential fields $U(d)$ defined as:

$$
U(d) = U_{\text{att}}(d) + \sum U_{\text{rep}}(d). \tag{8.8}
$$

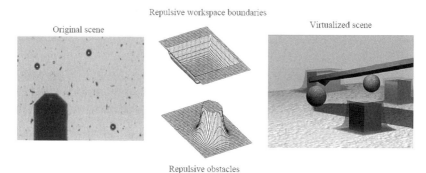

Figure 8.11. *Haptic and VR interfaces for real-time human/planner cooperation using potential fields for micromanipulation: (left) real images from the microscope; (center) integration of repulsive force fields at the boundary of the workspace and microsphere obstacles for guidance of planning microtasks and (right) 3D representation in a virtual environment*

The goal of the first potential field $U_{\mathrm{att}}(d)$ is to attract the robot towards the final state. For that purpose, we assigned to the map a potential field which is defined as a crescent distance function from the final to the current state. The second component $U_{\mathrm{rep}}(d)$ is repulsive with a potential field inversely proportional to the distance from the obstacles. The fields can be modified by changing one or two variables which can make them attractive for on-line modification by a human operator. The corresponding repulsive force is defined as the negative gradient of potential function, expressed as:

$$\overrightarrow{F}(d) = -\nabla U(d) \tag{8.9}$$

where $\nabla U_{\mathrm{global}}$ represents the Laplacian operator.

Potential fields are defined as one of the following classes, depending on their nature and objective.

8.4.2.2. *Potential field as attractive goal*

In order to assist the operator during object pushing motion, attractive potential fields such as:

$$
\begin{aligned}
U_{\mathrm{att}}(d) &= \frac{1}{2}\xi\|d - d_{\mathrm{goal}}\|^2 \\
F_{\mathrm{att}}(d) &= \xi\|d - d_{\mathrm{goal}}\|
\end{aligned}
\tag{8.10}
$$

have been implemented, where d_{goal} is the goal position. As the parabolic function tends to zero at d_{goal}, the AFM-based manipulator becomes closer to the goal configuration. The classical local minima problems associated with these attractive potential fields are avoided by operator manipulation skills during operation.

8.4.2.3. *Potential fields as repulsive forces*

In order to haptically guide the operator gesture during pushing tasks, repulsive potentials are important in order to repel the AFM-based manipulator from a boundary which is not crossed. These repulsive potentials can also be used to constrain the involvement of the human. In order to avoid collisions with other objects and impurities, a repulsive boundary can be used to disallow the human to manoeuver the AFM-based manipulator outside a given workspace. The boundary is represented as an inverted rectangle expressed:

$$U_{\text{boun}}(d) = A_b \frac{C_b(d)}{\exp^{-C_b(d)}} \tag{8.11}$$

where A_b is a scaling factor and $C_b(d)$ is defined:

$$C_b(d) = \left[\left(\frac{x - x_b}{a_b} \right)^{2d} + \left(\frac{b_b}{a_b} \right)^2 \left(\frac{y - y_b}{b_b} \right)^{2d} \right]^{\frac{1}{2d}} - 1 \tag{8.12}$$

where x_b and y_b specify the center of the rectangle. The dimensions a_b and b_b are derived from the width w and depth z of the rectangle, calculated as:

$$a_b = \frac{w}{2} \left(2^{\frac{1}{2d}} \right) \text{ and } b_b = \frac{z}{2} \left(2^{\frac{1}{2d}} \right). \tag{8.13}$$

During telemicromanipulation tasks, the operator can potentially collide with dust and/or sphere particles which are present in the configuration space. Due to the physical interaction properties of the dust (electrostatic force, van der Waals force and adhesive force), attractive forces can greatly disturb the manipulation operations. To deal with the problem of real-time collision-free path planning, virtual repulsive forces are generated around obstacles from discrete potential fields. The expression for this potential field is:

$$U_{\text{obstacle}}(d) = \begin{cases} \frac{1}{2} \eta \left(\frac{1}{d} - \frac{1}{d_0} \right) & \text{if } d \leq d_0 \\ 0 & \text{if } d > d_0 \end{cases} \tag{8.14}$$

where d is the penetration distance, d_0 is a positive constant which represents the action distance of the potential and η is a position scaling factor.

The combination of 2D path planning optimization [AMM 04] and the attractive and repulsive virtual potential fields gives a potential field map (Figure 8.12) for operator haptic guidance during pushing tasks. The idea of this kind of assistance fixture is to achieve guided motion paths of the AFM tip without touching the obstacles. Its role is to prevent the attraction of the AFM tip from the micro-objects under the adhesion forces (van der Waals force, electrostatic force and surface tension

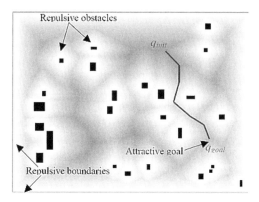

Figure 8.12. *C-space distribution of repulsive and attractive virtual potential fields; a virtual fixture is overlaid on the virtual environment for operator gesture guidance during micromanipulation tasks*

force). This virtual guide appears as an elastic mechanical impedance created at the contact moment between the AFM tip and the geometrical representation of the potential field.

A virtual fixture control mode is then introduced where virtual fixtures are placed in the environment based on the potential field map of the task knowledge. Virtual fixtures represent a task-dependent geometry overlaid on the environment (represented as a virtual line between the AFM-based manipulator tip and its target location for perceptual aid during micromanipulation tasks, as shown in Figure 8.12). It is typically attached to a movable micro-object to guide the AFM-based robot manipulator to the target location.

As a geometrical constraint in the task space configuration manifold (C-Space) the fixture imposes restrictions on the robot movements, therefore ensuring that the AFM-based robotic manipulator does not collide with the micro-object. Although their control properties have not been studied, the virtual fixture can be abstracted as a sliding surface. Here, a point in the C-Space that represents the configuration space of the AMF probe can move (or slide) along the sliding surface towards the goal defined by the attractive potential field defined in equation (8.10). Through interaction using the haptic interface, the operator is able to slide along the surface during pushing-based nanomanipulation towards the goal while feeling the virtual reaction force normal to this surface. The key requirement for application of the virtual fixture is microtask dependency, which has a major influence on its implementation.

8.4.3. *Model-based local motion planning*

During microscale tasks, the human operator should be provided with enough information about the task. When the AFM-based manipulator is closed to the microobject, visible resolution interaction is not accurate and the AFM tip induces visual occlusion of the object. Furthermore, manipulated objects are not stationary during micromanipulation tasks and the process of locating the objects and repositioning the AFM probe is not reversible due to non-linear mechanics. Model-based motion planning strategy in a microscale local region has therefore been coordinated with haptic-based guidance approach in order to attenuate the tremors and abrupt gestures of the operator during approach and/or contact phases.

A potential field surrounds the handled microspheres with a spherical geometry acting as a shock absorber potential field, defined:

$$U_{\text{sphere}}(d) = \begin{cases} \lambda \frac{\delta d}{\delta t} & \text{if } d \le d_0 \\ 0 & \text{if } d > d_0 \end{cases} \tag{8.15}$$

where δ is the partial derivative and λ is a position scaling factor.

Its simple geometry has the advantage of being symmetrical and continuous in 3D space, minimizing the risks of gesture jump.

Interaction forces among the AFM tip, particle and substrate before the tip pushes the particle can be seen in Figures 8.13a and b when the AFM tip is controlled in the z-direction. Based on modeling of interactive forces in an AFM-based robotic manipulation, the results provide insight into the effective compliant motion strategy during interaction with microsized objects. When the AFM tip closely approaches the microsized object, visible resolution of the 3D optical microscope as visual sensor is limited to observe the interaction of an AFM-based nanomanipulator. The user interface gives warning messages as feedback to the operator. At the contact point, the user interface provides force feedback through the haptic interface. The main components of the adhesion forces f_{adh} (van der Waals and adhesive) between an AFM cantilever and microsized object are given in detail in [AMM 04].

8.4.4. *Force feedback stabilization by virtual coupling*

The haptic rendering is based on a PHANToM Desktop interface. The internal operating loop of this interface requires an update frequency of around 1000 Hz. However, the mass-spring-damper (MSD) system update frequency does not exceed 15 Hz. This frequency difference does not ensure coherence between the systems, leading to instabilities of the user haptic rendering.

We have adopted a solution to use a virtual coupling model, defined in [ADA 98]. This approach consists of introducing a virtual passive link between the simulation

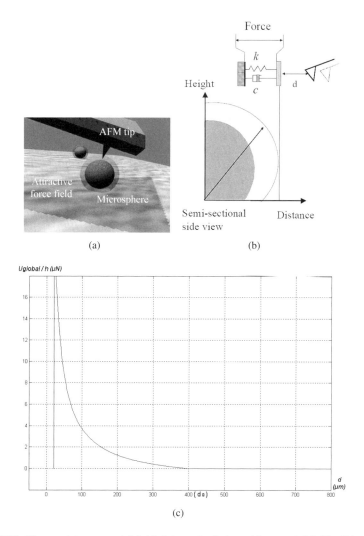

Figure 8.13. *The repulsive potential field: (a) manipulation with potential fields, (b) repulsive potential field representation and (c) repulsive potential field function*

model and the haptic interface in order to ensure the stability and the performance of the system (Figure 8.14a). When we combine the impedance display implementation with an appropriate virtual coupling network, we obtain the admittance matrix for the combined interface.

The linear two-port is said to be absolutely stable if there exists no set of passive terminating one-port impedances for which the system is unstable. Llewellyn's

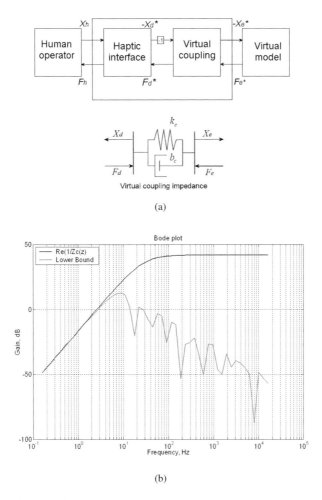

Figure 8.14. *Virtual coupling implementation (see color section)*

stability criteria [LLE 52] provides both necessary and sufficient conditions for absolute stability of linear two-ports. The conditions for absolute stability of the haptic interface are:

$$Re(Z_{\mathrm{di}}(z)) \geq 0, \frac{1}{Z_{\mathrm{cvi}}(z)} \geq 0 \qquad (8.16)$$

and

$$\cos(\angle ZOH(z)) + \frac{2Re(Z_{\mathrm{di}}(z))Re(\frac{1}{Z_{\mathrm{cvi}}(z)})}{|ZOH(z)|} \geq 1, \tag{8.17}$$

where $Z_{\mathrm{cvi}}(z)$ is the virtual coupling impedance (k_c, b_c), $ZOH(z)$ is a zero-order holder and $Z_{\mathrm{di}}(z)$ is the PHANToM impedance. The inequality (8.17) can be rewritten to obtain an explicit expression of absolute stability of the haptic interface:

$$Re\left(\frac{1}{Z_{\mathrm{cvi}}(z)}\right) \geq \frac{1 - \cos(\angle ZOH(z))}{2Re(Z_{\mathrm{di}}(z))}|ZOH(z)|. \tag{8.18}$$

The impedance display of the virtual coupling induces a limit on the maximum impedance which can be rendered. We use equation (8.18) to find the virtual coupling which makes the haptic interface absolutely stable. Using the design of the best performing model, absolutely stabilizing virtual coupling parameters are found such as $b_c = 0.008\,\mathrm{N\,(mm\,s^{-1})^{-1}}$ and $k_c = 2.5\,\mathrm{N\,m^{-1}}$ (as a thin red line). The left-hand side of equation (8.18) with the resulting values is plotted in Figure 8.14 as a bold blue line. We have:

$$\frac{1}{Z_{\mathrm{cvi}}(z)} \geq \frac{1 - \cos(\angle ZOH(z))}{2Re(Z_{\mathrm{di}}(z))}|ZOH(z)|. \tag{8.19}$$

8.5. Evaluating manipulation tasks through multimodal feedback and assistance metaphors

This section presents an experimental investigation carried out on nine people with different levels of expertise (experts, students and technicians). The tasks consist of handling several microspheres according to different micromanipulation strategies: (1) micromanipulation by adhesion (spatial displacement strategy) and (2) micromanipulation by pushing (planar displacement strategy). The manipulated microspheres are made of polystyrene with different diameters (50.0 μm and 20.3 μm). In the experiments, we considered the dust particles deposited on the substrate as potential obstacles that should be avoided during micromanipulation tasks.

8.5.1. Approach phase

A basic micromanipulation task consisting of moving the end-effector from an initial configuration, until contact with a microsphere to be manipulated, was conducted.

The specific task required that the operator pushes the microsphere while applying the smallest possible pushing force in a minimum completion time. We define the time to completion as the time from when the AFM tip enters a fixed zone of radius D centered at the micro-object corresponding to the attractive potential defined in equation (8.10). Practically, we note that the best effect is given at $D = 20\,\mu\text{m}$ since the force feedback is minimized at this point.

Figure 8.15 depicts the velocity of master arm by using several potential field representations. When the operator uses the sound potential field (Figure 8.15a) we observe that, after a short period of acceleration corresponding to the approach phase (effector/potential field), the operator gradually decreases the speed to reach the contact point. Figure 8.15b shows that, in the case of the shock absorber potential field, the speed values are relatively important ($140\,\text{mm s}^{-1}$) compared to sound potential field representation ($50\,\text{mm s}^{-1}$).

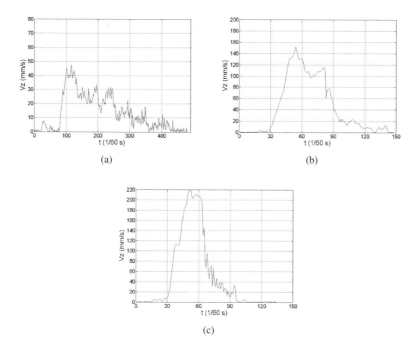

(a)

(b)

(c)

Figure 8.15. *Velocity during micromanipulation: (a) sound potential field, (b) shock absorber potential field and (c) shock absorber potential field with repulsive component*

As we can see in Figure 8.16, the execution time is reduced. When we add a repulsive force to a shock absorber potential field, the results of Figure 8.15b show that there is no influence on the behavior of the operator since the operator motion is strongly damped by the virtual guide. The main difference comes from the level of acceleration and speed values during the first phase of the motion (before the contact with the potential field).

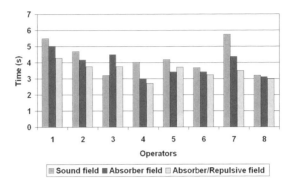

Figure 8.16. *Execution time*

These results underline the importance of the potential field in the regulation of gestures during the critical approach phase (Figure 8.17). The observations clearly show that the coupling between vision and audio feedback are not efficient for the quality (tremor) and performance (execution time) of gestures. The origin of these poor results is that the audio modality only introduces a qualitative perception of distance. The approach operation therefore requires an important cognitive effort for the integration of visual and audio perception. Moreover, the exploitation of the audio modality with a modulation scheme (amplitude, frequency, etc.) induces some stress during the operator manipulation.

The audio feedback is perceived unconsciously as noise. By introducing a shock absorber potential field, the subjects know that the gesture is secured in the close proximity of the target, ensuring a spontaneous gesture without tremor. The viscosity acts as a filtering system during the penetration phase.

Complementary experience shows that the use of auditory feedback reduces the risk of breaking the micro-object since the operator is applying progressively pushing forces. This step-wise motion is similar to 'sample-and-correct motion' that was observed in Fitts' law movement experiments [TOK 96] and Tokashiki microhandling experiments [EME 99]. This indicates that superimposing auditory feedback on visual and force feedback is a good strategy to minimize the strain on the operator when pushing the micro/nanoparticles. The combination of force and sound feedback adds flexibility to the visual feedback system. If a user does not want higher repulsive forces to interfere with the motion of their hand during the approach-retract phenomenon of the AFM tip, they can reduce them up to the sound level.

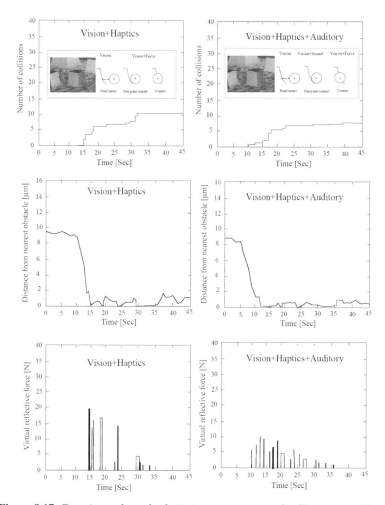

Figure 8.17. *Experimental graphs depicting time versus total collisions, AFM-based manipulator's clearance defining the distance with the obstacle and contact force acting on the micromanipulator: (left) with vision plus haptics and (right) with vision plus haptics plus auditory feedbacks*

8.5.1.1. *Displacement phase*

The objective of this second experiment is to characterize the combination of different manipulation guides in order to find the optimal fixtures to be adopted for micromanipulation tasks using adhesion. We assume that the microsphere is initially adhered to the AFM tip before initiating the displacement task. In this experiment, the operator must simply move the micromanipulator end-effector from its initial configuration to the final configuration by avoiding obstacles located in the microscene.

Figure 8.18a depicts the master's arm trajectory when the operator uses only the visual representation of the potential field. In this case, the operator moves the end-effector by avoiding geometrical contact with the visual representation of the potential field (intuitive visual control). The operator therefore regularly corrects the end-effector position in order to avoid contact with the visual potential fields. When considering potential fields with repulsive force feedback (Figure 8.18c), we note that the operator's gesture is controlled in a precise and direct way with less motion readjustments. The velocity curves shown in Figures 8.18b and Figure 8.18d confirm these initial observations.

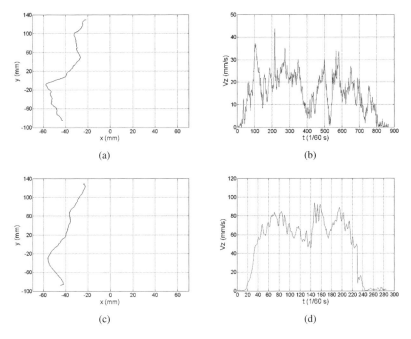

(a)

(b)

(c)

(d)

Figure 8.18. *Master's arm trajectory and velocity with (a), (b) visual potential field and (c), (d) visual and haptic potential fields during the microsphere displacement*

We note also that, in the case of the visual representation, operator motions are relatively slow with frequent acceleration and deceleration phases. On the contrary, haptic feedback greatly improves the operator gesture since they feel less stressed. The velocity achieved in this case is more important: around $v_z \sim 80 \, \mathrm{mm \, s^{-1}}$ compared to $v_z \sim 30 \, \mathrm{mm \, s^{-1}}$ in the previous case.

Finally, Figure 8.19 emphasizes the relatively important gain on the execution time. Figure 8.20 shows the operator trajectories when using the path planning module. A virtual line is drawn between the AFM-based manipulator tip and its intended target for perceptual aid during manual telemicromanipulation tasks. Figure 8.19 represents the trajectory guidance results based on sound feedback. It shows clearly the difficulty encountered by the operator in following the optimal path. Indeed, the operator frequently readjusts the end-effector's position close to the optimal path with respect to different sound modulations (amplitude, frequency and amplitude/frequency).

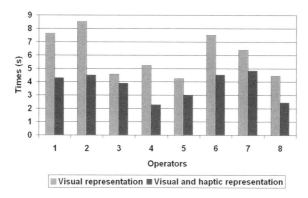

Figure 8.19. *Execution time with the visual and haptic representation of potential fields*

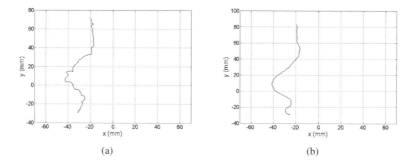

(a)	(b)

Figure 8.20. *Master's arm trajectory with (a) sound and (b) haptic representation of the optimal trajectory*

Trajectories obtained with haptic constraint are smoothed, as can be seen in Figure 8.20b. In the latter case, the operator gesture is being entirely guided by the haptic virtual guide. These haptically-generated paths are generated by the virtual reaction force between master and suggested virtual workpath during human operation. Furthermore, the execution time is less important than the sound mode.

Figure 8.21a compares the mean task completion time with the two representations of the potential field. A single micropushing task was repeated 30 times by six experienced human subjects. We observe that the execution of the micropushing task benefits most from the force feedback when comparing V+F and V feedbacks. Other results show a small improvement of execution time when we introduce the audio modality.

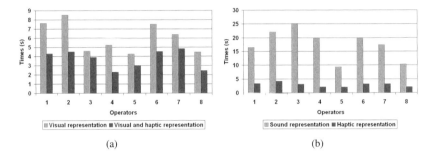

(a)   (b)

Figure 8.21. *Execution time for different configurations: (a) visual and haptic representation of potential fields and (b) sound and haptic representation of the optimal trajectory*

The displacement phase is a complex task, and requires the perception and simultaneous interpretation of several data and constraints. If the visual mode is the most suitable for the integration of spatial information, it presents some limitations in the case of considered context. In fact, the displacement phase involves controlling the gesture to reach the objective destination while avoiding obstacles (dust, other microspheres, ground, etc.).

The operator must take into account the kinematic limitation of the manipulator. The results of the experiment show that human operators cannot simultaneously and efficiently integrate this heterogenous information. Moreover, this information is dispersed in the scene at different locations without an intuitive coherence for the operator and with a possible occultation (effector, obstacles, etc.).

The introduction of the haptic potential field makes the manipulation secure. The gestures of the operator are protected from attraction to obstacles or any possible mistakes. The operator focuses on reaching the final objective. If the manipulated microsphere is too close to obstacles, the potential field applies an adequate force to readjust the movement. The trajectory of the operator gesture shows that the shape of the potential field allows a smooth transition when the operator collides with obstacles.

Other experiments which combine the visual and haptic rendering with audio feedback were carried out. The audio modality was exploited for the sonification in 3D of microword events (friction with ground, contact with potential field, etc.). The results of this experiment shows clearly that the audio feedback completes the perception of the task environment by informing the operator of the different events. The audio modality has the advantage of allowing the localization of the event source by exploiting the intuitive monoauricular audio localization mechanisms. The exploitation of the audio modality to display these events allows the visual and haptic modality to be discharged, considerably reducing the cognitive effort.

Figure 8.20 corresponds to the master's arm trajectory when the operator uses path-planning-based virtual fixtures. This assistance metaphor presents the optimal path to reach the final target by considering several constraints present in the scene (obstacles, kinematic limitations, etc.). The path is displayed through a multimodal representation. The exploitation of the audio modality to complete the visual feedback to help the operator to follow the trajectory presents a trajectory with an important amount of adjustments. The distance from the optimal trajectory is auralized through an amplitude and a frequency modulation.

The observations show that the audio modality is not relevant for a short distance perception. However, we observe that the audio modality plays an important role when the divergence is more important. Another reason for the important amount of adjustments is that the auditory modality is passive modality and cannot produce an active constraint on the operator gesture. The operator adjusts the displacement after a period of interpretation of audio feedback. The exploitation of the haptic modality for this metaphor introduces an active gesture regulation. In fact, the haptic modality allows the perception of distance while applying a constraint to move the master's arm on the right path. The result of this second experiment clearly shows the efficiency of the haptic modality.

Figure 8.21b confirms the developed observations. The mean execution time taken to exploit the auditory modality is too important. The exploitation of the haptic modality significantly reduces the execution time and improves the manipulation comfort. The addition of the audio modality to complete the haptic feedback is not relevant for close estrangement. However, some benefits can be obtained when we utilize an alarm for important estrangement or possible collision with obstacles.

8.6. Conclusion

The teleoperation scheme based on virtual fixtures and metaphors using vision, haptic and aural feedback enables the operator to transfer both motion, vision and human skills at the microscale. The different experiments that have been carried out in this study clearly show the interest of some virtual fixtures for operator guidance and assistance during manual telemicromanipulation tasks. The main advantage is that the operator concentrates only on the useful part of operational gesture, in this way improving the task execution, the execution time and the safety of the micromanipulation task. Furthermore, as the mental effort is reduced it allows an increase in operator endurance and expertise. A selection of the appropriate level of immersion has been proposed depending on the task requirements and the utility of the immersion techniques provided to the operator.

8.7. Bibliography

[ADA 98] ADAMS R., MOREYRA M., HANNAFORD B., "Stability and performance of haptic displays: theory and experiments", *Proceedings of the ASME Winter Annual Meeting Haptics Workshop*, Anaheim, USA, 1998.

[AMM 04] AMMI M., FERREIRA A., "Virtualized reality interfaces for tele-micromanipulation", *IEEE International Conference on Robotics and Automation*, New Orleans LA (USA), April 2004.

[AMM 07] AMMI M., FERREIRA A., "Robotic assisted micromanipulation system using virtual fixtures and metaphors", *IEEE International Conference on Robotics and Automation*, Roma, Italy, p. 454–460, April 2007.

[ARA 00] ARAI F., SUGIYAMA T., LUANGJARMEKORN P., KAWAJI A., FUKUDA T., ITOIGAWA K., MAEDA A., "3D viewpoint selection and bilateral control for bio-micromanipulation", *IEEE International Conference on Robotics and Automation*, San Francisco, CA, p. 947–952, April 2000.

[AUG 94] AUGUSTINE-SU S., FURUTA R., "A specification of 3D manipulations in virtual environments", *Topical Workshop on Virtual Reality Proceedings of the Fourth International Symposium on Measurement and Control in Robotics*, Houston, Texas, p. 64–68, November 1994.

[BET 04] BETTINI A., MARAYONG P., LANG S., OKAMURA A., HAGER G., "Vision-assisted control for manipulation using virtual fixtures", *IEEE Transactions on Robotics*, vol. 20, num. 6, p. 953–956, 2004.

[BOW 09] BOWMAN D., *Navigation in Virtual Environments*, Course: Navigation, University of Virginia, USA, 2009.

[EME 99] EME T., HAUERT P., GOLDBERG K., ZESCH W., SIEGWART R., "Micro-assembly using auditory display of force feedback", *Proceedings SPIE*, Boston, MA, p. 203–210, 1999.

[FAH 02] FAHLBUSCH S., SHIRINOV A., FATIKOW S., "AFM-based micro force sensor and haptic interface for a nanohandling robot", *IEEE/RSJ International Conference on Intelligent Robots and Systems*, Lausanne, Switzerland, p. 1772–1777, October 2002.

[FER 04] FERREIRA A., CASSIER C., HIRAI S., "Automated microassembly system assisted by vision servoing and virtual reality", *IEEE/ASME Transactions on Mechatronics*, vol. 9, num. 2, p. 321–333, 2004.

[FOK 05] FOK, LIU, LI, "Modeling of haptic sensing of nanolithography with an atomic force microscope", *IEEE International Conference on Robotics and Automation*, Barcelona, Spain, April 2005.

[ISR 92] ISRAELACHVILI J., *Intermolecular Forces*, Academic Press, San Diego, 2nd edition, 1992.

[KAW 01] KAWAJI A., ARAI F., FUKUDA, "3D attitude control system for bio-micromanipulation", *International Symposium on Micromechatronics and Human Science*, p. 197–202, 2001.

[KUN 06] KUNCOVA-KALLIO J., KALLIO P., "Lab automation in cultivation of adherent cells", *IEEE Transactions on Automation Science and Engineering*, vol. 3, num. 2, p. 177–186, 2006.

[LI 04] LI G., XI N., YU M., FUNG W., "Development of augmented reality system for AFM-based nanomanipulation", *IEEE/ASME Transactions on Mechatronics*, vol. 9, num. 2, p. 358–365, 2004.

[LI 05] LI G., XI N., CHEN H., POMEROY C., PROKOS M., "Videolized atomic force microscopy for interactive nanomanipulation and nanoassembly", *IEEE Transactions on Nanotechnology*, vol. 4, num. 5, p. 605–615, 2005.

[LIE 02] LIEBLING M., BLU T., CUCHE E., MARQUET P., DEPEURSINGE C., UNSER M., "A novel non-destructive reconstruction method for digital holography microscopy", *IEEE International Conference on Microscopy*, p. 625–628, 2002.

[LLE 52] LLEWELLYN F., "Some fundamental properties of transmission systems", *Proceedings of IRE*, vol. 40, 1952.

[LYN 07] LYNCH N., ONAL C., SCHUSTER E., SITTI M., "A strategy for vision-based controlled pushing of microparticles", *IEEE International Conference on Robotics and Automation*, Roma, Italy, p. 1413–1418, April 2007.

[MAK 01] MAKALIWE J., RIQUICHA A., "Automatic planning of nanoparticle assembly tasks", *IEEE International Symposium on Assembly and Task Planning*, Fukuoka, Japan, p. 288–293, May 2001.

[MAR 05] MARCHI F., URMA D., MARLIÈRE S., FLORENS J., BESANÇON A., CHEVRIER J., LUCIANI A., "Educational tool for nanophysics using multisensory rendering", *WorldHaptics 2005*, Pisa, Italy, March 2005.

[OHB 00] OHBA K., ORTEGA J., TANIE K., RIN G., DANGI R., TAKEI Y., KANEKO T., KAWAHARA N., "Real-time micro environmental observation with virtual reality", *International Conference on Intelligent Robots and Systems*, p. 487–490, 2000.

[SEK 05] SEKULER R., BLAKE R., *Perception*, McGraw-Hill, New York, 2nd edition, 2005.

[SIT 00] SITTI M., HASHIMOTO H., "Two-dimensional fine particle positioning under an optical microscope using a piezoresistive cantilever as a manipulator", *Journal of Micromechatronics*, vol. 1, num. 1, p. 25–48, 2000.

[TOK 96] TOKASHIKI H., AKELLA P., KANEKO K., KOMORIYA K., TANIE K., "Macro-micro teleoperated systems with sensory integration", *IEEE International Conference on Robotics and Automation*, Minneapolis, Minnesota, p. 1687–1693, April 1996.

[VOG 06] VOGL W., MA B., SITTI M., "Augmented reality user interface for an atomic force microscope based nanorobotic system", *IEEE Transactions on Nanotechnology*, vol. 5, num. 4, p. 397–406, 2006.

Chapter 9

Six-dof Teleoperation Platform: Application to Flexible Molecular Docking

Carrying out a molecular docking task with a force feedback with 6-dof requires us to address three major difficulties. Software designed for applications such as pharmaceutical must be adapted. The initial difficulty therefore consists of the protein's conformational change response time, which is not real time. The control scheme therefore risks being unstable. The scale difference between the forces and the displacements of the user's and the molecule's environment, as well as the stiffness of the intermolecular forces, creates a real problem with regard to the interpretation of the forces. Further, the molecular simulator assesses interaction energy; consideration must therefore be given to its conversion into force. The remote operation platform sets up and authorizes a force feedback with 6-dof, taking into account these difficulties. We propose: the reuse of molecular simulation software integrating an energy minimization process calculated from any force field interfaced with a haptic organ providing 6-dof haptic feedback; a wave-variable control scheme capable of attenuating the considerable amplitude of the forces and making communication passive, delayed by the calculation of the protein's conformation change (homothetic coefficients provide the concordance between the physical magnitudes of the two worlds); and a conversion of the interaction energy into the force to be felt. The latter is provided by a parameterized model using the method of least squares to update its parameters. Its analytical derivative provides the interaction forces.

Chapter written by Bruno DAUNAY and Stéphane RÉGNIER.

9.1. Introduction

The first step in the design of new drugs is the study of therapeutic targets responsible for a disease. Generally, these targets are part of a biological entity responsible for the disease such as a virus, a parasite or a bacterium. The targets are mostly proteins. Consequently, proteins are often the chosen targets for the design of a drug. Once the protein responsible for a disease and its 3D structure are identified, e.g. by crystallography, the aim is to inhibit its action.

Proteins may have several binding sites in their native conformation. The drug (ligand) has to be chosen so that its interaction with the target, at specific places, modifies the 3D conformation and therefore its initial function. The conformational change may lead to irreversible inhibition (the protein is chemically destroyed) or to reversible inhibition (the protein is linked with the drug). The binding process inside the protein's binding site is called molecular docking.

It is possible to model the interactions (or bonds) between the ligand candidates and the protein. The bindings depend on the different molecular groups involved. The bonds can be ionic, hydrogenous, van der Waals or a combination of these. The proteins and other organic compounds are stable in their environment. To simulate the conformational change of a protein is equivalent to simulating the geometrical effects induced by a bonding disturbance. The disturbance can be induced, for example, by the ligand's approach. The interaction energies are modeled according to the desired precision using quantum mechanics or models that only aim to minimize the complexity of involved phenomena. The motivation for this simplification is that it decreases the computational time of the molecular simulation. The native state of a protein is energy stable (at a steady state). It is therefore necessary to minimize the total energy introduced to simulate the conformational variation induced by an external interaction.

The wide diversity of proteins and of their physico-chemical properties of simulation leads to a wide diversity of interaction models, each specific to a particular property to simulate. Once the total energy of the system is computed, dedicated algorithms calculate the conformational change. Among them, molecular dynamics explores the space of the possible conformations and the minimization methods optimize the initial conformation for its energy to be minimal.

The docking software identifies the position and the orientation of the ligand, which optimally fits the protein. While the ligand evolves in the binding site, the total energy of the system is minimized to guarantee the stability of the molecular system's energy. Due to the geometric and the chemical description of the protein, the molecules are displayed using a database of ligands that can interact with the binding site of the target. Molecules which do not match the physico-chemical properties necessary for an interaction with the binding site are first deleted from this database. The next step consists of determining, among the remaining molecules, if an attachment with the binding site is possible. If this condition is satisfied, the docking algorithms quantify the attachment affinity according to a cost function.

Most of the algorithms include two components. The first is a technique to search for the optimal position of the ligand in the binding site. The second is a function to quantify each possible binding position in order to classify and compare the different ligands. The candidates are therefore selected according to new criteria such as solubility, dissolution kinetics or toxicity.

The software used only gives visual information of a 3D model of the ligand and the protein. This visualization allows the user to empirically design the geometric structure of ligands that fit the binding site. During the ligand design, the user can improve its geometry by adding or removing atoms.

Such an approach is not totally satisfying. The visual information provided by the computer does not directly render the molecular forces between the ligand and the protein. Empirical modification of the ligand's geometry therefore assumes a strong knowledge of the binding site's attractive or repulsive areas.

This difficulty can be addressed by the use of haptic feedback. By coupling the 3D model of the ligand to a haptic device, the user should feel the interaction forces exercised by the protein and determine if the insertion process of the docking is possible. A 6-dof haptic coupling allows the user to feel the forces and the torques during the process. Once the process is validated, the comparison between the affinity of different candidates and the binding site is possible. The haptic feedback is then an important element in helping the user to define the best geometry.

This emerging approach of interactive systems faces several obstacles. The molecular simulations are not real time because of the complexity related to the calculation of stable conformations. The bilateral coupling is then dealing with instabilities. All the interaction models describe the binding using energy. The optimization method uses the energy as a performance criteria. It is however quite complicated to derive the chosen interaction model to obtain the forces and the torques of the interaction. Finally, the wide diversity of the interaction models and of the optimization methods make the teleoperation platform dependent on the initial choice of the interaction model and of the optimization method.

The chapter is divided into three sections, each dedicated to a specific aspect of the nanoworld and, more specifically, to the molecular simulation and its bilateral coupling with the macroworld.

The energy evaluation is not compatible with real time because of the number of degrees of freedom simulated. Moreover, the instability of the molecular forces is high. Starting from these considerations, the teleoperation platform is presented. It is composed of a first part dedicated to molecular simulation using existing software. The second part is a *Virtuose* (Virtuose 6D35-45 from Haption company, http://www.haption.com), a haptic device able to ensure both force and torque haptic feedback. The initial objective is to achieve a docking between a ligand and a protein without any restriction of the conformations.

Section 9.2 is dedicated to the study of the haptic device using a homothetic force-position coupling. The objective is to identify the difficulties associated with the control of a molecular system. The relation between the haptic device's displacements and the ligand's displacements is realized using a constant coefficient during the teleoperation. In a similar manner, the molecular efforts are expressed in the operator space using a force coefficient determined with respect to the molecular dynamics. The computing time for the molecular simulation is too long to ensure the communication stability between the haptic device and the simulation. Moreover, the interaction forces have a highly variable profile. A new control scheme is therefore envisaged to reduce the stiffness of the van der Waals forces and to ensure the communication is stable.

Section 9.3 takes into account the stability problem described previously. A new control scheme using wave variables is presented. The wave variables are studied in the same way as a spring damper between the molecular simulation and the haptic device in order to minimize the highly variable profile of the forces and the torques. The advantage of such a control scheme consists of its ability to overcome the instability problem generated by the simulations delays. This control scheme, which is new for the considered application, must preserve the teleoperation platform stability and must decrease the high variability of the intermolecular forces. This control scheme will also make it possible to consider haptic metaphors in order to enhance the user's perception.

The conformational simulation of molecular systems is performed using the energy calculated from the force field. The interaction models represented by the molecular mechanics (hybrid methods and force fields) depend on the biochemical properties and the size of the proteins. This diversity could be a drawback if the forces sent back to the haptic device are directly calculated with these methods. In fact, it would be impossible to use another interaction model without changing the control scheme. Moreover, the energy cannot be computed according to the variation of the haptic device's position.

Section 9.4 describes a method to convert energy into force without the need for its derivation. The interaction energy supplied by the simulator is approximated using a model depending on the parameters to be estimated. The analytical derivation of the new model provides the forces and the torques of the ligand–protein interaction. The coupling between the new model and the previously defined wave variables is finally presented.

The conclusion shows that the proposed solutions cannot lead, for instance, to a finalized product. Anticipated future research, such as a thorough investigation of the transparency and the addition of haptic or visual metaphors, suggests that the proposed platform (the term platform refers to the haptic device, the control scheme and the molecular simulator) could achieve its original objectives. The platform can be extended to other applications assuming that they are based on energy. The teleoperation platform, initially created for molecular docking simulations, could therefore also be used for other micro-applications.

9.2. Proposed approach

The objective is to insert the interactive teleoperation platform into the design of the ligand. Once the virtual screening operation is realized, ten or more ligands still remain geometrically optimized. The affinity test of the candidates for the considered receptor has to be possible using the software responsible for the virtual screening. The teleoperation platform then has to be compatible with the existing software. The question concerning the reuse of existing methods for the molecular simulation of the remaining ligands is crucial. These simulations, as well as the software, have their own restrictions but seem to be compatible with the work of pharmaceutical engineers.

This section includes the various elements and restrictions involved in finding a solution for haptic feedback in molecular docking simulations. Section 9.2.1 concerns the modeling and the simulation of the molecular behavior. Section 9.2.2 is focused on the protein flexibility. In fact, a rigid-rigid approach would lead to quick calculation of the interaction. However, the simulated behavior would not reflect reality. That is why a study concerning the use of such flexible simulations is proposed.

Section 9.2.3 deals with the reuse of simulation software. However, this implies that the real-time considerations for the control scheme stability are taken into account. Section 9.2.4 answers the force feedback expectations.

9.2.1. *Molecular modeling and simulation*

Molecular modeling consists of finding positions (conformations) for which the molecular energy is minimum. Many methods are applicable such as quantum mechanics, empirical or hybrid methods. At the molecular scale, the gradients of these energies provide a high complexity for the proportional bilateral coupling scheme. Classical minimization methods can be applied to determine the conformation. The molecular simulation therefore takes into account many classical methods, including long computation time, which are a problem for the control scheme.

The advantages of the empirical (force field) approach are faster computation time and a supervision of the energy terms used in the total energy equation. It is possible to consider large molecules (more than hundred atoms) due to the simplicity of the analytical form of the energy terms and their adaptability. However, molecular mechanics formalism implies that molecular bindings are flexible. It is therefore not possible to model binding breaks. Atoms are defined as spheres with a specific charge calculated from empirical methods. Consequently, it is impossible to model phenomena that include high variations or depend on electronic densities.

However, the molecular simulation has to be in real time to feel the molecular interactions on a haptic device. An acceptable frequency is around 1 kHz or more. Moreover, a ligand–protein interaction does not need the creation nor the destruction of bindings. This approach, although less precise than quantum mechanics, is preferred to guarantee the control stability.

The simulation goal is to reach, at any time-step, the conformation of the lower potential energy for a given position and orientation of the ligand. The energy minimization based on classical optimization methods has to be preferred.

9.2.2. *Flexible ligand and flexible protein*

To predict the interactions between biological entities, most of the docking methods usually consider the proteins as rigid bodies [LEE 04, MEN 92, NAG 02, PAT 86, STO 01, TOM 94, WOL 07]. Atoms are fixed in the global coordinates and there is no conformational changes. These methods are not suitable since they usually fail if the protein has to change its conformation to allow the docking.

Protein flexibility is of prime importance in cellular mechanisms (contrary to rigidity, the flexibility concerns the atoms' ability to change their positions). The protein changes its shape to fit its targets, to make specific interactions, to avoid steric effects or to enhance the surface complementarity allowing hydrogen bonds. The proteins can also change their conformations during enzymatic reactions.

Figure 9.1 illustrates the principle of the flexibility of a ligand. Some atoms are considered to be fixed due to the specificity of the backbone (to conform with reality). When the interaction between the ligand and the protein change the total energy of the two molecules, the position of the atom groups that can rotate around their bond is modified. Here, the atom groups centered on P1 move around the bond P2. P1 is not activated in this case because the resulting total energy would be lower.

Generally, two movements can be distinguished. The first corresponds to large-amplitude movements for which several parts of the protein move related to each other. The second is low-amplitude movements, induced by the protein in its stable conformation.

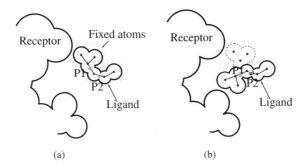

Figure 9.1. *Conformational change of a ligand in contact with a protein binding site (dotted lines represent a set of fixed atoms): (a) ligand in contact with the binding site and (b) conformational change of the protein according to its torsional angles*

Molecular docking simulations have to represent this flexibility for both the ligand and the protein. The molecular dynamics and the minimization process are useful in simulating such a flexibility. The energy minimization method is chosen to simulate the conformational change of the considered system. In fact, the aim is not to compute the whole conformational space of the protein but only to minimize the interaction energy between the ligand and the protein. Molecular dynamics methods do not exactly suit this objective.

The real-time restriction due to the use of a haptic device implies that we should consider an empirical method for the interaction modeling. These models are quicker to compute the conformational changes but less accurate. The interactions will then be modeled using a force field which can be chosen from the existing field.

The teleoperation platform will then include an energy computed using a force field, itself optimized using a minimization process.

Once the interaction modeling has been chosen (a force field) and the optimization method selected (energy minimization), creating software is questionable since many programs are optimized for this application. Because of the wide software diversity, all able to model and simulate the protein behavior, it has been decided to use an existing program known as 'Molecular Operating Environment'. The platform must then be software-independent in order to be usable with any molecular simulator.

9.2.3. *Force feedback*

Because of the relatively low success rates of the docking for fully automated algorithms, including a human operator in the loop would appear to be a solution. It has been shown [BIR 03, OUH 88, OUH 89, PER 07] that haptic feedback can provide additional information to the user in order to understand the interactions between a ligand and a protein. The operator would then be able to feel the repulsive or the attractive areas and define the best geometry of the ligand. The design becomes interactive and each modification of the geometry can be tested on-line for accurate design.

To choose 6-dof haptic feedback (meaning to feel the translations and the rotations) may seem unnecessary for a ligand protein docking. However, several applications need the torques to be felt as depicted in Figure 9.2. It is therefore necessary for our applications for the teleoperation platform to allow the torques to be felt.

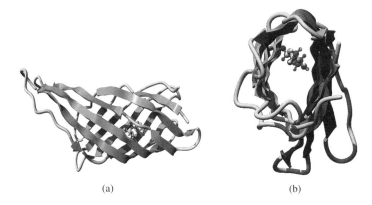

(a)   (b)

Figure 9.2. *The use of the torques is required to study the force feedback of the deformation of a molecule inside a transmembrane channel: (a) glucose molecule inside a transmembrane channel and (b) front view*

Figure 9.2 depicts one of the possible applications requiring 6-dof haptic feedback. In fact, when the protein (glucose) entered the transmembrane channel, it could be interesting to study its mechanical properties and especially its deformation along its major axis. The torques can give additional information.

Due to the need for 6-dof haptic feedback, a specific haptic device called *Virtuose* has been chosen. Provided by Haption company (www.haption.fr; Figure 9.3), it can generate forces of up to 35 N. Its workspace is around $0.90 \times 1\,\mathrm{m}^2$.

Several problems are incurred due to the specificities of this haptic device:

– the computation time induced by the energy evaluation and minimization seems to be too long to guarantee the control scheme stability;

– the molecular interactions are described using a force field and the interaction forces and torques are not easily computable; and

Figure 9.3. *Haptic device Virtuose coupled to the molecular simulator software in a 3D environment: (a) ligand manipulation and (b) Virtuose*

– a molecular docking has to be realized using flexible ligand and flexible protein, increasing the computation time.

The platform has to be independent of the interaction models used. In fact, a conceived platform for a particular force field is dependent on the physicochemical properties that are implemented. The proteins responsible for a disease do not all have the same properties and the tool must be robust against these specificities.

The simulation method does not need to be modified. The conceived platform must be independent of the interaction models and should use several algorithms to minimize the energy.

9.2.4. *Summary*

The molecular docking problem is well defined. The aim is to optimize the position and the orientation of several ligands inside the binding site of a molecule. It is also to optimize the geometry of the candidates in order to optimally fit the expected binding site. The affinity will modify the protein's 3D structure and hence its biological properties. To feel the affinity of several candidates for a binding site can help to choose the best ligand and hence to enhance the drug efficiency.

Previous studies concerning force feedback in molecular docking were based on a molecular dynamics simulator. They usually considered rigid ligand as well as a rigid binding site [SAN 03]. As the problem became more complex and the computational time increased, some approximations were performed such as a low number of atoms to be simulated [NAG 02], precalculation of the forces using 3D grids [BAY 01, LEE 04] and a haptic feedback of only 3-dof [MOR 07, WOL 07], neglecting the importance of the torques for many applications. Finally, no research was conducted in the field of haptic metaphor at a molecular scale. The coefficients governing the transmission are fixed for both the displacements and the forces.

In view of this, we conceived a platform for general applications using existing simulation software (without the need for specific optimization) and 6-dof force feedback. The following section deals with the problems to be overcome for such a general platform. Specific control schemes are studied, taking into account the specificities of the docking such as the delay for the force computation or the high variable profile of the forces and the torques.

The next section is a first description of the coupling of a haptic device to a molecular simulation. It deals with a control scheme for a flexible ligand around a binding site of a protein and draws a parallel between two worlds with different properties.

9.3. Force-position control scheme

The platform, as described previously, is composed of several parts. The first is the haptic device *Virtuose* allowing the forces and the torques to be felt. The second part comprises simulation software called MOE. It is able to model the molecular interactions and simulate the conformational change of the protein to a stable protein. The interactions are modeled using a force field and the potential minimum is reach using minimization techniques. The main drawback of the software is that it is not real time. The third part, the bilateral control scheme of the ligand which ensures the communication between the haptic device and the simulation, deals with the study of this control scheme.

The following section deals with the study of a first homothetic control scheme applied to molecular docking. First, the platform is precisely described. Secondly, the homothetic coefficients are studied as well as their influence on the macro feeling of the molecular interactions. Finally, the conclusion deals with the problems encountered and proposes an evolution for the control scheme to guarantee the stability regarding the simulator delays.

9.3.1. *Ideal control scheme without delays*

An ideal control scheme would reproduce the action of a rigid body between the haptic device displacements and the slave displacements in the virtual scene. However, for stability issues, this virtual coupling is not conceivable. An explanation could be that an infinite gain representing the stiffness of the rigid body could not be set using sampled systems. The virtual coupling corresponds to a spring damper between the measured movement (by the haptic device) and the simulated movement (virtual scene). If the simulation imposes a stiff constraint, the user will only perceive the stiffness of the virtual coupling.

9.3.1.1. *Ligand control*

Let us consider a coupling by only regarding the translations. The control scheme described in Figure 9.4 uses velocities and positions and is described:

$$F = KX + C\dot{X} \text{ such that } F = Z\dot{X} \text{ using impedance} \tag{9.1}$$

where F represents the wrench of the applied forces (Figure 9.4), K is the stiffness of the coupling, C is the damper and X and $\dot{X}$ are the positions and velocities of the master or the slave device in the simulation.

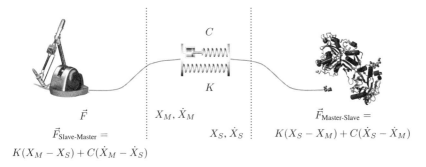

Figure 9.4. *Virtual coupling principle: the ligand is considered as a slave which is servoed through a spring damper by the Virtuose*

X_M is the measured position of the haptic device (the master arm). Likewise, the molecule position X_S is measured.

9.3.1.2. *Principle*

In this case, the controller's input is a position or a velocity which is set as the *Virtuose* output. The user imparts a force to the *Virtuose* which interprets it as a position or a velocity through the use of sensors. This position or velocity is sent to the slave. Then the force is:

$$F_{\text{Master-Slave}} = K(X_S - X_M) + C(\dot{X}_S - \dot{X}_M).$$

This force is sent to the environment which sends back a new position for the slave X_S as well as a new velocity $\dot{X}_S$. The controller then sends a force to the master:

$$F_{\text{Master-Slave}} = K(X_M - X_S) + C(\dot{X}_M - \dot{X}_S).$$

The choice of the gain values K and C depends on the sampling period and the stiffness and weight of the object manipulated by the user in the simulation. These gains guarantee the contact feeling. If they are too low, the user will feel a soft contact. On the contrary, if they are too high the system will be unstable.

Once the force values $F_{\text{Slave-Master}}$ have been calculated, the torques Γ to apply to the motors are obtained using the Jacobian matrix of the haptic device:

$$\Gamma = \mathbf{J}^t F_{\text{Slave-Master}}.$$

9.3.1.3. *Scaling factors*

The *Virtuose* is designed to be manipulated by a human operator in a range of around 100 radians. The applied efforts can be up to 35 N. In return, the size of a molecule's binding site is around 10 Å. The ligand cannot be manipulated for higher displacements. The forces brought into play are in the range of nanoNewtons.

Whatever the control scheme, it is necessary to set scaling factors responsible for the forces and displacement scaling between the operator world and the simulation scene.

According to Figure 9.5, the force coefficient K_f is chosen with respect to the maximum force of the simulation and the maximum force that the operator applies to the haptic device. The position scaling factor K_h is calculated using the ratio between the maximum displacement of the ligand and the maximum displacement of the haptic device.

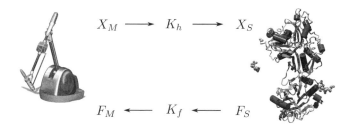

Figure 9.5. *Homothetic control scheme principle*

9.3.2. *Environment*

As for the control scheme, the environments can be divided into two groups:

– an impedance, converting velocities or positions into forces (the ligand is then servoed regarding the position), and

– an admittance, when forces are converted into positions or velocities.

The docking simulation using MOE is an impedance: it uses positions and sends back an interaction force.

9.3.3. *Transparency*

Considering a device which simulates an object's weight, the virtual environment computes this weight and sends the force to the haptic device. The user feels not only the force but also the inertia of the haptic device. The user then handles something heavier than the virtual object. The goal is to counterbalance the additional force. The generalization of this technique is called transparency. It consists of identifying all the haptic device disturbances. The control scheme must compensate for the disturbances to feel only the desired forces.

When the ligand is in contact with its environment, a relation links the force F_h, set by the molecule to the ligand, to the ligand's velocity $\dot{X}_S$:

$$F_h = Z_e \dot{X}_S$$

where Z_e represents the impedance sent by the molecule to the ligand. Likewise, a relation links the force F_M set by the operator to the *Virtuose* and its velocity $\dot{X}_M$ by considering the impedance Z_M:

$$F_M = Z_M \dot{X}_M.$$

The condition for the operator to accurately feel the ligand's interactions with the protein is that the two impedances are identical. By the mean of the homothetic factors,

$$Z_M = -\frac{K_f}{K_h} Z_e.$$

However, the molecule-transmitted impedance to the ligand is difficult to quantify. It is represented by the evaluation of the force field. This can vary according to the protein being simulated. This relation cannot provide an analytic solution for the tuning of the haptic device gains.

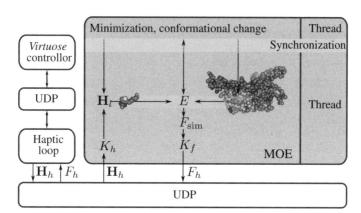

Figure 9.6. *Platform architecture*

9.3.4. *Description of a docking task*

Figure 9.6 depicts a simulation task. The haptic loop obtains the *Virtuose* positions and the orientations expressed as a homogenous matrix $[4 \times 4]$, $\mathbf{H}_h$. The haptic loop sends the information to the molecular simulator using UDP protocol.

The ligand–protein interaction is computed, set into a force suitable for the *Virtuose* and sent to the haptic device. Meanwhile, the minimization process updates the atom positions of both the ligand and the protein. It is an 'asynchronous' control scheme since the ligand's displacement is assumed to be rigid. The minimization process then updates the new atom positions. The forces are computed by considering two rigid entities.

9.3.4.1. *Displacement scaling factor*

$\mathbf{H}_h$ represents a macroscopic displacement. A scaling factor responsible for the correspondence between the haptic device's macroscopic displacements and the ligand's microscopic displacements has to be calculated. $\mathbf{H}_h$ is then expressed in the molecule coordinates and multiplied by a coefficient $\mathbf{K}_H = \{\mathbf{K}_D, \mathbf{K}_R\}$ (equation (9.2)).

$\mathbf{K}_H$ makes it correspond to the translations and the rotations in the two worlds. However, if it is necessary for the translations to be adapted using a coefficient, the rotations are identical in the two worlds. In fact, the low angular variation of the *Virtuose* grip does not require an adaptation from the macroscopic world to the microscopic world. The rotation matrix which characterizes the rotation scaling is set to the identity.

K_D is the matrix containing the translation scaling factors regarding the different axes. All the coefficients are set to the same value for the user convenience. They are set to K_h (Figure 9.5).

K_R is the matrix containing the rotation scaling factors regarding the different axes. They are all set according to the identity $\mathbf{K}_R = \mathbf{I}$.

The result $\mathbf{H}_l$ (concatenation of the rotation $\mathbf{R}_H$ and the translation $\mathbf{X}_H$ of the *Virtuose*), represents the microscopic displacement of the ligand associated with the effector. The teleoperation factors are linear to avoid a non-linearity addition (specific non-linear scaling factors would be more appropriate in order to resolve the damping problem encountered in the haptic feedback and may be included).

Because of the ligand flexibility, the displacement of the ligand is a composition of the haptic device's displacement and the minimization result. The global evolution of the position of the ligand atoms is then described by equation (9.2) while the binding site evolution is modified by the minimization process i.e. equation (9.3):

$$\mathbf{H}_l = \left[\begin{array}{cc} \mathbf{R}_L & \mathbf{X}_L \\ 0 & 1 \end{array} \right] \qquad (9.2)$$

where

$$\begin{cases} \mathbf{X}_L = \mathbf{K}_D\ \mathbf{X}_H\ \mathbf{X}_{\text{Energy}}^{\text{Ligand atoms}} \\ \mathbf{R}_L = \mathbf{K}_R\ \mathbf{R}_H\ \mathbf{R}_{\text{Energy}}^{\text{Ligand atoms}} \end{cases}$$

and

$$\mathbf{H}_{\text{Binding site}} = \mathbf{H}_{\text{Energy}}^{\text{Binding site atoms}}. \qquad (9.3)$$

$\mathbf{H}_{\text{Ligand}}$ and $\mathbf{H}_{\text{Binding site}}$ represent the positions and orientations of the ligand and the binding site in the simulation, $\mathbf{K}_D$ is the displacement factor, $\mathbf{K}_R$ is the rotation factor (set to the identity matrix), $\mathbf{X}_H$ and $\mathbf{R}_H$ are the position and orientation of the *Virtuose* and $\{\mathbf{X}, \mathbf{R}\}_{\text{Energy}}^{\text{Ligand atoms}}$ and $\mathbf{H}_{\text{Energy}}^{\text{Binding site atoms}}$ are the position and the rotation, respectively, representing the conformational modification induced by the energy applied to the ligand and the binding site.

$\mathbf{K}_D$ represents the ratio between the maximum of the *Virtuose* displacement and the desired maximum displacement in the microscopic coordinates.

9.3.4.2. *Force calculation*

Considering sample time and a trajectory along any axis with $\overrightarrow{x_k}$, the force can be computed as:

$$\overrightarrow{F}_{\text{Haptic}}.\overrightarrow{x_k} = \frac{E_i - E_{i-1}}{x_{k_i} - x_{k_{i-1}}} \qquad (9.4)$$

where E_i and x_{k_i} are the evaluated energy at step i and the haptic device displacement (along $\overrightarrow{x_k}$) expressed as the molecule coordinate, respectively. The torques are computed using an angular variation:

$$\overrightarrow{M}_{\text{Haptic}}.\overrightarrow{x_k} = \frac{E_i - E_{i-1}}{\theta_{x_{k_i}} - \theta_{x_{k_{i-1}}}} \tag{9.5}$$

where θ_i represents the device orientation at step i. The wrench to feel is then composed of the forces and the torques computed using equations (9.4) and (9.5).

However, such an approach is open to criticism. Deriving the energy assumes that its value regarding the three-space direction is known. Due to the platform's configuration (which is force-field independent), it is not possible to obtain such values. Only the resulting value containing all the axis information is available. It is then not possible to make the energy correspond to the displacement axes. To use the previous equations (equations (9.4) and (9.5)) leads to the computation of the wrong force/torque, produced by the force field for a given ligand/protein position.

Another drawback of this method is the generated instabilities. In fact, this method is only suitable if the haptic device positions are defined. Yet, when the haptic device is fixed, the variation of position is nil. Equations (9.4) and (9.5) are no longer defined. To solve this problem in a first approximation when the haptic device is fixed, the previous force is applied. Another approach is studied in section 9.4 and is more suitable.

9.3.4.3. *Effort scaling factor*

The computed efforts are set in the molecular coordinates. In order for the forces and torques to be felt, a scaling factor K_f, responsible for the bilateral forces and torques scaling, is applied. It is considered isotropic for the forces and the torques. K_f is defined (here, only in 1D):

$$K_f = \frac{F_h}{F_{\text{sim}}} = \frac{\text{Maximal force/torque admissible on } \textit{Virtuose}}{\text{Maximal force/torque of the simulation}} \tag{9.6}$$

where the maximum force admissible on the *Virtuose* is 5 N and the maximum force of the simulation is pre-determined using a molecular dynamic simulation between the ligand and the protein for the stable configuration.

9.3.5. *Influence of the effort scaling factor*

This section shows that the interaction forces profile is highly variable (for both amplitude and frequency) when manipulating a flexible ligand in a flexible binding site. In fact, during the manipulation, the atom positions vary. The time necessary for the interaction energy and the forces to be computed leads some atoms to collide, resulting in infinite forces being computed.

Figure 9.7 shows the energy variation and the force profile obtained during the manipulation of the biotin inside the flexible streptavidin binding site.

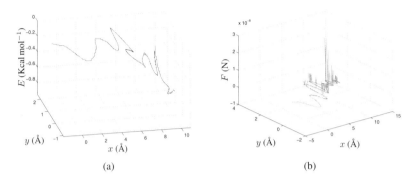

(a)   (b)

Figure 9.7. *Manipulation of the biotin in the binding site of the streptavidin with* **z** *constant: (a) energy computed and (b) force computed (blue curve: force computed along the $\vec{x}$ axis and red curve: force computed along the $\vec{y}$ axis) (see color section)*

The force profile derived from the energy appears to be unstable. While the forces acting on the *Virtuose* $\vec{y}$ axis are greater than the initial expected order, the forces acting on the $\vec{x}$ axis remain of the order 10^{-10} N. The effort scaling coefficient, initially calculated for a maximum force of -3.5×10^{-10} N, makes it difficult to feel such forces where the regions are highly variable. In fact, when the scaling factor is chosen to feel the efforts of the order of 10^{-8} N, forces lower than 10^{-10} N are difficult to interpret. Conversely, to predict an effort with maximum scaling factor of the order of 10^{-10} N would saturate the device motors if a greater effort is calculated.

To preserve the device safety, a cutting force is computed. The forces greater than the desired forces are felt using infinite stiffness simulating a wall. The physical explanation of this process is straightforward. If during the molecular dynamics the interaction forces are in the region of 10^{-10} N, then the moved atoms have an internal constraint preventing them penetrating the van der Waals radius. Theoretically, the simulated ligand position minimizes the energy. During the ligand manipulation and without constraints for the molecule displacements, some van der Waals radius may interpenetrate and produce infinite efforts. In order to guarantee the separation, it is preferable to send an infinite stiffness to the device rather than an infinite effort to the user, which is a source of instability.

The force profile felt during a ligand–protein docking manipulation is depicted in Figure 9.8. The maximum force admissible on *Virtuose* is 5 N. Using molecular dynamics, the maximum estimated force of the biotin–streptavidin interaction is $5 \times$

10^{-10} N. The effort scaling factor is then:

$$K_f = \frac{5}{5 \times 10^{-10}} = 1 \times 10^{10}.$$ (9.7)

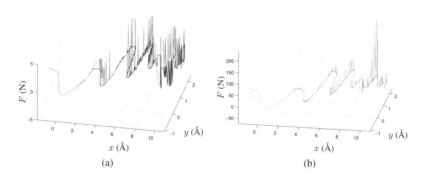

(a)   (b)

Figure 9.8. *Manipulation of the biotin in the binding site of the streptavidin with $\vec{z}$ constant: (a) limitation of the forces to 5 N, (b) without limitation (simulation) (blue curve: component of $\vec{x}$; red curve: component of $\vec{y}$) (see color section)*

Figure 9.8b shows the force profile that is theoretically sent back to the haptic device for such a scaling factor. Without a limitation for the sent efforts, the device would have to apply forces of the order 200 N. Consequently, this limitation is necessary to guarantee the device safety but alters the docking feeling (Figure 9.8a).

The major problem for feeling the forces is not so much the infinite stiffness sent back to the device when a force limitation is detected, but the force profile instability itself. According to Figure 9.8a, once the limited effort is reached the forces tend towards zero. This highly variable force generates an instability for the haptic device. After having applied a high effort, the ligand can be attracted towards a repulsive area, each moving the ligand towards the opposite area. This oscillation cannot be controlled by the user.

9.3.6. Influence of the displacement scaling

9.3.6.1. Low displacement scaling factor

Figure 9.9 depicts the results obtained during a ligand manipulation in a receptor using a low displacement scaling factor. An entire displacement of the *Virtuose* along the $\vec{x}$ axis corresponds to a displacement of 0.001 Å along the same axis in the binding site. The minimization process is activated and the device power is switched off (there is no force feedback).

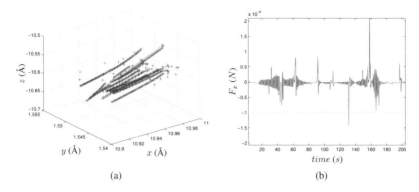

(a)   (b)

Figure 9.9. *Biotin manipulation inside the streptavidin binding site according to a linear position setting: (a) center of mass displacement (blue) during a conformational change (red: initial position) (see color section) and (b) forces computed during a minimization process on $\vec{x}$ (horizontal lines: compare with Figure 9.10b)*

Figure 9.9a relates the flexible ligand's center of mass during a linear position displacement. As long as the interaction energy has no variations, the displacement of the center of mass is linear according to the desired direction (such as a rigid body). When the ligand's displacement reaches $0.03\,\text{Å}$, the interaction energy is modified. The minimization process imposes a new set of coordinates for the ligand. Consequently, the position of the center of mass is modified. Once the conformation is minimized, the ligand is still controlled by the linear displacement. The calculated force profile is depicted in Figure 9.9b.

It is possible to distinguish an oscillation around its equilibrium position, which corresponds to the minimum of energy. This oscillation makes the force profile difficult to interpret without loss of transparency. Although the interaction force is of the order $10^{-8}\,\text{N}$, which corresponds to a force scaling factor without loss of force information, the generated oscillation would make the manipulation unstable.

The objective is to choose the best ligand geometry for the considered binding site. Such an oscillation cannot provide additional information to the operator concerning the best interaction forces generated by different geometries.

9.3.6.2. *High displacement scaling factor*

For a high displacement scaling factor, an entire displacement of the *Virtuose* corresponds to a displacement of $0.1\,\text{Å}$ the force profile has higher amplitudes. The magnitude, represented by the green line ($F_x = 10^{-8}\,\text{N}$), compares the two profiles shown in Figures 9.9b and 9.10b. In fact, a force scaling factor limiting the user feeling to this value would lead to the saturation of the haptic device. Even if the scaling factors make it possible to feel such a force profile, which is the addition of attractive and repulsive forces, it cannot lead to an accurate interpretation of the protein force field.

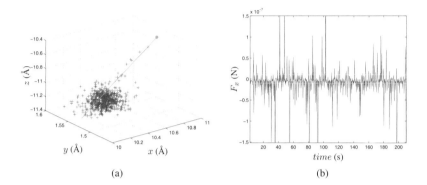

(a)   (b)

Figure 9.10. *Biotin manipulation inside the streptavidin binding site according to a linear position setting: (a) center of mass displacement (blue) during a conformational change (red: initial position) (see color section) and (b) forces computed during the manipulation*

9.3.7. *Summary*

The high amplitude of the forces is due to several factors. The first is the computation time needed by the minimization process and the van der Waals radius calculation. During a manipulation using a high scaling factor, if the user calculates several van der Waals radii to interpenetrate (the minimization process does not have enough time to avoid this configuration), the resulting forces may be high. Consequently, the ligand may be suddenly moved far away and can again interpenetrate other van der Waals radii. Such a configuration cannot be controlled by the user.

A low displacement scaling factor can provide a good force feeling after filtering and addition of viscosity. The main drawback is the delay in completing the desired task. Providing a displacement of 0.001 Å for the entire *Virtuose* is difficult to achieve because of the need for large displacements.

Conversely, a high displacement scaling factor leads to a highly variable force profile. Although this would then be impossible to understand, the docking task is possible.

9.4. Control scheme for high dynamical and delayed systems

The previous section demonstrated several results including the haptic device instability. The computation time needed for the minimization process is high and does not guarantee the exchange of information between the haptic device and the simulation part at a rate of milliseconds. Moreover, the efforts calculated by MOE have high variable amplitudes. These two characteristics make the system unstable.

This section offers solutions to the previous problems. On the one hand, the high amplitude of the efforts have to be decreased in order to prevent the haptic device from oscillating between several positions which have infinite stiffness. On the other hand, the control scheme has to be stable regarding the delays.

Wave variables can be a way to solve the problem. A solution consists of considering the wave variables as a virtual damper between the molecular simulation and the haptic device. Because they act on velocities, the idea is to introduce into the control scheme a damper factor which will decrease the amplitude of the effort.

Although the wave variables guarantee the stability of a delayed communication, they generate coupling stiffness. The transparency is then modified.

The loss of transparency can be a solution to decrease the high amplitude of the efforts. Whatever their variation, a modification of the control scheme transparency then ensures the haptic device considers the contacts as if they were soft contacts. The maximum efforts are no longer felt as hard contacts, ensuring stable manipulation. The results obtained are analyzed and compared to the previous results.

9.4.1. *Wave transformation*

Wave variables are derived from the well-defined scattering parameters. Niemeyer [ADA 98, HAR 07, HAN 03, NIE 91, NIE 96, NIE 04] demonstrates that time delay is a passive element of a control chain if it is considered in the wave domain. If all components of the transmission are passive, as well as the haptic device and the simulation, then the entire process consisting of sending the information by the haptic device, its transformation in the wave domain, its interpretation by the simulator and its feedback become stable and robust whatever the delay.

In the wave domain, including a delay τ (and considering Figure 9.11) the transmission is defined:

$$\begin{aligned}
\mathbf{U}_{\text{Slave}}(t) &= \mathbf{U}_{\text{Master}}(t - \tau) \\
\mathbf{V}_{\text{Master}}(t) &= \mathbf{V}_{\text{Slave}}(t - \tau)
\end{aligned}$$

where $\mathbf{U}$ and $\mathbf{V}$ are the forward and backward waves (six components), respectively.

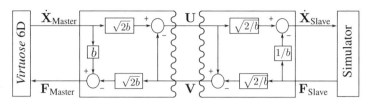

Figure 9.11. *Wave transformation (**U** and **V**) of information (velocity **Ẋ** and wrench **F**) from master to slave in a time-delayed τ transmission; b is a stiffness factor*

In order to interpret the information provided by the wave variables, it is necessary to successively encode and decode the wave. This is carried out by the two bijective expressions (equations (9.8) and (9.9)) for encoding, which imply equations (9.10) and (9.11) are true for decoding:

$$\mathbf{U}_{\text{Master}}(t) \;=\; \left(b\dot{\mathbf{X}}_{\text{Master}}(t) + \mathbf{F}_{\text{Master}}(t)\right)/\sqrt{2b} \tag{9.8}$$

$$\mathbf{V}_{\text{Slave}}(t) \;=\; \left(b\dot{\mathbf{X}}_{\text{Slave}}(t) - \mathbf{F}_{\text{Slave}}(t)\right)/\sqrt{2b} \tag{9.9}$$

$$\dot{\mathbf{X}}_{\text{Slave}}(t) \;=\; \sqrt{2/b}\,\mathbf{U}_{\text{Slave}}(t) - 1/b\mathbf{F}_{\text{Slave}}(t) \tag{9.10}$$

$$\mathbf{F}_{\text{Master}}(t) \;=\; b\dot{\mathbf{X}}_{\text{Master}}(t) - \sqrt{2b}\mathbf{V}_{\text{Master}}(t) \tag{9.11}$$

where the wave impedance b is an arbitrary constant which determines the stiffness of the transmission and $\dot{\mathbf{X}}$, $\mathbf{F}$, $\mathbf{U}$ and $\mathbf{V}$ are the velocity (six components) and wrench (six components) for the forward and backward waves, respectively.

The molecular docking uses the *Virtuose* positions. The first control scheme using wave variables has to send the positions to the simulator. There is no need to modify the simulator, ensuring platform independence.

The major problem to be solved is the high variations of the forces. The idea of sending the haptic device position directly to the simulation and to use the wave variable as a damper is then justified. The decoded wave variable velocity will be used, through a damping factor, to soften the high variations of the forces.

9.4.2. *Virtual damper using wave variables*

Figure 9.12 represents the control scheme using the wave variables as a damper. The haptic device positions and the orientations $\mathbf{X}_v$ are sent to the molecular simulator using UDP protocol. An effort $\mathbf{F}_s$, calculated in the device coordinates using the appropriate scaling factor, is sent back to the device. The damping factor B softens the generated efforts. The efforts to feel are computed by:

$$\mathbf{F}_v = \mathbf{F}_s - B\dot{\mathbf{X}}_v \qquad (9.12)$$

where $\mathbf{F}_v$ is the effort to send to the user using the wave variables.

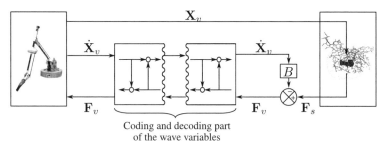

Figure 9.12. *The wave variables used as a virtual damper*

9.4.2.1. *Variable encoding and decoding*

The realized coupling between the *Virtuose* and the molecular simulator is depicted in Figure 9.13. The wave variable definitions are modified to keep the physical meaning:

$$\mathbf{U} = \frac{b\dot{\mathbf{X}}_v - \mathbf{F}_v}{\sqrt{2b}} \qquad (9.13)$$

and

$$\mathbf{V} = \frac{b\dot{\mathbf{X}}_v + \mathbf{F}_v}{\sqrt{2b}}. \qquad (9.14)$$

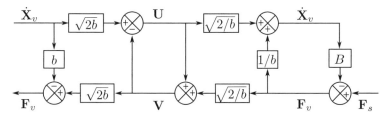

Figure 9.13. *Wave variables encoding and decoding*

Consequently, the admittance loop which encodes the efforts coming from the simulation into an energy and which decodes the energy coming from the device into a velocity, is modified. Starting from this modification, the physical values of the device and the simulation can be encoded or decoded according to Figure 9.13. The returned variable $\mathbf{V}$ can therefore be expressed according to the force to be sent to the *Virtuose*, $\mathbf{F}_v$:

$$\mathbf{V} = \mathbf{U} + \sqrt{\frac{2}{b}}\mathbf{F}_v. \tag{9.15}$$

In order to avoid internal instabilities, the algebraic loop calculating the *Virtuose* velocities from the wave variables is analytically calculated. The *Virtuose* velocity has to be written according to the efforts sent by the simulation. It is necessary to know its encoding into wave variables. The *Virtuose* velocity $\dot{\mathbf{X}}_v$, computed with respect to the force to send back $\mathbf{F}_v = \mathbf{F}_s - B\dot{\mathbf{X}}_v$, is (according to equation (9.13)):

$$\dot{\mathbf{X}}_v = \sqrt{\frac{2}{b}}\mathbf{U} + \frac{\mathbf{F}_v}{b}. \tag{9.16}$$

Substituting for $\mathbf{F}_v$, we have:

$$\dot{\mathbf{X}}_v = \sqrt{\frac{2}{b}}\mathbf{U} + \frac{\mathbf{F}_s}{b} - \frac{B}{b}\dot{\mathbf{X}}_v \tag{9.17}$$

which yields the decoded velocity:

$$\dot{\mathbf{X}}_v = \frac{1}{B+b}\left(\sqrt{2b}\mathbf{U} + \mathbf{F}_s\right). \tag{9.18}$$

The force encoding to send back to the user is defined from the definition of $\mathbf{V}$. According to equation (9.15), the backward wave is then written:

$$\mathbf{V} = \mathbf{U} + \sqrt{\frac{2}{b}}(\mathbf{F}_s - B\dot{\mathbf{X}}_v). \tag{9.19}$$

Substituting the *Virtuose* velocity with the decoded velocity (equation(9.18)), the returned variable is:

$$\mathbf{V} = \mathbf{U} + \sqrt{\frac{2}{b}} - \sqrt{\frac{2}{b}}\frac{B}{b+B}\left(\sqrt{2b}\mathbf{U} + \mathbf{F}_s\right). \tag{9.20}$$

Finally, the variable encoding the simulation effort into an energy is written:

$$\mathbf{V} = \left(1 - \frac{2B}{b+B}\right)\mathbf{U} + \left(\sqrt{\frac{2}{b}} - \sqrt{\frac{2}{b}}\frac{B}{b+B}\right)\mathbf{F}_s. \tag{9.21}$$

The contact stiffness depends on the system's parameters, here represented by b, B and by the delay τ which is between the encoding of $\mathbf{V}$ and its decoding. The wave variables act as a damper between the device and the simulation. [NIE 96] shows that it can be modeled using an equivalent stiffness and inertia for a control scheme without filtering. The delay softens the stiffness of the communication, therefore increasing the inertia. It is important to consider the tuning of b and also to reduce the delay to ensure stability.

9.4.2.2. Results

The results presented here show the influence of the damping factor B on the control scheme stability.

9.4.2.2.1. Low damping factor

Figure 9.14 shows the haptic device response for a null damping factor B and for fixed effort and displacement factors $K_D = 2 \times 10^{-9}$ and $K_f = 5 \times 10^7$. The docking manipulation is performed between the biotin and the streptavidin. The simulation energy is not dissipated; only the factor b is acting.

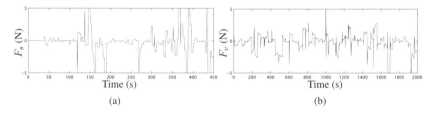

Figure 9.14. *Interaction force between the biotin and the streptavidin on $\vec{x}$: (a) forces sent by the simulation and (b) forces sent to the master*

The low damping, easily shown in Figures 9.14a and b, is due to the stabilization factor b and to the loss of transparency induced by the delay. The docking simulation is possible and the biotin fits the streptavidin receptor. However, the generated force profile to feel is still highly variable (Figure 9.14b). It cannot guarantee easily understood information on the forces acting inside the streptavidin. It is not possible to distinguish the best ligand, i.e. the ligand having the higher affinity.

9.4.2.2.2. High damping factor

By increasing B, the forces sent back to the device look more stable in comparison to the previous results. However, it is important to pay attention to the data of Figure 9.15.

Because of the high value of the damping factor ($B = 50$), the variation of the forces have a low influence on the user feeling. In fact, it is mainly constrained by

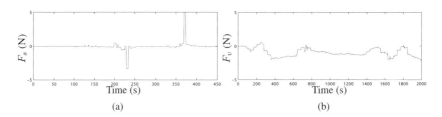

Figure 9.15. *Interaction force between the biotin and the streptavidin on $\vec{x}$ (damping factor $B = 50$, displacement scaling factor $K_D = 2 \times 10^{-9}$ and effort scaling factor $K_f = 5 \times 10^7$): (a) forces sent by the simulation and (b) forces sent to the master*

the induced viscosity. The viscosity constrains the user to set small displacements. The molecular simulator has enough time to compute the interaction energy and the interaction forces, before the van der Waals radii interpenetrate each other. The low displacements then generate the low force variations.

Figures 9.15a and 9.15b seem to show different results. However, a high viscosity prevents the user from making rough movements, restricting the variations of the forces. A high viscosity implies low displacements. The felt efforts correspond to the damping and not actually to the intermolecular forces, however. The forces shown in Figure 9.15b mainly represent the effect of the viscosity.

Due to the addition of viscosity in the control scheme, the molecular docking is possible. The interaction efforts vary little, but the force feeling is not transparent. It is therefore not possible to distinguish the addition of the viscosity and the efforts.

9.4.3. *Wave variables without damping*

The control scheme is modified: the *Virtuose* velocity is sent to the simulation instead of its position.

9.4.3.1. *Molecular simulator*

The molecular simulator presented previously uses the *Virtuose* positions for the display of the ligand and the calculation of the interaction energy. However, the wave variables are based on the velocity. They have to be interpreted by the simulation. The control scheme is modified as depicted in Figure 9.16.

9.4.3.1.1. Velocity integration

The velocity $\dot{\mathbf{X}}_v$ (six components) calculated at the *Virtuose* end-effector is denoted as matrix $\mathbf{T}_v$. It comprises the linear *Virtuose* velocity $\dot{\mathbf{X}}$ and the angular

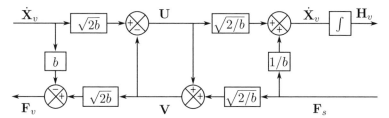

Figure 9.16. *Wave variables control scheme*

velocity Ω, and is defined:

$$\mathbf{T}_v = \begin{bmatrix} \Omega & \dot{\mathbf{X}} \\ 0 & 1 \end{bmatrix}. \tag{9.22}$$

The matrix $[\mathbf{T}_v]$ defines the velocity homogenous matrix. The matrix Ω is antisymmetric and written as $[\Omega]$, defined:

$$[\mathbf{T}_v] = \begin{bmatrix} [\Omega] & \dot{\mathbf{X}} \\ 0 & 1 \end{bmatrix}, \quad \text{with } [\Omega] = \begin{bmatrix} 0 & -\Omega_3 & \Omega_2 \\ \Omega_3 & 0 & -\Omega_1 \\ -\Omega_2 & \Omega_1 & 0 \end{bmatrix} \quad \text{and } \dot{\mathbf{X}} = \begin{bmatrix} \dot{X}_1 \\ \dot{X}_2 \\ \dot{X}_3 \end{bmatrix}. \tag{9.23}$$

$\mathbf{T}_v$ can be written using the position's homogenous matrix $\mathbf{H}_v$ of the *Virtuose* [MUR 94]:

$$[\mathbf{T}_v] \approx \dot{\mathbf{H}}_v\, \mathbf{H}_v^{-1}. \tag{9.24}$$

The discretization of equation (9.24) can be written:

$$[\mathbf{T}_v]\, \mathbf{H}_{v_k} = \frac{1}{t} \left[\mathbf{H}_{v_{k+1}} - \mathbf{H}_{v_k} \right] \tag{9.25}$$

where t represents the sampling period and k the process iteration. The haptic device position at time-step $k+1$ is, according to equation (9.25):

$$\mathbf{H}_{v_{k+1}} = [1 + t[\mathbf{T}_v]]\, \mathbf{H}_{v_k}. \tag{9.26}$$

However, the velocity measurement appears to be noisy; a drift is observed. Moreover, the integration implies drift on the calculated position. During the manipulation, the *Virtuose* has to be re-centered in order to avoid this effect (it can be compared to a mouse for a computer in this case).

9.4.3.1.2. Ligand position

The device end-effector O, calculated on its basis B, is written as $^B\dot{\mathbf{X}}_O$. The ligand velocity L in the graphical display F is written as $^F\dot{\mathbf{X}}_L$.

From equation (9.26), according to the coordinates, it is possible to write:

$$^F\left(\mathbf{H}_{v_{k+1}}\right)_L = \left[\mathbf{1} + t\,^F(\mathbf{T}_v)_L\right]\,^F(\mathbf{H}_{v_k})_L. \tag{9.27}$$

Yet, according to the *Virtuose* velocity, the ligand velocity expressed in the *Virtuose* basis is:

$$^B\mathbf{T}_O =^B \mathbf{N}_F\,^F\dot{\mathbf{X}}_L \tag{9.28}$$

where

$$^B\mathbf{N}_F = \begin{bmatrix} ^B\mathbf{R}_F & ^B[\mathbf{X}]_F\,^B\mathbf{R}_F \\ 0 & ^B\mathbf{R}_F \end{bmatrix}$$

and

$$^B[\mathbf{X}]_F = \begin{bmatrix} 0 & -X_3 & X_2 \\ X_3 & 0 & -X_1 \\ -X_2 & X_1 & 0 \end{bmatrix}.$$

$^B[\mathbf{X}]_F$ is the position of the *Virtuose* coordinates basis, according to the simulation display screen, with components $(\vec{x},\ \vec{y},\ \vec{z})$ defined by $^B[\mathbf{X}]_F = [X_1\ X_2\ X_3]^t$.

Knowing that the *Virtuose* is assumed to be at the center of the display screen (i.e. $^B[\mathbf{X}]_F = \mathbf{0}$), $^B\mathbf{N}_F$ is written as:

$$^B\mathbf{N}_F = \begin{bmatrix} ^B\mathbf{R}_F & \mathbf{0} \\ \mathbf{0} & ^B\mathbf{R}_F \end{bmatrix}. \tag{9.29}$$

The ligand velocity, displayed in the screen, is therefore:

$$^F\dot{\mathbf{X}}_L =^F \mathbf{N}_B\,^B\dot{\mathbf{X}}_O. \tag{9.30}$$

$^F\dot{\mathbf{X}}_L$ is converted into a matrix $^F\mathbf{T}_L$. At time-step $k+1$, the new ligand position is computed (substituting equation (9.30) into equation (9.27)) with knowledge of the initial step:

$$^F(\mathbf{H}_{v_0})_L = \begin{bmatrix} 1 & \mathbf{X}_{cdm} \\ \mathbf{O} & 1 \end{bmatrix} \tag{9.31}$$

where $\mathbf{X}_{cdm}$ is the position of the center of mass written in the display screen. The rigid displacement is then:

$$^F\left(\mathbf{H}_{v_{k+1}}\right)_L = \left[\mathbf{1} + t[^F\mathbf{T}_L]\right]^F(\mathbf{H}_{v_k})_L. \tag{9.32}$$

The setting sent to the simulation is $^{F}\left(\mathbf{H}_{v_{k+1}}\right)_{L}$. However, the ligand is flexible during the simulation. The previous displacement has to be modified using the position's variation induced by the minimization process. Assuming that the simulator computes the matrix of the updated position of the atoms i.e. $^{F}\left(\mathbf{H}_{MOE_{k+1}}\right)_{L}$, the ligand displacement is then:

$$^{F}\left(\mathbf{H}_{Total_{k+1}}\right)_{L} =^{F}\left(\mathbf{H}_{v_{k+1}}\right)_{L} {}^{F}\left(\mathbf{H}_{MOE_{k+1}}\right)_{L}. \tag{9.33}$$

This last matrix is applied to the ligand. The device displacement therefore generates a rigid displacement and the new ligand position is then updated. This method is referred to as asynchronous and applied to the ligand (first the rigid displacement and second the minimized atom displacement).

9.4.3.2. Results

Figure 9.17 shows the master response (Figure 9.17b) regarding the docking simulation excitation (Figure 9.17a).

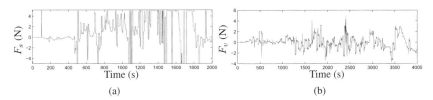

(a)   (b)

Figure 9.17. *Interaction force between the biotin and the streptavidin on $\vec{x}$ (displacement scaling factor $K_D = 1 \times 10^{-9}$ and effort scaling factor $K_f = 5 \times 10^{7}$): (a) forces sent by the simulation and (b) forces sent to the master*

The forces from the simulation which are computed in the user world, through the use of the scaling factor K_f, are saturated at 5 N in order to protect the haptic device (Figure 9.17a). The effort scaling factor does not make the maximum force of the simulation correspond to the maximum force admissible on the haptic device. A better resolution of the forces is obtained during the ligand displacement inside the binding site of the protein. The major drawback is the saturation of the haptic device.

The forces from the simulation are softened. They are mainly due to the equivalent stiffness of the control scheme and depend on the delays. This enables the setting values sent back to the user to be softened.

The main advantage of this method is that it allows additional work on the macro-feeling of the interaction forces. In fact, the efforts sent back to the user are not filtered out due to the viscosity. The felt efforts are equivalent to the computed efforts. It is then possible to discriminate the ligands according to their geometry and thus their affinity. However, additional work on the macro-feeling of the interaction forces are still needed. The simple homothetic scaling factors, computed at the beginning of the simulation, do not allow for low and accurate displacements inside the binding site as well as large displacements to leave the binding site.

The forces sent back to the device through the use of the wave variables do not have the same variations as the forces computed by the simulation. It is then possible to focus the attention on the scaling factors. Their effects are softened if the previous control scheme is considered.

9.4.4. *Summary*

The wave variables make the control scheme stable regarding the delays. The main advantage lies in their transparency properties. This low transparency softens the high variable profile of the interaction forces.

The control scheme investigated first suggests using the wave variables as a virtual damper. This softens the amplitude of the efforts. The obtained result allows for a flexible ligand to fit the binding site of a flexible protein. The interaction forces sent back to the haptic device are proportionaly soft through the use of an adjustable coefficient B. The coefficient value is high; this results in low ligand displacements and stable force feedback. Geometrical distinction for the highest affinity is not possible, however. The docking is possible but felt efforts do not help the user understand the transportation of the ligand inside the binding site.

The second control scheme aims to solve this problem. In fact, it filters and softens the efforts using its characteristic impedance b and communication delays. The settings sent to the haptic device are not altered. The force feeling represents the real interaction between the ligand and the binding site. It is then possible to search for the attractive or repulsive areas. However, the efforts sent to the device are still noisy. A possible solution is to add a low-pass filter to limit the force variations.

The high force amplitudes and high frequencies may be due to their definition. The spatial derivation of the energy is a rough approximation of the efforts, which may lead to instabilities. Another method to convert the energy into efforts has to be studied.

The final approach studied in this chapter proposes modeling the binding site energy in order to provide an analytical solution for the efforts. This model would directly interact with the haptic device, allowing the delay problem to be overcome.

The approach consists of creating a new energy model depending on the position and the orientation of the device in order to derive the interaction energy. This field will interact with the haptic device and with the simulator. It will guarantee a real-time answer. This new model provides a force-field-independent platform.

9.5. From energy description of a force field to force feeling

9.5.1. *Introduction*

As described in section 9.3.4.2, the forces and torques calculated from the interaction energy are a spatial derivation of the haptic device position.

Deriving the energy relative to the variation of the position or the angle variation of the haptic device is not a good way to obtain the interaction wrench. The results are not the exact wrench of the interaction efforts because of numerical divergences.

The force profile obtained using this method is depicted in Figure 9.18. This force profile cannot be clearly interpreted by the user. In other words, the affinity difference between two ligands for the same binding site cannot be determined. The need for a smooth and correct force profile means a different method must be adopted. Given that energies depending on specific directions cannot be calculated from classical molecular simulators, we decided to calculate an energy field in which each term provides an analytical solution for the relevant forces and torques. First, an energy model is predetermined. Its parameters have to be estimated to ensure convergence between the model and the molecule energy field. Second, the wrench interaction is determined using a derivation of this analytical model. These two points are discussed in the following.

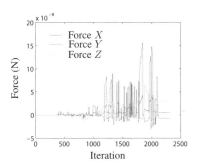

Figure 9.18. *Force profile around the minimized ligand position along the x, y and z axes using the simple derivation method*

9.5.2. *Energy modeling of the interaction*

To build an energy model depending on parameters to be identified, from which the derivation has no singularity, appears to be a solution to easily convert the energy provided by the minimization process into a wrench. The predetermined energy model is compared to the interaction energy to ensure its convergence. At the equilibrium position, the energy field has no large variations for a specific protein conformation, ensuring good convergence for the model. Energy barriers are filtered out due to the latence of the model convergence. If they do occur, they are no longer felt by the user.

Our method involves approaching the energy calculated by the minimization process (E^{meas}) using potential-containing terms ($\widehat{E}(\mathbf{p}, \mathbf{R}, \theta)$), each of which depend on the parameters to be estimated and represented here by θ. The potential gradient at each of the ligand position $\mathbf{p}$ and orientation $\mathbf{R}$ is equal to the interaction forces and torques ($\mathbf{F}(\mathbf{p}, \mathbf{R})$):

$$\forall (\mathbf{p}, \mathbf{R}) \; \nabla_{(\mathbf{p}, \mathbf{R})} \widehat{E}(\mathbf{p}, \mathbf{R}, \theta) = \mathbf{F}(\mathbf{p}, \mathbf{R}).$$

This new potential has to be compared to the interaction energy using a root-mean-square method to determine its parameters at each of the positions and orientations of the ligand.

As shown in Figure 9.19, the interaction energy field looks like a polynomial function (quadratic function). The shape of the function to be estimated must approximate the polynomial function in order to ensure the algorithm's convergence. A comparison with a quadratic function is made, validating the choice of quadratic terms for the predicted energy.

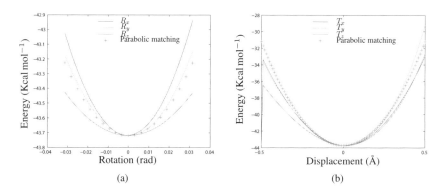

Figure 9.19. *Energy field evaluation between the ligand (biotin) in the minimized streptavidin complex: (a) rotation of the ligand around its equilibrium position and (b) translation of the ligand around its equilibrium position (see color section)*

Let us consider the function described by equation (9.34) as a potential to be evaluated. Let i be the current object frame and e the equilibrium frame. We then have:

$$\widehat{E}_i(\mathbf{p}, \mathbf{R}, k_t, \mathbf{p}_e, g_0, \mathbf{R}_e) = \frac{1}{2}k_t||^i\mathbf{p} - ^i\mathbf{p}_e||^2 - g_0\mathrm{tr}(^i\mathbf{R}^T\mathbf{R}_e) + c \qquad (9.34)$$

where $\mathbf{p}$ is the position of the ligand center of mass (haptic device position), $\mathbf{R}$ the haptic device rotation and k_t and g_0 are arbitrarily set as spring constants. The latter are chosen as a diagonal matrix in order to provide different gains according to the displacement direction; translations (Figure 9.19b) and rotations (Figure 9.19a) have different values according to the displacement axes. $\mathbf{p}_e$ and $\mathbf{R}_e$ are the equilibrium position and orientation of the estimated potential and c is a positive constant to be estimated (initially set to zero).

The function has two terms (considering a null constant); their derivation is used to find the forces and the torques. The estimated potential parameters are found by solving the problem:

$$\min_\theta \sum ||E^{\mathrm{meas}} - \widehat{E}(\mathbf{p}, \mathbf{R}, \theta)||^2 = \varepsilon^2 \to 0 \qquad (9.35)$$

where θ represents the parameter set $(k_t, \mathbf{p}_e, g_0, \mathbf{R}_e)$, E^{meas} is the interaction energy provided by the minimization process, $\widehat{E}(\mathbf{p}, \mathbf{R}, \theta)$ is the estimated energy calculated using equation (9.34) and ε is the quadratic error between the estimation and the measure.

Since $\widehat{E}(\mathbf{p}, \mathbf{R}, \theta)$ does not depend linearly on its parameters, equation (9.35) has to be linearized i.e.

$$E_{i+1}^{\mathrm{meas}}(\mathbf{p}, \mathbf{R}) = \widehat{E}_{i+1}(\mathbf{p}, \mathbf{R}, \theta) + \frac{\partial E_{i+1}(\mathbf{p}, \mathbf{R}, \theta)}{\partial\theta}\delta\theta \qquad (9.36)$$

where i represents the step number. The measured potential can then be expanded in order to evaluate the estimated gradient of the potential with regard to its parameters θ:

$$\begin{aligned}
E_{i+1} =\ & \widehat{E}_{i+1} + \frac{1}{2}||^{i+1}\mathbf{p} - ^{i+1}\mathbf{p}_e||^2\delta k_t - k_t(^{i+1}\mathbf{p} - ^{i+1}\mathbf{p}_e)^T\delta\mathbf{p}_e \\
& - \ \mathrm{tr}\,(^{i+1}\mathbf{R}^T\mathbf{R}_e)\,\delta g_0 + 2g_0\left[as\,(^{i+1}\mathbf{R}^T\mathbf{R}_e)^{V\,T}\right]\delta\theta_e
\end{aligned}$$

where $as\,(^{i+1}\mathbf{R}^T\mathbf{R}_e)^V$ is the antisymmetric part of the equilibrium rotation matrix, written as a vector. The predicted gradient is then written:

$$\begin{aligned}
\nabla_\theta\widehat{E}_{i+1} =\ & \Big[\ +\frac{1}{2}||^{i+1}\mathbf{p} - ^{i+1}\mathbf{p}_e||^2, -k_t(^{i+1}\mathbf{p} - ^{i+1}\mathbf{p}_e)^T, \\
& -\ \mathrm{tr}\,(^{i+1}\mathbf{R}^T\mathbf{R}_e), +2g_0\left[as\,(^{i+1}\mathbf{R}^T\mathbf{R}_e)^{V\,T}\right]\ \Big].
\end{aligned} \qquad (9.37)$$

By taking equation (9.37) into consideration, equation (9.36) can then be rewritten as:

$$
\begin{bmatrix}
\nabla_\theta \widehat{E}(i, p(i), \theta(i-1)) \\
\nabla_\theta \widehat{E}(i-1, p(i-1), \theta(i-2)) \\
\vdots \\
\nabla_\theta \widehat{E}(i-m, p(i-m), \theta(i-m-1))
\end{bmatrix}
\begin{bmatrix}
\delta k_t \\
\delta \mathbf{p}_e \\
\delta g_0 \\
\delta \mathbf{R}_e
\end{bmatrix}
=
$$

$$
\begin{bmatrix}
E^m(i, p(i)) - \widehat{E}(i, p(i), \theta(i-1)) \\
E^m(i-1, p(i-1)) - \widehat{E}(i-1, p(i-1), \theta(k-2)) \\
\vdots \\
E^m(i-m, p(i-m)) - \widehat{E}(i-m, p(i-m), \theta(i-m-1))
\end{bmatrix}.
\tag{9.38}
$$

Each parameter can be updated from equations (9.38) and (9.39), using a recursive or not, weighted or not, root-mean square method:

$$
\theta(i+1) = \theta(i) + \delta\theta/G.
\tag{9.39}
$$

That is to say,

$$
\begin{cases}
k_t(i+1) & = & k_t(i) + \delta k_t/G \\
p_e(i+1) & = & p_e(i) + \delta p_e/G \\
g_0(i+1) & = & g_0(i) + \delta g_0/G \\
R_e(i+1) & = & R_e(i)\exp^{[\delta \mathbf{R}_e/G]}.
\end{cases}
\tag{9.40}
$$

G is a positive constant responsible for the algorithm convergence speed. If the protein–ligand binding energy landscape is rough (large user displacement), a high value for G only enables the operator to feel a low-energy approximation. This provides smooth haptic feedback, whereas a low value will lead to unstable and non-comprehensive feedback representing the exact rough profile. G is an on-line adaptive factor that can limit the unstable effects during a docking operation. The operator's perception does not reflect the reality; rather, it shows a trend and is one of the major points of the method.

The larger the size of the matrix of the predicted gradient, the more precise the estimation of the parameters. However, the calculation time needed for the inversion of the matrix will also be greater. The size of the matrix will then have to be a compromise between the short computational time needed for real-time haptic feedback and the precision of the model. These approximations will depend on the computer used.

9.5.2.1. *Limits*

This last step (equation (9.40)) provides updated values for the approximated energy to be obtained. This estimation should provide a close representation of the energy field provided that the shape of the estimator is not too remote from the measured field.

The algorithm also depends on the initial conditions and on the excitation type. For initial conditions that are very remote from the solution, the algorithm will take a long time to converge. An estimation of the solution could be a good way of ensuring the convergence, knowing that the forces are calculated from the estimation. This implies ensuring the convergence at each time-step.

The estimated gradient matrix shape is important, as updated parameters are provided by its inverse. A guarantee of its existence is that there are no linear combinations of the lines. In other words, if the ligand is fixed (the haptic device is consequently fixed), the matrix will be singular. During the ligand manipulation, if such a case appears, the ligand has to be moved around its current position to prevent the estimated gradient from being uninvertible. This is automatically done (in the background) when the ligand is fixed to prevent altering the user perception.

9.5.2.2. *Application*

In order to feel the docking forces, the force-field first has to be approximated. The operator will then interact with the approximated model, which is updated at each time-step.

Figure 9.20 depicts the approximate force fields in a minimized streptavidin complex; Figure 9.21 depicts the graphical representation of this simulation. The interaction energy has to be approximated using a polynomial function. Graphically, the interaction surface can be represented by the yellow sphere and the orientation of the half sphere. The forces felt then correspond to the distance between the real haptic device position and the yellow sphere, and the torques correspond to the orientation difference between the haptic device rotation and the half sphere (in an approximate way). For each ligand manipulation, all the parameters of the model are updated to obtain the potential minimum position and its orientation, knowing that forces and torques are obtained for these parameters.

9.5.3. *The interaction wrench calculation*

Once the interaction energy is predicted, its gradient is used to calculate the forces. The new gradient is obtained not from the parameters but from the position and the orientation of the haptic device. Unlike the direct derivation, the forces obtained are defined whatever the haptic device displacement. They are computed from the energy

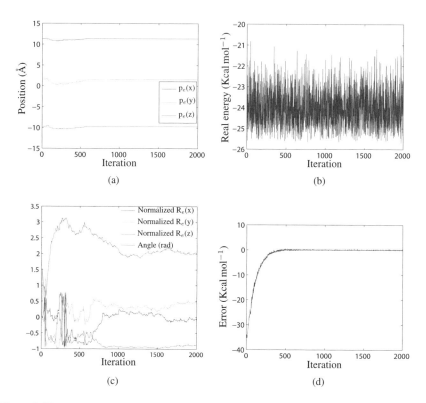

Figure 9.20. *Approximation of the force field in a minimized streptavidin complex: (a) position of the potential minimum; (b) measured interaction energy; (c) orientation of the potential minimum; and (d) estimation error (see color section)*

model considering its derivation regarding the position $\mathbf{p}$ and the rotation $\mathbf{R}$ of the haptic device. The wrench is calculated at the center of mass of the protein:

$$\mathbf{F} = \left[k_t(\mathbf{p} - \mathbf{p}_e), 2g_0 \left(as(\mathbf{R}^T\mathbf{R}_e)^{VT} \right) \right].$$

Figure 9.22 shows the forces and torques obtained during a ligand manipulation inside the binding site using the wave variable coupling. The ligand is turned around within its equilibrium position, resulting in the torques being felt.

Figure 9.22a represents the profile of the forces obtained from the derivation of the real energy. The amplitude of the forces seems very high. This result has to be compared to Figure 9.22b. In fact, this last graph plots the forces we obtained after having approximated the energy. It is clear that, because of the small variation in the parameter set, the force profile looks smoother and is therefore haptically comprehensive. The torques are shown in Figure 9.22c.

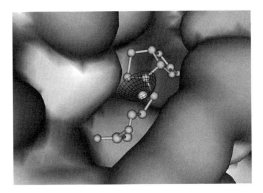

Figure 9.21. *Graphical interpretation of Figure 9.20. The yellow sphere represents the predicted interaction potential minimum (Figure 9.20a), represented by the colored surfaces. The potential orientation is determined by the orientation of the half sphere (Figure 9.20b) (see color section)*

Interestingly, unlike the results obtained with direct energy derivation, the results here show that the forces inside the active site seem to vary very little. The forces inside the active site are well depicted and do not seem to have the same profile as those obtained from the derivation of the real energy. The results are also due to the stability of the control scheme with regard to the delayed response and the chosen communication transparency (dictated by the choice of b). This makes it possible to establish a parallel between the microworld and the macroworld.

Additionally, these results make it possible to perform further research on the issue of force factor, in contrast to the first method in which the forces are unstable.

9.5.4. *Summary*

This section has shown that it is not easy to convert the energy into forces. We have proposed modeling the energy of the binding site locally using a function depending on parameters to be estimated. Using the root-mean-square method, the estimated parameters allow the energy model to approach the real binding site energy profile. This modeled energy, for which the shape is predetermined, provides an analytical solution for the forces. The method is proved to be convergent if the model matrices are well conditioned.

The local model of the energy has the advantage to be force-field independent. In fact, only the energy provided by the simulator is used for the calculation of the estimation parameters. The shape of the energy model has to be close to the energy to model. A shape that is far from the binding site energy will make the process diverge. The shape of the energy model also has to be determined according to an estimation of

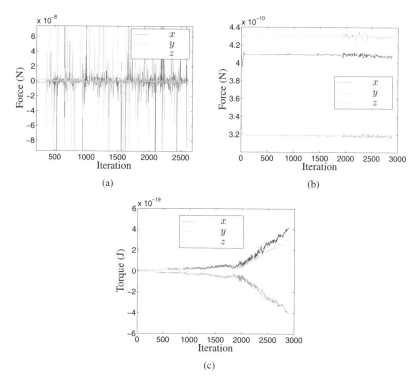

Figure 9.22. *Forces and torques during a ligand rotation inside the active site: (a) forces calculated considering the derivation of the real energy, (b) forces obtained after approximating the energy field and (c) torques calculated after approximating the energy field (see color section)*

the shape of the binding site energy. A solution could be to use a general form using the power as a parameter to estimate. This highly non-linear shape will introduce a divergence problem which will need more attention, however.

The choice of a root-mean-square method as an optimization process was due to its simplicity and its resolution. However, it is only suitable for real-time processes if only a few parameters have to be estimated. Recursive root-mean-square method would be the best compromise.

Due to this interaction model, the docking can be considered. The energies used for the minimization of molecular systems are approximated using a model which provides an analytical solution for the forces to be felt. The optimization algorithm has to provide a quick estimation to guarantee the stability of the control scheme. The main advantage is that, by the mean of a forgotten factor or by the modification of the size of the predicted gradient matrix, the high variations of the forces are filtered out. The manipulation then looks stable.

The presented method was implemented using MOE and a wave variable control scheme without a damping factor. The efforts are felt according to the translation and the rotation of the *Virtuose* (Figure 9.23). The force profile is stable and the bilateral control scheme ensures the scaling of the physical values between the user world and the molecular world.

Figure 9.23. *Manipulation of the biotin around the binding site of the streptavidin*

9.6. Conclusion

To deal with the force feedback problem in molecular simulations, a teleoperation platform has been proposed. The objective is to manipulate a ligand inside a protein binding site according to 6-dof. Several problems appeared:

1) A lot of protein simulators exist and many models can determine the shape of the molecular system. It is therefore important for the platform to be software and force-field independent.

2) To use an existing software program implies considering its properties. To be specific, the considered software is not real time and the conformational search requires a long computation time. The control scheme has to overcome this problem.

3) Interactions are described using energy. This energy is minimized to produce the protein's conformational changes. It is therefore hard to directly derive the energy to compute the interaction forces. The energy contribution along each displacement axis is not known. A method had to be created to ensure the conversion of the energy into forces.

4) The force profile is highly and suddenly variable. This is firstly because of the non-linear forces and secondly because of the conformational change during the docking. The control scheme had to consider this property in order to provide forces

which could be easily understood by the user. Also, the scaling factors had to be well defined.

To solve these problems, several methods have been proposed.

The displacement and effort scaling factors, determined at the beginning of the simulation, are set to the control scheme. The first is determined arbitrarily and the second by using molecular dynamics. The amplitude and the variations of the efforts are amplified since the molecular system is flexible. The highly variable profile is softened using wave variables which have firstly been used as a virtual damper. The decoded velocity is multiplied by an adjustable damping coefficient and added to the force sent back by the simulation. Even if the control scheme allows the force instability to be softened, its main drawback is that it is not possible for the user to make the difference between the viscosity and the forces.

The wave variables were then used as a communication channel between the simulator and the device. The forces sent back to the haptic device are softened due to the loss of transparency. In fact, the communication stiffness mostly depends on the delays. The contacts are soft and the forces are understandable, however. There are no haptic device oscillations between positions which have infinite stiffness. The control scheme is therefore stable regarding the delays.

The specificity of the force-field and the wide variety of optimization methods imply that the platform must not be specific to a particular system. Moreover, the interactions are described using energy. The interaction forces have to be computed from this energy without any knowledge of its influence along the displacement axis. The idea is to use a model of the binding site energy. The shape is predetermined and allows the forces and the torques to be analytically computed. This is a guarantee that the platform is independent of the force-field used. The energy model depends on parameters to be estimated, which are modified by the computed binding site energy. The haptic device is coupled to the model and gives real-time information while its parameters are updated separately. This process avoids the need for the molecular simulator to be optimized. The force profile looks smoother, leading to the possibility for additional work on the macro-feeling of the molecular forces.

The work presented in this chapter is a first step towards the haptic-based molecular simulation world. In fact, this application offers specificities that are not always compatible with the haptic feedback systems. It is therefore possible to feel the forces and the torques of a docking simulation using a haptic device. To discriminate the ligands' affinity to a binding site is still a difficult problem. The loss of transparency and the high protein flexibility alter the user's perception. The next step consists of adapting the scaling factors to the dedicated task. Non-linear adjustable scaling factors must replace the constant factors to ensure little displacements inside the receptor and large displacements outside.

In order for the platform to be useful, additional work is needed:

– If the parallel between the nanoworld and the macroworld is realized using a homothetic control scheme, it is necessary to add haptic metaphors for the user to really understand the binding site energy. This is still an open problem. The loss of transparency is not necessarily a drawback if it can enhance the user's perception. In fact, there is no need to feel the entire profile. The high stiffness of the forces can therefore be modeled using a stable function near the contacts (e.g. van der Waals forces). The addition of visual metaphors and of augmented reality tools can increase the user's perception.

– The teleoperation platform uses a haptic device called *Virtuose* which has not been conceived for micro-applications. Additional work on the dedicated tools is needed. The devices have to be conceived for the molecular specificities, i.e. a permanent conformational change and small sizes. Attention has to be paid to the inertia and the stiffness of these devices which must be minimized.

– The scaling factors are constant and predetermined. The task is then predetermined since it is not possible to provide a high resolution of forces implicated in large displacements. Non-linear scaling factors are a solution to make the force feedback independent of the task.

This platform can be useful for other energy-based applications for two reasons. The first is that it uses a predetermined function to model the binding site and the parameters are estimated. The second is that the forces and the torques are analytically computed. Every system that uses energy to describe the interactions can therefore be integrated to the platform. For example, it is then possible to feel the interaction between two DNA strands. The haptic system can characterize any biological entity assuming that they are described using energy. It is now possible to quickly explore molecular or microscopic environments.

9.7. Bibliography

[ADA 98] ADAMS R., HANNAFORD B., "A two-port framework for the design of unconditionally stable haptic interfaces", *IEEE/RSJ International Conference on Intelligent Robots and Systems*, p. 1254–1259, 1998.

[BAY 01] BAYAZIT O. B., SONG G., AMATO N. M., "Ligand binding with OBPRM and user input", *International Conference on Robotic and Automation*, p. 954–959, 2001.

[BIR 03] BIRMANN S., WRIGGERS W., "Interactive fitting augmented by force-feedback and virtual reality", *Journal of Structural Biology*, vol. 144, p. 123–131, 2003.

[HAN 03] HANNAFORD B., HIRZINGER G., PREUSCH C., RYU J., "Time domain passivity control with reference energy behavior", *IEEE/RSJ International Conference on Intelligent Robots and Systems*, p. 2932–2937, 2003.

[HAR 07] HART J. S., NIEMEYER G., "Design guidelines for wave variable controllers in time delayed telerobotics", *Second Joint EuroHaptics Conference and Symposium on Haptic Interfaces for Virtual Environment and Teleoperator Systems (WHC'07)*, p. 182–187, 2007.

[LEE 04] LEE Y. G., LYONS K. W., "Smoothing haptic interaction using molecular force calculations", *Computer-aided Design*, vol. 36, p. 75–90, 2004.

[MEN 92] MENG E. C., SHOICHET B. K., KUNTZ I. D., "Automated docking with grid-based energy calculation", *Journal of Computational Chemistry*, vol. 13, num. 4, p. 505–524, 1992.

[MOR 07] MORIN S., REDON S., "A force-feedback algorithm for adaptive articulated-body dynamics simulation", *International Conference on Robotics and Automation*, p. 3245–3250, 2007.

[MUR 94] MURRAY R. M., LI Z., SASTRY S. S., *A Mathematical Introduction to Robotic Manipulation*, CRC Press, 1994.

[NAG 02] NAGATA H., MIZUSHIMA H., TANAKA H., "Concept and prototype of protein-ligand docking simulator with force feedback technology", *Bioinformatics*, vol. 18, p. 140–146, 2002.

[NIE 91] NIEMEYER G., SLOTINE J. J. E., "Stable adaptive teleoperation", *IEEE Journal of Oceanic Engineering*, vol. 16, p. 152–162, 1991.

[NIE 96] NIEMEYER G., Using wave variables in time delayed force reflecting teleoperation, PhD Thesis, Massachusetts Institute of Technology, September 1996.

[NIE 04] NIEMEYER G., SLOTINE J., "Telemanipulation with time delays", *International Journal of Robotics Research*, vol. 23, num. 9, p. 873–890, 2004.

[OUH 88] OUH-YOUNG M., PIQUE M., HUGUES J., AL., "Using a manipulator for force display in molecular docking", *Proceedings of International Conference on Robotics and Automation*, p. 1824–1829, 1988.

[OUH 89] OUH-YOUNG M., BEARD D., JR F. P. B., "Force display performs better than visual display in simple 6DOF docking task", *Proceedings of International Conference on Robotics and Automation*, p. 1462–1466, 1989.

[PAT 86] PATTABIRAMAN N., LEVITT M., FERRIN T. E., LANGRIDGE R., "Computer graphics in real-time docking with energy calculation and minimization", *Journal of Computational Chemistry*, vol. 6, num. 5, p. 432–436, 1986.

[PER 07] PERSSON P. B., COOPER M. D., TIBELL A. L., AINSWORTH S., YNNERMAN A., JONSSON B., "Designing and evaluating a haptic system for biomolecular education", *IEEE Virtual Reality*, p. 171–178, 2007.

[SAN 03] SANKARANARAYANAN G., WEGHORST S., SANNER M., GILLET A., OLSON A., "Role of haptics in structural molecular biology", *Symposium on Haptic Interfaces for Virtual Environment and Teleoperator Systems*, p. 363–366, 2003.

[STO 01] STONE J., GULLINGSRUD J., GRAYSON P., SCHULTEN K., "A system for interactive molecular dynamics simulation", *ACM Symposium on Interactive 3D Graphics*, p. 191–194, 2001.

[TOM 94] TOMIOKA N., ITAI A., "Green: a program package for docking studies in rational drug design", *Journal of Computer-aided Molecular Design*, vol. 8, num. 4, p. 347–366, 1994.

[WOL 07] WOLLACOTT A. M., MERZ JR K. M., "Haptic applications for molecular structure manipulation", *Journal of Molecular Graphics and Modeling*, vol. 25, num. 6, p. 801–805, 2007.

List of Authors

Irfan AHMAD
GIPSA-Lab
Control Systems Department
Grenoble Universities
France

Mehdi AMMI
University of Paris-Sud 11
LIMSI-CNRS
Orsay
France

Gildas BESANÇON
GIPSA-Lab
Control Systems Department
Grenoble Universities
France

Sylvain BLANVILLAIN
GIPSA-Lab
Control Systems Department
Grenoble Universities
France

Scott COGAN
FEMTO-ST Institute
CNRS
Besançon
France

Eric COLINET
CEA-LETI
Minatec
Grenoble
France

Bruno DAUNAY
LIMMS/CNRS
Institute of Industrial Science
University of Tokyo
Japan

Abdelbaki DJOUAMBI
Département d'Electronique
Faculté des Sciences Technologiques
University Oum El Bouaghi
Algeria

Antoine FERREIRA
Institut PRISME
Equipe Systèmes Robotiques Interactifs
ENSI Bourges
France

Pierre GRANGEAT
CEA-LETI
Minatec
Grenoble
France

Yassine HADDAB
AS2M Department
FEMTO-ST Institute
CNRS - UFC - ENSMM - UTBM
Besançon
France

Hui HUI
FEMTO-ST Institute
CNRS
Besançon
France

Guillaume JOURDAN
CEA-LETI
Minatec
Grenoble
France

Chady KHARRAT
CEA-LETI
Minatec
Grenoble
France

Michel LENCZNER
FEMTO-ST Institute
CNRS
University of Technology of Belfort Montbéliard
France

Philippe LUTZ
AS2M Department
FEMTO-ST Institute
CNRS - UFC - ENSMM - UTBM
Besançon
France

Pascal MAILLEY
CEA-LETI
Minatec
Grenoble
France

Emmanuel PILLET
FEMTO-ST Institute
CNRS
Besançon
France

Micky RAKOTONDRABE
AS2M Department
FEMTO-ST Institute
CNRS - UFC - ENSMM - UTBM
Besançon
France

Nicolas RATIER
FEMTO-ST - Institute
CNRS
National Engineering School of Mechanics and Microtechnology
Besançon
France

Stéphane RÉGNIER
Institut des Systèmes Intelligents et Robotique (ISIR) UMR CNRS
Pierre and Marie Curie University
Paris
France

Youssef YAKOUBI
Laboratoire J.L.
LIONS - UMR CNRS
Pierre and Marie Curie University
Paris
France

Alina VODA
GIPSA-Lab
Control Systems Department
Grenoble Universities
France

Index